Alice Thomas Ellis

The mother of seven children, Alice Thomas Ellis
has a distinguished career as a novelist (she is
currently working on her eleventh novel)
and journalist.

In this, her first full-length work of non-fiction,
her provocative and idiosyncratic view of life will
outrage, amuse, entertain and challenge readers.

SCEPTRE

Serpent on the Rock

ALICE THOMAS ELLIS

SCEPTRE

For Richard Cohen

Copyright © 1994 by Alice Thomas Ellis (Anna Haycraft)

First published in 1994 by Hodder and Stoughton
A division of Hodder Headline PLC

The right of Alice Thomas Ellis (Anna Haycraft) to be identified
as the Author of the Work has been asserted by her in accordance
with the Copyright, Designs and Patents Act 1988.
First published in paperback in 1995 by Hodder & Stoughton
A Sceptre Paperback

10 9 8 7 6 5 4 3 2 1

British Library Cataloguing in Publication Data

Ellis, Alice Thomas
Serpent on the Rock
I.Title
282.09417

ISBN 0 340 63796 X

Printed and bound in Great Britain by
Cox and Wyman Ltd, Reading, Berkshire

Hodder and Stoughton
A Division of Hodder Headline PLC
338 Euston Road
London NW1 3BH

Acknowledgements

I would like to thank the many people who took time to talk to me.

I am grateful too to Janet, Nicky and Linden who alone know how much I owe to them.

Keren Levy, who chose the pictures, wishes to remain anonymous.

Illustration Credits

Sun Worship, *Karen Davies*

The Brompton Oratory: interior and exterior, *Architectural Association*
Modern Catholic church exterior, *Architectural Association*
'Scooped-out' look of modern Catholic church interior, *Richard Einzig/1978: Arcaid*

Annie Murphy at a press conference, *Frank Spooner Pictures/Gamma*
Bishop Casey: before . . ., *Rex Features*
Bishop Casey: after . . ., *Frank Spooner Pictures/Gamma*

New style nuns sitting around a table, *Network Photographers*
A novice is prepared for the taking of her final vows, *Eve Arnold – Magnum Photos Limited*

Two women priests, *Rex Features*
Father John and Bishop Clement, *Rex Features*
Traditional nuns getting down to work, *David Hurn – Magnum Photos Limited*

A French street priest, *E. Prequ – Sygma*
Armagh Cathedral interior, *Photograph by John Brooks/ Jarrold Publishing from 'St Patrick's Cathedral, Armagh', Irish Heritage Series, published Eason & Son Ltd*

Christa, *sculpture by Edwina Sandys*

On The Obligations and Rights of All Christ's Faithful.

'[Christ's faithful] have the right, indeed at times the duty, in keeping with their knowledge, competence and position, to manifest to the sacred Pastors their views on matters which concern the good of the Church.'

From Canon 212, *The Code of Canon Law*

Contents

Preface

There be three things which are too wonderful for me,
yea four which I know not;
the way of an eagle in the air;
the way of a serpent upon a rock;
the way of a ship in the midst of the sea;
and the way of a man with a maid.

Proverbs 30:19

I hold by the Ould Church, for she's the mother of them all – ay, an' the father, too. I like her bekaze she's most remarkable regimental in her fittings. I may die in Honolulu, Nova Zambra, or Cape Cayenne, but wherever I die, me being 'fwhat I am, an' a priest handy, I go under the same orders an' the same words an' the same unction as tho' the Pope himself came down from the roof av St. Peter's to see me off. There's neither high nor low, nor broad nor deep, nor betwixt nor between wid her, an' that's what I like. But mark you, she's no manner av Church for a wake man, bekaze she takes the body and the soul av him, onless he has his proper work to do. I remember when my father died that was three months comin' to his grave; begad, he'd ha' sold the shebeen above our heads for three minutes' quittance of purgathory. An' he did all he could. That's why I say ut takes a strong man to deal with the Ould Church, an' for that reason you'll find so many women go there. An' that same's a conundrum.

From Rudyard Kipling, *Life's Handicap*

I was born in Liverpool, a city which Carl Jung once dreamed was at the centre of the world. My grandfather, a Finn, had been a sea captain until he retired, became a naturalised Englishman and a Mason and bought himself two pubs in the heart of Liverpool 8, now known as Toxteth. One, The Alligator, was flattened in the Blitz but the other, The Nook, still stands, bearing on its outer wall a plaque announcing that it is the centre of the Chinese quarter. My grandfather died by his own hand before I was born and The Nook had been sold. The family had moved out, some into Nelson, some into Canning Street. The city was then still lively, with contrasting areas of affluence and great poverty. I remember, vaguely, crowded streets and markets, noisy horse-drawn drays and the smell from the breweries mingling with the fog. Throngs of people were daily ferried across the Mersey to their places of work and there was all the hurry and confusion of a maritime city. I have faint memories of feeling intimidated by the noise and the hordes: a fear of being lost.

Many movements and new cults were flourishing at that time: my father was a member of the early Labour Party and a friend of Walter Citrine, then one of its leading lights. Citrine's sister, known to me as Auntie Bell, used to let me feed the milkman's horse with lumps of sugar, and his son, a phrenologist, felt my bumps and pronounced me a person with a strong moral sense. (As far as I am aware he made no other diagnosis and I have often had cause to doubt his infallibility.) Perhaps it is these early memories and a concomitant sense of loyalty which have disabled me – although I am apolitical and don't see that it matters much *sub specie aeternitatis* which party is in power – from voting Conservative.

My father also, under the influence of a family called Bhaer – Otto, his son Julius and his wife Clare – became a member of the Church of Humanity. I don't know why the German Bhaers had ended up in Liverpool but their presence contributed to my childish sense of the cosmopolitan nature of the place: not that I was aware of this, but they served exotic dishes such as curry and spaghetti when I was accustomed only to steamed plaice and rice pudding. The smell of curry still evokes in me images of sophisticated Germans rather than the Raj.

My parents were married in this Church and were then, so I am told, required to live together in the house of a fellow member for a year before consummating their union. This they duly did. People now find this extraordinary and can scarcely believe it possible.

When I was born I was received into the institution, Julius Bhaer standing not, I suppose, as godfather but as my sponsor. The actual church building was adorned outside with a low relief of mother and child: not Christ and the Virgin, but any mother and child, since this relationship was regarded as the highest, most perfect form of human love. Inside were ranged busts of admirable human beings. I can't remember who they were but I believe Plato was one of them. As a wedding present my Mama and Papa were given a volume of the letters of the founder, Auguste Comte (the positivist), and his lady friend Clothilde de Vaux. Throughout my life I have sporadically attempted to read this work and been defeated: where it is not incomprehensible or boring it is unwittingly comic, with Comte referring to his ex-wife as 'the unworthy one', agitating himself because Clothilde has spoken to another man, or castigating himself for his suspicions. I cannot imagine what my mother made of it. Her only noticeable input is an inscription on the fly-leaf giving the date of the civic ceremony of the wedding. This served to inoculate me against humanism.

Comte, so I am told, thought of people as belonging to two basic types, believers in God and non-believers. Non-believers would instantly become adherents of the Church of Humanity and in the course of time all religions would merge into one 'Catholic Church', which by then would have assimilated Comterian ideology, so that eventually religious and non-religious, Catholics and humanitarians, would be indistinguishable one from another and there would be only one sociologically controlled, worldwide Religion of Humanity. I am often puzzled by the thought processes of great thinkers, since between the premise and the conclusion the path becomes indistinct. I would have said that Comte was a great wishful thinker if I had not observed much of Christianity endeavouring to transform itself into a branch of sociology. Nevertheless other religions have, so far, resisted the tendency.

My father's favourite sister, Amy, had married a Catholic and had six children; they all lived in Canning Street with the family portraits, tapestries and some ghosts. Many other relations – and I had a lot of them – were already Catholic, and as I grew older and went to stay with them they would take me to church.

When I was young I was acutely aware that it was necessary to be good. Somebody must have told me so, or perhaps I picked it up from the high-minded people by whom I was surrounded, or perhaps it was due to the conclusion of the phrenologist which had seeped into my consciousness, but I was not a pious child. At the start of the Second World War my mother and I went to live in Wales and I became

acquainted with the local children. Most of these were the off-
spring of regular church- or chapel-goers and sooner or later I
accompanied them to virtually every place of worship in the vicinity.
This served to inoculate me against Protestantism and Handel: the
Messiah was always being performed while the rain fell ceaselessly
on the chapel roof. I went to Sunday school too and collected
great quantities of illustrated Bible tales printed on separate leaf-
lets. The pictures were all carefully historical, with Jesus and the
disciples dressed in biblical mode except for some unconvincing
and strangely repellent representations of the 'Good Shepherd',
still clad in long robes, but surrounded by children in modern
dress. I had no religious sense at all, although I sometimes asked
God for favours on the off-chance.

When I went to grammar school, I annoyed the Scripture mistress
with a theory, which I thought original, that His followers had felt the
times required a prophet and a teacher and had therefore nominated
Christ. Also, for some reason, I had developed an antipathy to the
Salvation Army. The Scripture mistress said that was intolerant and
they did very good work. I'm sure she was right but they still make
me feel shy, as do the newer Jesus Army and the televangelists.

When I went back to Liverpool I no longer found it intimidating;
at seventeen my early childhood seemed lost in the mists of time. I
enrolled at the College of Art. I was surprised a while later when what
seemed like everyone in the entire western world started comporting
themselves as if they were second-year art students, sleeping around,
smoking pot and wearing funny clothes. My year had done all that
and grown out of it – with a few exceptions who are now mostly
dead. Liverpool then was one of the most beautiful cities in the world,
filthy dirty yet magical. One evening, leaving the Philharmonic, I was
startled by an all-pervasive scent of flowers. I don't know where
it came from. A judge had described the area where I lived as
the worst square mile in the world. There was prostitution – I
remember still the cry from the alley behind our house in Canning
Street, 'Lemme go and I'll give you your pound back' – and crime,
and my cousin was stopped in Rodney Street by the police, who
insisted on searching his cricket bag for drugs. Bessy Braddock, the
larger-than-life Labour MP, detested the police, who, she claimed,
in their thirst for promotion were in the habit of kicking from under
them the legs of drunks, thus rendering them incapable and subject

to arrest. But I had no sense of fear or evil: the people had a wit and a liveliness and a confidence and were unlike anyone else.

Another aspect of Liverpool life and culture when I was a girl was the apparent lack of any race or colour prejudice. It may have existed but I was never aware of it. People say that the city grew wealthy on the slave trade and point to iron rings in the docks to which they say the slaves were shackled, although others claim these were merely a device to tie the ships up. Whatever the truth about these rings, and there is no doubt that the slave trade flourished here, the mix of races usual in a great sea port had led not to self-conscious tolerance but unquestioning acceptance of a great variety of people.

Soon after this the greed of the unions and the corruption of the City Council started Liverpool's tragic decline – and soon after that it became famous only as the home of the Beatles. Now it is notorious for darker reasons. Then the churches were full, always open and a source of constant interest as well as solace. There was sectarian strife – I knew a grandmother who followed the Holy Day processions with the handle of her sewing machine under her shawl in order to protect her altar-boy grandson against possible attack from Orangemen – but it seldom got out of hand. The parish priest, who kept singing birds in the presbytery, had laid out a formal Italian garden behind the church and employed an ex-art student to decorate the church itself with murals. I was engaged to help in filling in the borders.

It is presently *de rigueur* to claim that Catholicism thirty-odd years ago was repressive, hidebound and frightening, but I found in it great richness and an abundance of people who made me laugh: a release from fear and the vague oppression of a childhood shadowed alike by the joyless strictures of Protestantism and the horrors of fairy-tale and terrifying legend.

Just as film and pop stars so often claim to have suffered sexual and physical abuse in their childhood, so almost everyone who went to a convent school now claims to have been clouted with rulers by sadistic sisters, to have had her innocently burgeoning sexuality blighted for ever by disapproval, to have had her potential genius stunted and to have been told off for wearing unsuitable shoes because her parents were too poor to buy the regulation sort. They seem all to have been wild, free spirits, elfin-faced gamines brimming with originality and always in trouble for talking to the milkman or turning somersaults in the cloisters. I suppose it's as good an excuse for one's present state as any. I went to a secular school, suffered the same prohibitions and lack of respect for my little self and see no reason to whinge about it now.

I had a happy childhood apart from some aspects of school and Sunday evenings. At the age of about seventeen I became a member of the Labour Party at the behest of an activist in the room above mine in our lodging house in Canning Street, but she and her fellow workers talked about dialectical materialism without ever explaining precisely what they meant by this term and failed to hold my interest. This served to inoculate me against the extreme Left, and the evenings which we spent drinking cocoa made with condensed milk, discussing the meaning of life, ended without our ever reaching any satisfactory conclusion.

Then after due time and instruction I became a Catholic because I no longer found it possible to disbelieve in God. This surprised some of my family and friends (though not those who were Catholic, since they found it only natural), for it seems I had not previously given the impression of being a person with a serious approach to life. I felt entirely at home with the conviction, aims and rituals of the Church and secure in the certainty that it was immune from frivolous change and the pressures of fashion; primarily concerned with the numinous rather than with the social and political concerns of its members. After a while I became a postulant in a religious community until I had to go to hospital with what was diagnosed as a slipped disc.

Before this misfortune I was one of thirty or so postulants in the Novice House. It was large and clean, and the lives we led were very simple. We got up early, leaping out of bed at the first sound of the handbell (wielded by a nun who had got up even earlier), washed, dressed and went to chapel. This rising at the crack of dawn was the most extreme mortification of the flesh I had experienced. The days were divided between prayer, lessons, recreation and meals. The food was also simple: bread and marg (jam on High Holy Days) and mugs of tea formed breakfast, while dinner at midday consisted of meat or fish and vegetables followed by fruit from the orchard. We were required to eat everything all up regardless of preference or inclination. One girl could not abide fish, while I had a deep dislike of liver. We coped by cutting up the loathsome substances into tiny bits and swallowing them whole. People today see this as barbaric cruelty but we had been brought up during the war when there wasn't a lot of choice and you tended to eat up everything on your plate anyway since there wasn't anything else.

The professed nuns wore a habit of black robe and scapular with wimple, veil and guimpe, while the postulants were clad in black frocks and stockings and an attenuated sort of veil with a strip of white cloth around the forehead. We added blue cotton aprons when performing menial tasks and wore ordinary black coats out of doors. Instant obedience was expected of us: if you were in the middle of, say, applying a flat wash to a water-colour and the bell rang for chapel you had to put down your brush on the instant and speed silently away. This tended to spoil your painting but it really didn't matter very much. We were encouraged, once a week, to meditate on the hour of our death with the proviso that the nervous could think about something else if it upset them too greatly, and were recommended certain devotional works to read in the chapel; those of us who found some of the sentiments too sweet were permitted to choose something more palatable. All our letters, both incoming and outgoing, were read by the Novice Mistress, a circumstance which fills many people with horror, though I can't see why. If you have nothing to hide why should not your life be an open book? If you have, then, contrary to popular opinion, a convent is probably not the place for you. Not, that is, until you have shriven your conscience, tidied up your ways and made amends. The whole point of the religious life, it seemed to me, was to purge yourself of your own will and desires and become not self- but God-centred. This notion is now out of favour, as people, women especially, are abdured to 'affirm' themselves, whatever that means.

The doctors gave it as their opinion that without surgery my spinal complaint, while not life-threatening, was probably incurable and I limped back into the world, since it appeared that I would be unable to take a proper part in an active community. I shall be eternally grateful to the nuns who forbade a wild-eyed surgeon to practise his skills on me, for in the course of time and after a few lapses my back healed. I got married in the church of our local Franciscan friary in Wales and settled down, anxious to do my best to be a Catholic wife and mother, imagining that while not easy it would be simple. Ha.

After the Second Vatican Council of 1963 attitudes to religion changed so remarkably that I frequently found the Church unrecognisable. A priest I had known for years, who had always given every appearance of sanity and sanctity, cast off clerical garb, requested us to call him in future by his Christian name and spoke of the widest possible ecumenism in the warmest possible terms: he professed himself delighted with the prospect of universal singing and dancing in the aisles and round the altar and gave an overwhelming impression of goofiness. I was startled, for he was an elderly person, and elderly persons are not usually changeable. It filled me with a strange feeling, a sense of the possibility of impermanence, of ultimate worthlessness and the prospect of the triumph of chaos and old night.

When the family first moved into our current house in north London, the parish church, while not from the exterior a thing of beauty, nevertheless was clearly a place of Catholic worship. There were statues, a sanctuary light, a smell of incense, a painting behind the altar and an air of hush and solemnity. There were many priests resident in the presbytery, regular confessions, missions and full congregations. I had at that time four small children and sometimes failed to attend Sunday Mass. When I did, taking the children with me, they had a tendency to disappear under the pews, emerging at various points and having to be reclaimed. It was very tiring. One day, after I had failed to attend a previous Sunday's services, a Christian Brother came to the door and demanded to know why I had missed Mass. 'But Father,' I said, by way of excuse, 'I have so much to do with the babies and the building' – we were living in the rubble while the house was reconstituted around us – 'and I have so little time.' 'Time for everything but to save your own soul,' he observed. Far from being cast down I was enchanted by this remark, finding in it a reassuring reminder of the reality and gravity of Faith. That, I considered, was what the priest was for, to put the fear of God into the straying sheep.

Shortly after this came the changes consequent upon the Second Vatican Council. I went into the church one day to find the congregation singing *Kumbaya*. I didn't go back there for years, and no priest came to look for me.

For some time I didn't go to church at all. On the few occasions when I forced myself into our local place of worship, I found evidence of confusion and uncertainty. One of the priests had had a nervous breakdown, which did not surprise me, while most of the others had become remote and ill-tempered, and this did not surprise me either. Sometimes, according to whose whim I know not, the church would be painted white and all the statues removed. At others the colours would have been restored and the saints put back *in situ*.

As time passed, matters got, if anything, worse. The old priests were replaced by a succession of younger men who notably lacked gravitas and tended to go round in stone-washed jeans, and there usually seemed to be only one in residence where once there had been eight or more. During services odd parishioners would announce 'hallelujah' at unexpected moments and the laity seemed to be in charge, trotting up and down bearing the Host, reading the lessons and performing as Ministers of the Eucharist. Communion in the hand became commonplace and I found the whole business variously comic, irritating and dispiriting, with an overall sense of misrule. When I bothered to enquire what was going on the almost invariable response was that that was the way things were done in the early Church. This dubious answer fails to reassure me, for no one can know precisely how matters were ordered 2,000 years ago, and throwing out centuries of accretion is vandalism. It makes the work of our most recent ancestors seem like a waste of time, and the innovators not progressive but destructive: 'progress is the insult we pay to our ancestors.'

A hundred years ago Max O'Rell, a Frenchman and a master at St Paul's, wrote of his mistrust of the *unco guid*, a Scottish term which roughly translates as *bien-pensant*. He says: 'The worst type of Anglo-Saxon *parvenu* is probably the *unco guid* or religious *parvenu*. He is seldom to be found among Roman Catholics: that is among the followers of the most ancient Christian religion, but among the followers of the newest forms of "Christianity". This is quite natural. He has to try to eclipse his fellow Christians by his piety, in order to show that the new religion to which he belongs was a necessary invention. He casts left and right little grimaces that are so many forced smiles of self-satisfaction. "Try and be as good as I am," he seems to say to all who happen to look at him, "and you will be as happy" – and he smiles and smiles. He has a small soul, a small heart and a small brain.' Unfortunately in the past thirty years the *unco guid* have infiltrated Catholicism. The rictus is now epidemic in many Catholic churches, accompanying the handshake which is customary in the new Mass.

I felt bereft and consequently resentful. I was so annoyed that in 1977 I stirred out of my habitual indolence and wrote a book called *The Sin Eater*: I put it in the form of a novel, since novels give better scope for ungoverned rage than more sober works and I had to do something rather than sink into despair. The heroine was not a nice woman, for I was also fed up with women whining about their powerlessness. Women did the cooking, I reasoned, and thus held the power of life and death, apart from being the only people who could give birth. They were not the innocent, helpless victims that some claimed. For instance, my mother was the youngest of seven sisters and it would have been a rash man who attempted to oppress any one of them. Rose, as I called my creation, was a Roman Catholic who felt freed by the changes in the Church, not to express herself as a child of God liberated from the old constraints, but to behave as badly as she liked, given over to original sin.

She said of the Church: 'They modernised it. . . . They fell victim to the municipal line of thought which goes: "That's beautiful. It must be old. We'd better knock it down"'; and 'At the consecration they do a sort of advertiser's announcement. You think for a moment they're telling you God's blood is untouched by human hand, a sort of guarantee of wholesomeness – though I'd always been led to believe it was feet. But they're actually explaining it is *made* by human hands. They're very honest, you see. They don't want to feel they're putting anything over on anybody. I think it's meant for the enlightenment of the credulous, who previously thought it came straight from Heaven in vast ethereal tankers. And they're creeping up on transubstantiation, circling it with a net. It'll be the next to go, and then heigh ho for the gates of Hell'; and 'The P.P. [parish priest] comes from time to time to rebuke me but I take no notice. . . . I tell him I stand exactly where I always stood, while the Church has ebbed from me. I tell him I was a true obedient daughter of the Church but this is beyond a joke and I will not make a fool of myself because fools decree it should be so. Or words to that effect, you understand. . . . The last time I went to Mass – and it *was* the last time – there was the P.P. facing the congregation, standing behind his table and joining in the singing of the negro spirituals and the pop songs and Shall-we-gather-at-the-river. There has always been a hint of catering about the Mass but previously the priest had the dignity of a master chef busying himself with his *specialité*. Now he seems like a singing waiter in charge of an inadequate buffet. One is tempted to stroll up and ask for a double martini and enquire who on earth forgot to put the doings on the canapés. I wonder why they didn't keep the real Mass for me and just bring in this one for the kiddies and the mentally subnormal . . . ? It is as though one's revered, dignified and darling old mother had slapped on a mini-skirt and fishnet tights and started ogling strangers. A kind of menopausal madness, a sudden yearning to be attractive to all. It is tragic and hilarious and awfully embarrassing. And of course those who knew her before feel a great sense of betrayal and can't bring themselves to go and see her anymore.' This, of course, was written before Political Correctness arrived on our shores.

Rose speaks of the parish priest: 'To do him justice, he still does dress in the proper fashion. He hasn't taken to going round in jeans and a T-shirt and a little cross on a chain round his neck imploring people to call him Roger, and he hasn't left the Church to marry and devote his life to re-writing theology to conform with his own lusts and itches, and drivel on about the self-transcending nature of sex, like all those treacherous, lecherous Jesuits, mad with the radiant freedoms of contemporary thought. But it isn't enough. Now the Church has lost its head, priests feel free to say what they think themselves, and they don't have any thoughts at all except for some rubbish about the brotherhood of man. They seem to regard Our Lord as a sort of beaten egg to bind us all together.'

These were more or less my sentiments in regard to the innovations, and I have since seen little reason to revise them.

As time passed I began to find other Roman Catholic churches where order had been regained, if not retained. It became clear that the Church was in schism although I met few priests who would admit that this was so. Most smilingly insisted that all was well. A few years ago I wrote an article entitled 'Where's the Church I knew and loved?' The response was great. I received hundreds of letters from people who had been asking themselves that very question and could find no satisfactory answer. They all said that their queries were ignored, brushed aside and no one would speak for them. Those who made their feelings plain were accused of nostalgia at best, fascism at worst. Many of the discarded lunacies of the 1960s still persist in the Church, which, bizarrely, now seems to present a final resting place for some of the madder '-isms', Marxism, modernism, militant feminism and New Ageism being the most obvious; while a Church of England type of atheism is also evident in some quarters, together with some of the wilder degrees of Protestantism. It is extremely confusing, especially for those who clearly remember the Church as it was.

Then in May 1992 came the affair of Bishop Casey and the suggestion that his lapse was a fatal blow to Catholicism. 'Does this herald the end of the Catholic Church?' cried many, seemingly unaware of the vicissitudes the institution has gone through in its long history and ignoring the real threats of erosion and dilution. I decided that this might be an interesting moment to have a closer look at what was going on; so I set off on a sort of quest, although this is not quite the correct word: it implies a search for truth and I had found that in the Church. Now something had gone wrong and I saw my role, not as that of a knight pursuing the Grail, but more as that of an amateur sanitary inspector in search of the source of the whiff in the drains.

I

In Search of the Bishop

When Irish eyes are smiling . . .
Irish ballad

The Bishop and Annie Murphy – Making a sin of sex –
On the road in Ireland – Our first huge breakfast – The
prevalence of bungalows – The old priest – The new church
architecture – The eternal Church – The hotel owner's wife
– Fleeing from the postmistress – On being Kitty Kelley –
The Nuremberg rally – Bishop Casey's confession – Return
to Liverpool   The right style – On not being a theologian
– God's absence and God's presence.

'I Taught Virgin Bishop How To Love' (*Sun* headline, 16 May 1992).
The British press, diverted for a while from the miserable intricacies
of the marriage of the Prince and Princess of Wales, had fallen upon
this mundane item of news and wrung from it every last drop of
speculation and prurience. Later on in the article Annie Murphy,
the woman in the case, describes herself as a 'forbidden fruit', and is
quoted as saying: 'Eamonn told me he had not been with a woman.
He was forty-six and a virgin. I was experienced and obviously took
the lead, but it was difficult. He was not a man, he was a novice –
and it progressed slowly.' She continues: 'I'd tease him sometimes
about celibacy and say he'd have to run to the confessional. Then
I'd grab the keys to the confessional box and hide them.'

She goes on in this roguish vein: 'Eamonn was ordaining some
priests and I put on a black cloak and went into the church. He was
telling them they would have to be celibate and then he locked eyes
on me. He began tripping over his words. He could hardly get them
out. Later I told him I'd felt like snatching his mitre hat off his head
and dancing on it because he'd been such a hypocrite.'

There are no keys to the confessional and the matter of celibacy is generally dealt with at the time of ordination to the diaconate.

She also says: 'When he came to my room the first time it was no surprise. I was expecting a sexual relationship almost straight away. But he wasn't a man who came to your bed and made love that night. He was in his forties and a virgin. I can see the humorous side now but then it was marvellous. Eamonn often said he was sinning. But I'd reply, "Yes, but are you enjoying it?" He would say, "Yes." It was just great fun to be with him.'

Opinions on Annie Murphy vary: some see her as scheming and manipulative, others as a pathetic victim. An article in the *Sunday Times* of 10 May read: 'Nobody, it seemed, would point a finger at the bishop for his human error – until the Friday morning broadcast when Annie Murphy's thin, trembling voice changed everything. "Falling in love with him", she whispered, "was like gliding on gossamer wings. We were like two little children. But the descent into hell began once the baby was born." The bishop was reluctant to acknowledge the child. "He had a terrible fear of his son . . . he touched him like he was on fire."'

Nevertheless, by one means or another, from September 1974 the Bishop of Galway paid Annie Murphy US$175 a month, having first responded to her demands 'belligerently and begrudgingly'. He offered $100 a month until she threatened to go to the Vatican and make her child a ward of the Church. In 1990 he handed over $115,000, and a further lump sum of $150,000 was discussed but came to nothing. Annie Murphy, rather confusingly in view of her earlier requirements, said she didn't want the money. 'I didn't demand money from Eamonn. He offered and we refused it.' The article concludes with a remark made by an old man to an Irish poet on the subject of sex: 'It's the loveliest little thing in the world, and they had to go and make a sin of it.'

I decided to go to Ireland and see what they thought about it all there. As I can neither drive nor type and have no sense of direction, I suggested to Janet, who is an essential element in our family life, having been nanny to our youngest children, and now, all things considered, being mine, that it might be fun if she came too. Then we thought we might as well make a party of it and take along our friend Al as the driver – for he has a remarkable talent for finding empty parking spaces and adequate hostelries.

We spent the first night of our quest in a small pink-washed hotel in County Wexford, separated from the sea by a harbour wall and a narrow road. In the morning I crossed the road to look more closely at the sea and saw not a fishing boat but a horse wading through the water, for this was serious hunting country and we got the impression that nearly everything else was of secondary importance. Riding boots, hats, whips and representations of horses took up the spaces between the many portraits of relations on the walls, and we felt the inhabitants were only marking time until they could rush out and get on with the proper business of life. The young owner brought us breakfast of cereal, orange juice, soda bread, toast and marmalade and plates of bacon (two rashers), eggs (one), sausages (two), tomato (half) and a choice of tea or coffee. We enjoyed it a lot.

Afterwards I collared her between the kitchen and the horses and asked what her views were on the present state of the Church. She said that she couldn't claim that hers was a really staunch Catholic household and I asked what she meant. Did they miss Mass or Holy Days of Obligation? 'Dear God, no,' she said, shocked. She meant they didn't go every day to church and very seldom twice. What I should do, she told me, if I wanted to know about the religion was to go and see the farmers and the country shopkeepers who would have a very different view of the situation from that of the city people. Could she give me any names, I asked. She looked at me as though I were crazy. Just ask anyone, she said. I would find them in the fields and in the lanes. So we got in the car and set off.

'Stop at any church,' I said to Al the driver, and he said it was a funny thing but he hadn't noticed many: he would have thought the place would be sinking under them. After a while he gave a cry of gratification, having observed a forbidding-looking stone edifice. We stopped and went in. 'I think', said Janet, noticing certain signs as we approached the door, 'that this is one of ours' (she is a Methodist). 'Or rather it was,' she added, for it seemed to be in use as a polling station (it was Maastricht polling day), and anyway when it wasn't serving that purpose it was the local badminton club. The interior was painted a sinister green and contained only two officials: no players, no voters and certainly no worshippers. 'Good start,' said Janet.

Our next stop was at a country pub, standing by itself just off the road. It had suffered the common fate of such establishments the world over. Having been a small, traditional hostelry off the beaten track, unchanged over many years, it had suddenly realised what it could make from the tourist trade and was now pretending to be what it had once unselfconsciously been: there were dressers and harps and ancient advertisements and odd-looking implements that no one could remember the purpose of. The only people in the bar were Americans, Germans and us, admiring the old flagged floor and dubious beams. 'Go round,' invited the barmaid, 'and see the place.' In a back room we discovered the rest of the staff sitting at a table and on stools at yet another bar. 'Oh, sorry,' we said, 'we've disturbed your lunch.' 'Not at all,' said a lady, who, I gained the impression, was the most important member of the staff, probably the manageress; 'it's our breakfast.' 'Tell me,' I said, 'what do you think of the state of the Catholic Church and what do you make of Bishop Casey?' 'Oh,' she said, 'my Dad was shattered by the changes. He's always saying the Latin had more meaning.' This reflects Janet's point of view: she holds that it's like opera – that as long as they're singing in some foreign language you get carried away by the beauty of the music, but once you understand the words you can no longer suspend disbelief and quite often give way to hilarity. This view is not as trivial as some think; there are matters to which only one mode of expression is suited and which lose integrity in translation.

'And Bishop Casey?' I prompted. She cheered up at this and the other girls joined in. 'He's only human,' they said charitably, 'but he should have owned up years ago.' I asked what they thought about celibacy laws for priests and my friend, who appeared to be the spokeswoman, as befitting her status, said she thought they should all be married and then they'd know what it was like. She was one of those women you wouldn't cross in a hurry and I detected a note of vengefulness in this remark, as from one who feels that too many men have too easy a time. She went on to say that more went on in life than we knew, and what about all those uncles and their nieces? I was going to press her to explain further what she meant by this but she had remembered a joke. 'They say the Bishop of Galway has gone off to Peru to take up a position as a missionary.' Here everyone rolled off her stool laughing, so we said goodbye and left, pausing only to admire the practical china dresser with the barred space for chickens at the bottom.

We were to find the combination of compassion, ribaldry and regret common in the people to whom we talked – a different response from that of the English press, having no tinge of breathless horror, no smacking of the brow with the palm of the hand and gasp of outrage. The Irish, I was told, have known their priests well for years. They are sorry when they fall but they are not particularly astonished.

Back on the road we ourselves were struck with wonder: not so much at the beauty of the countryside but at the number of new bungalows. There was not an old building to be seen for miles except for a few ruins decaying into the earth. Everywhere there were bungalows, all built to the same basic plan with some variation as to the quantity of arches in front (the winner had six) and some evidence of individual eccentricity in the choice of coloured stone. It was as though a master salesman had travelled the country and everywhere had succeeded in selling his wares. He had also apparently carried with him packets of seeds which he gave to everyone who bought a bungalow: these seeds gave rise to a tree called a Japanese poplar which flourishes exuberantly in Irish soil. It has leaves of pink and cream and looks like a larger version of the ubiquitous poinsettia which casts a gloom over Christmas. We quite liked the first one we saw but after a while we got to hate them.

Al rebuked me when I expressed dismay at the paucity of old cottages, reminding me that when the tower blocks went up in London the first occupants were grateful to be free of damp and darkness and rat-infested backyards and glad of modern kitchens and light. Disillusion set in later but the principle was sound, he said. I still think we should hang on to the old for as long as we can and seek to improve rather than destroy it. But then I think that about almost everything. We would see a handsome stretch of wall and a pair of imposing gateposts or an ancient hedge, then we'd look beyond them and see, not a mellow house, but another bungalow. It is sad that the picturesque should have become unliveable in. Later I heard a story about an Englishwoman who had bought a piece of land with an old thatched cottage which she set about restoring. Her neighbours were annoyed at this, considering that she was lowering the tone of the district. More, after a while they suspected that she was playing an elaborate joke on them, mocking and reminding them of an impoverished past.

The towns seem less changed from the old days, with their flat frontages and strong colours, blue and pink and green and yellow.

While we were in Ireland we enjoyed the continental type of heat which seems to be becoming more usual in our northern climes and it added to the sense of foreignness. We had the feeling that comes to the stranger – that a life that he can never share or understand is going on in secret quarters, behind closed doors, yet the people when we spoke to them were invariably friendly, welcoming and courteous. Once we said that we felt further from home than if we were in France (as indeed we were in pedantically geographical terms), and agreed that this was a good thing as the EC is imposing a dispiriting homogeneity on its member nations. What perverse element is it in human nature – I mused – that causes the Church on the one hand to banish the universal Latin and prevail upon its people to pray in the vernacular, while politicians try to persuade us of the benefits of a common currency on the other?

We came to Macroom in County Cork and parked the car. In the streets they were preparing for the Feast of Corpus Christi and the annual procession. We stopped outside a shop to look in the window, wondering what sort of shop it was. It clearly sold ironmongery and rat-poison and things for farmers and gardeners, but the owner had cleared half his window to make space for the statue of Christ and garlands of red paper roses. He did it every year for when the procession went by. In devotional terms it had the edge over the Regent Street Christmas illuminations. The ironmonger was getting on in years. I wrote on the back of an envelope, 'Is the old religion still alive in the minds of the old?' Not the most brilliant of *aperçus* but it seemed significant at the time in view of my vague impression that where there had been one religion there were now two, or possibly more.

That night in a hotel bar I asked three girls what they thought about the state of the Church. They were puzzled, as though it had never occurred to them to wonder about it, and they made me feel as if I had asked a silly question. Then I did ask a silly question. 'Do you remember the faith as it was?' I enquired. 'No,' they responded, which was not surprising as they were each aged only about twenty. 'Do you like the present Mass?' I went on. 'Yes,' they said, growing increasingly bewildered. So I asked them what they thought about Bishop Casey. Had he shaken their faith? They must have been getting bored with me but they replied again with perfect politeness that they hadn't given him much thought. He was only one man, after all, and no, he hadn't shaken their faith in the least. I let them go and bought myself a drink.

Al had to rely greatly on the Irish Tourist Board offices, since we were spending every night in a different place and virtually every bungalow offered B&B, making choice difficult. He said the young women employed in them were helpful and efficient and we said that it was just as well until we remembered that almost every other institution we had dealings with was conspicuously lacking in these qualities, and any person encountering efficiency and helpfulness was richly entitled to express some surprise.

After a certain amount of to-ing and fro-ing we settled on a farm-house, a real one standing amidst fields, with a farmyard harbouring cows and chickens. Many of the bungalows were also described as farmhouses but they failed to convince, largely because there was little evidence of livestock in their vicinity and the word 'farmhouse' conjures up a vision to which they failed to approximate. Our chosen refuge was an old building rather on the lines of a Welsh longhouse, though not as attractive. The Welsh do not have much visual sense but they did have access to a lot of stone, and houses built of local materials are almost always satisfying. I couldn't work out what the basic fabric of this house was because the exterior had been rendered in a cream-coloured substance.

Inside, the old fireplace had been removed and central heating installed. As I lamented this fact Al reminded me that maintaining and cleaning those old fireplaces must have been extremely hard work. He finds me impractical and given to fits of misplaced aestheticism. We were shown into a sitting-room floored with a flowered carpet and containing an inordinate number of chairs covered in brown Dralon. I opened my mouth to speak but thought better of it and looked instead at the family photographs on the wall and in an alcove: grandparents and great-grandparents, relations who had entered the priesthood, wedding groups. Through the window came the smell of new-mown hay and the sound of birds singing and cows lowing.

In the morning we gathered in the dining-room and were served with half a grapefruit, cereal, toast and marmalade, two rashers of bacon, one egg, half a tomato and two sausages, and a choice of tea or coffee. Despite a small feeling of _déjà vu_ we enjoyed it. I spoke to our hostess and told her I was researching a book on the Church, asking if she had any thoughts on the matter, especially in relation to the Bishop of Galway. She smiled and sighed and said he had been very foolish but had done such a lot of good work. She took our plates out to the kitchen, then hastened back to express an anxious hope that all the good he had done would not be forgotten. Suddenly she looked at me sideways and enquired whether I was a member of Opus Dei. I denied it and I think she was disappointed.

Since she was of an age to remember the old Mass I asked what she thought of the changes and she said she hadn't really minded. What *really* worried her and the old people was the question of Adam and Eve. There had been great distress when it was suggested that they were not actual historical figures. I wondered who had been silly enough to tell them this. The business of Bishop Casey seemed to have been of little import compared with this troubling revelation. Perhaps the locals had had one of those misguided priests who insist on stuffing the ears of the congregation with theological and biblical minutiae which can baffle the most attentive and informed listener.

Having partially digested the matutinal cholesterol we jumped back in the car and set off yet again, coming in the course of time to a small and apparently deserted town. The school was closed because it was the Feast of Corpus Christi. We went into a shop where we found the owner and the priest's housekeeper. Don't ask me how I knew it was she: one just always does. They are unmistakable. I asked if I could see the parish priest and she said it was an unfortunate thing but he'd gone to London. It was a terrible shame, she said, because he was a very intelligent man and could have told me anything I wanted to know. However, if I liked she would take me to meet the old parish priest who was now retired, seeing as how he was ninety-one years old. I accepted this offer and was ushered into his study where he was reading a newspaper but welcomed me kindly, telling me first that he had designed the presbytery himself without the benefit of an architect and did I know that he was ninety-one years old? I expressed astonishment and he looked gratified. It seems sometimes that a kind of second childhood can come not as a blight but as a blessing. He reminded me of a good and well-loved child, secure in an innocent vanity, untouched by wickedness or doubt.

Yet he had lived through troubled times. When he was four he had been lifted up to look through the window and see the police constable passing, an incident which had clearly made a great impression on him. He said that the town was now a 'respectable' place which it had not been when he first arrived, and then he remembered a time when all the people, poor as they were, had given pennies for the purchase of guns which were hidden from the authorities in all manner of ingenious ways. 'We're never conquered,' he said. 'We're going to win all the time. Even at my age I'm not a bit afraid to face anything. When you've got faith in the Lord, setbacks only make you better. People are great – just too often misunderstood.'

I was confused, uncertain here whether we were discussing the matter of victory in temporal or eternal terms. He had an expression of serenity, of quiet happiness, and explained that he still retained an interest in everything, including football, and was certain that one day there would be a peaceful, united Ireland. I think when he spoke of hope that it was this that was foremost in his mind. He told me a story about two parishioners and two chickens. One, as far as I could gather, had killed the chicken of the other, whereupon the aggrieved owner had plucked the live chicken of the party of the first part. As a penance he was made to gather up all the feathers in a high wind and give them back. I'm not sure I've got the point of that story but it has a satisfyingly rural element.

The housekeeper told us that the old church had been blown up in the Troubles. We went to look for the ruins but couldn't find them. I hadn't mentioned Bishop Casey to the old priest because I did not feel he would be interested.

We had to move on. I was reading Agatha Christie in the back of the car when I came upon a reference to hot scones, dripping with butter. 'If you see anything like a roadside café,' I said to Al, 'stop immediately.' 'We haven't seen one so far,' he said tersely, 'and we've done a few hundred miles.' Then, as if by a miracle, we saw a sign proclaiming teas and behind it a thatched cottage. We quickly parked and went in.

We asked directions to the church but although we followed them meticulously we didn't find it. Al repeated his opinion that they were curiously elusive. I said there was no problem if they were new. If you visited a place where you knew the Catholic church had been recently constructed, you only had to ask for the most diabolically ugly building in town, bar none. After a few more miles we came to one. 'That's got to be one of yours,' said Janet, and it was. Circular, with a lot of carpet and glass and seats arranged round a pagan-looking lump of something which I suppose was the altar, and the Blessed Sacrament housed in a brass Dalek to one side. '*Dear God*,' said Janet. We couldn't find the parish priest, not really knowing where to look for him.

We went on to another town, where we found the kind of church I am more accustomed to with the presbytery adjacent, and I tracked down the priest.

I asked my usual question, which by now was beginning to lose meaning for me and feel like dry husks in my mouth. 'What do you think of the state of the Church?'

He regarded me calmly and asked me what I meant.

'Well,' I said carefully, 'is it not in some confusion?'

'Not really,' he said, 'not for me. I follow what the Pope says because he is the Vicar of Christ.'

I found this novel, since most people in England, Catholics especially, are ambivalent in their attitudes to the Pontiff.

'We preach the word of God,' he said. 'After that it's for the people to make their own response. I don't know why they worry so about the Church – we're only passing through. It's Christ's Church and eternal. I just do the best I can and I have no worries. Not about the Church. In Ireland and in England,' he went on, 'we are very insular in our views. We are prisoners of history because we're only human, but the Church still survives.' He told me with sudden animation that there was a great increase in vocations in Korea but here in the west of Ireland people only talked about money. He said you couldn't trust the government, they hadn't got a democracy and the Ministers of Finance should be in gaol. Money-lending, interest, debt were the favoured subjects of conversation and all that most of the older people thought about. The young were more honourable, and angry because they had no say. He was glad that much of the poverty had been eased and the people had the new, lovely homes to live in.

My attention wandered here as I reflected that if only they'd uproot the dreaded Japanese poplars and grow indigenous creepers up the walls the overall effect of startling brand-newness wouldn't strike one as so odd. I emerged from this reverie to hear the priest saying that he'd like to live for ever, that he loved life and enjoyed a round of golf. I am always surprised to hear people talking like this as I do not feel the same way. The love of life is enviable, admirable and biblical too. Shamed by his enthusiasm, I changed the subject to one of my other worries and asked what he thought about the Charismatic movement. 'I don't think about it,' he said.

Later, I reflected that I had met two happy men that day and as far as I could tell it was their faith which had given them contentment, combined with an ability to concentrate on what was of immediate significance to them. The golfing priest seldom read the world press – which could be described as de-press – and so wasted no time or energy filling his mind with horrors. He said we should not go around in blinkers, but nor was there any virtue in immersing oneself in tales of depravity and cruelty if one were powerless to offer material help. 'Think on those things that are lovely and of good report' is something I frequently reminded myself but it's easier said than done. I didn't mention Bishop Casey to this priest either.

Back to the car, which was beginning to feel as the shell must feel to the snail. The girls in the Tourist Board office had recommended that we stay the night in a country-house hotel well off the road. It was nearly booked up and could only offer us rooms in what had been the servants' quarters. We're not fussy, so we accepted and went for a walk round the gardens before dinner, stopping now and then to swipe the blackcurrants.

Over a glass of sherry in the drawing-room I engaged the owner's wife in conversation. She was English and Church of England but took a close interest in all that affected her husband's country. What she took an even closer interest in, as we were to discover, was the subject of sexual morality; but we began decorously enough with talk of the current referendum. Then she said that the next referendum in the autumn was to be on abortion and it would tear the heart out of the country. She spoke of the rape case involving a child of fourteen. This was the first time I had heard the subject of abortion mentioned and I had not introduced the topic myself because I felt it was not a fit subject for discussion – not because it is too distressing or distasteful but because abortion is one of those subjects on which people of opposing views will never agree and there is no point in talking about it. Few people who have made up their minds are ever swayed by argument. Women are more flexible than men, but on abortion even they, when they have decided their attitudes, will seldom be persuaded to change them. The brute force of the vote is all that is left. My own reaction would have been to kill the man and have the baby, but I suppose that's impractical.

Our hostess observed that in the opinion of the local postmistress the girl was always to blame and I got the impression that, in this small community, what the postmistress said carried considerable weight. She did not permit her attitude to sexual immorality to be clouded by notions of human frailty, tolerance or forgiveness and I got a mental picture of her – stern, cold and Calvinistic. Our hostess, whom I shall call Jean, said in a tone pitched between fascination and despair that twenty-odd local girls got pregnant in the previous year (three of them by the same local lad, who had now fled to England) and no family could be found to undertake the care of a single one of these unmarried mothers. I was not as surprised at this as Jean seemed to be. Wayward girls and small babies can put a considerable strain on a household. Jean belonged to an organisation which, as far as I could gather, worried a lot about the situation and did what it could to help. Here Jean went to boil the potatoes and her husband to pick the parsley. After dinner the talk was of horses until it returned to teenage single mothers. 'You see,' said Jean, squinting with concentration, 'the trouble is they reject the Church's teaching on no sex before marriage, and then they go on to accept its teaching on birth control, so what can you do?' 'Why is that?' someone asked politely. 'They think that if it just *happens*,' explained Jean, 'it isn't such a sin. Not as though they'd *planned* it.' This aspect of human nature is one that the rationalist finds supremely irritating.

Next morning we sat down to breakfast: orange juice, cereal, two rashers of bacon, two sausages, one egg, half a tomato, soda bread, toast and marmalade, tea or coffee. We ate most of it and looked for Jean to say goodbye. 'And the year before last,' she was saying gloomily to some other guests, 'there were even *more* unmarried mothers.'

We set off to the post office, partly to buy the Sunday papers but mostly because I wanted to look at the postmistress. She was standing behind the counter, precisely as I had pictured her, wearing an air of terrible authority while a young woman dealt with the buying and selling. I wondered if this was because she herself didn't work on the Sabbath or whether she was always too grand to deal directly with the public.

'Go on,' urged Janet, 'ask her about the unmarried mothers.'

'You must be joking,' I said.

After peering round a rack of postcards for a clear look, Janet saw the wisdom of my words and we fled.

Reading the papers in the back of the car I came across a small headline: 'Novelist in hot pursuit of bishop'. How disgusting, I mused, my eye passing idly down the page. 'Alice Thomas Ellis is presently touring Ireland . . .' it said, going on to compare me with Kitty Kelley, the no-holds-barred biographer of Frank Sinatra and Nancy Reagan. 'Well,' I said to Al, 'we might as well turn round now and go home', for I had arranged to meet various eminent clerics and other distinguished persons and it was clear to me that not one of these individuals, if he had any sense, would now touch me with a bargepole. I could hear the slam of palace doors all over the republic and cold words of contemptuous dismissal. 'Don't be silly,' said Janet and the driver, 'all you have to do is explain you're not bothered about the bishop and you're writing a book about the Church and celibacy and stuff.'

I was quite sure that some literary hyena would undertake the task of describing the circumstances of the bishop's fall in prurient detail, but I would not care to endanger my immortal soul, nor what little reputation I have, by doing it myself.

We arrived in Mullingar and went to Mass. The church was crowded and there was standing room only. The service began with a woman singing a song I didn't recognise, then the priest came on. 'In the name of the Father and of the Son and of the Holy Spirit,' he began and added the sacred words, 'Good morning, everyone.' The congregation dutifully chorused 'Good morning, Father.' Here a thought occurred to me. If the Catholic Church ever has female priests will we have to call them Mother? And why, if so many people want women to take up positions of authority in the Church and play a greater part, is there a general if vague attitude of disapprobation towards such figures as Mother Abbess and Mother Prioress who are now regarded in some circles as autocratic anachronisms? Why, when so many religious have modified or discarded the habit in favour of secular skirts, shirts, cardigans or anoraks, do women aspiring to the priesthood want to dress in the style of their male counterparts in dog collar, surplice and stole?

We left early because the service wasn't doing anything for me. This is doubtless reprehensible but I felt I might as well have been at a

garden fête or parish jumble sale: there was no feeling of reverence or
awe but a general matiness, unconvincing and somehow depressing.

Janet, however, had gained a different impression. She was unusually
silent as we approached the car park until she suddenly said, 'That
was absolutely terrifying.' 'Why?' I asked, surprised. 'It was blind,
mindless obedience.' It transpired that she had also felt oppressed by
the number of people. 'But Janet,' I said, 'you've been to dozens of
Masses before.' She said this one was different: it had reminded
her of a Nuremberg rally. Talking further we concluded that the
traditional Mass had been unequivocally an occasion for the worship
of God at which the devout concentrated on matters eschatological
and the less committed thought about something else. Janet said
that she had only experienced such a crowd once before when
she had been present at a Cup Final, and that had frightened
her too: she had detected an enthusiasm in the church which had
been less religious than tribal. I thought she had read too much
into it; she said she was glad to be out in the fresh air.

We went to visit friends in Tuam: John and Norah, a young couple
with six children, the baby glaring at us from its pram in the way
of babies while the rest played in the garden, the gate to the road
fortified by a number of bicycles.

We had had trouble finding the place, for the houses were not
numbered and we had to ask some builders up on a roof if they
knew where the O'Connors lived. They conferred amongst themselves
until deciding that the O'Connors lived in the old O'Shea house a bit
further down. Two priests had earlier guided us to the street, knowing
the O'Connors well, but not their precise location. We thought that
life must be difficult for the postman.

John and Norah looked tired, as any young couple with six
children must. They said their faith was unshaken but Casey had
done a lot of harm to the Church and should have resigned rather than
live the life of a hypocrite. He had done more damage by that than by
the sin, and by staying on for seventeen years had blackened everyone
else in the Church. John said that Annie Murphy had given too
much detail to the press, and having kept silent for seventeen years
should have continued to do so. The thing was, said Norah, that if
you decide to keep a secret, whatever your motive – be it loyalty or
merely discretion – you should keep it all your life. Otherwise there
isn't any point in silence. Why should her son, as he was claiming,

suddenly feel the need of a father after all these years? On the other hand, Norah continued, it sounded as though she really was in love with the bishop, who was a man of great charm, although no oil-painting. When Annie Murphy had arrived at the airport in Ireland he had taken her hand and, not having been reared in the country where she would have understood that many priests are like this, warm and outgoing, she had misconstrued the gesture and been enchanted by the thought of capturing a bishop. Then again, too many women appeared to think it might be clever to ensnare a member of the clergy: there was a young priest in town and the girls flocked round him like flies, never leaving him alone. They don't have the same respect for the cloth that they did once, Norah added. This was not surprising when members of the clergy elect to go around in jeans and jumper, thus rendering themselves, from the highest possible motives, indistinguishable from the laity, but in Ireland the priests appear to dress in the traditional fashion, so the lack of respect must spring from some other cause. One possible reason was a failure to agree about certain basic issues. Norah said she had been advised by one priest that she could practise contraception without a single qualm of conscience. A second told her that under no circumstances was she even to consider it, while a third admitted frankly that he hadn't the faintest idea what she should do.

Janet, who was exceedingly well brought up, said she would as soon pinch the altar plate as make a pass at a priest. We thought about it in silence for a time. The priest-hunter or man-eater has been around for a long while but is now less readily recognised than once she was. Western society, with its innocent trust in the sacred quality of sex, imagines that the female circling the cleric has fallen hopelessly in love with him and must not be denied her satisfaction. The situation is often more complicated than this. Wherever there are clusters of males – from schools and universities to barracks and ports – there will be females in predatory mood intent on conquest. Pop groups and now clergymen are particularly at risk since co-education and the running down of the armed forces have led to a shortage of defined communities of men. But whereas pop stars may be regarded as fair game, being well able to look after themselves, priests are more like a protected species in a game reserve and the woman intent on bagging one is a poacher rather than a big-game hunter. 'If I had seduced a priest I should feel as shame-faced and uneasy as if I were wearing the pelt of some rare and vulnerable beast,' I said eventually. 'I don't see that it would give one a sense of achievement,' 'Well, of course it wouldn't,' said Janet scornfully.

'Would you like to meet the bishop?' enquired John. 'I'll just give him a ring.' Sadly the bishop was not at home but it was instructive to realise how easily available are Irish bishops to their flock; in England it is necessary to write letters and make appointments. Also, on reflection, few English Catholics seem to find it necessary to visit their bishops with any great frequency. I did once try to ask an English archbishop a pointed question but his secretary wouldn't allow it.

Our time in Ireland was drawing to an end. We heard some more jokes – 'How do you play safe chess? Put a condom on the bishop' and 'Casey confessed to Cardinal Sin, "Bless me, Sin, for I have fathered."' We also had yet another meal of bacon, eggs, etc. By now the question uppermost in my mind was: why did the Irish breakfast never vary? I felt there must be some EC directive on the matter, and asked our last hostess what it was all about. Why, for instance, could one not sometimes have fish? She was astounded by the suggestion and said that one simply never did. It was consoling to know that there are some things about which there is absolute certainty.

*   *   *

On the boat back to England, a vessel which resembled in many respects a floating motel or motorway café and was not dissimilar in some aspects to the modern churches we had seen, with carpet-tiles, plastic and potted plants, I wondered if I had learned anything. Perhaps only what I knew already – that there was confusion in the Church and great differences of opinion, attitude and approach, combined with a widespread disinclination to admit that this was so. Some of these differences were exemplified by the communications on the parish noticeboards – which varied from offers of secular help for every conceivable human misfortune, such as alcoholism, suicidal depression and inability to relate to the neighbours, to a handwritten letter from a woman informing the community that she had just been visited by Our Lady who had warned her that dire consequences would follow if the people voted Yes for Maastricht. Some parishes offered Benediction, others did not, some had many statues, others none. In some the Eucharist was housed centrally, in others to the side, and the style of celebration of Mass varied according to the whim of the priest.

In one matter, however, I found unity: I had met not one person who believed that Bishop Casey had single-handedly brought the Rock of Peter crashing to the ground. Whatever was amiss with the Church, and it would be vain to pretend that all was well, stemmed from some other cause or causes, and had begun long before the bishop's activities had initiated the latest debate on celibacy.

I went back to Liverpool to see what had happened there. I had long been baffled as to how a religion which had inspired the building of Chartres could also have led to the committing of Liverpool Cathedral, but I found few people who shared my opinion of it. Most professed themselves perfectly contented with the awful thing. There was something about its appearance, apart from its datedness, which worried me for reasons I couldn't quite fathom until I realised it resembled nothing so much as one of those annoying attachments which come with the recherché items of kitchen equipment which you buy in a moment of enthusiasm and then can't remember the use of – the things that grate as they grind as they chop, or possibly the thing that goes in the dishwasher to facilitate the application of salt. The Parliament Building in Wellington has a similar effect: it looks like the vital component of a vacuum cleaner but New Zealanders seem quite fond of it, referring to it as 'the Beehive'. I suppose if you live in the vicinity of these edifices the shock wears off after a while.

Visiting some people I had not seen for years I found again that smiling determination to deny that there is anything awry in the Church – despite the fact that the Vatican and many theologians are seldom in accord and that there is laxity, confusion and an abundance of what used to be called heresy until it was decided that this was rude and everyone was entitled to his own opinion. They asked if I did not remember how stern the old regime had been, how as a postulant all my letters both incoming and outgoing had been read by the Mistress of Novices, how we had not been permitted close friendships or any personal freedom and had been discouraged from meeting the glances of passing strangers. I remember not minding any of these rules, finding them quite within the terms of the way of life I had undertaken. I saw the inadvisability of exclusive relationships within a community, had no clearer idea then than I have now of precisely what personal freedom means or entails, and appreciated the unwisdom of making eyes at passers-by. Now, of course, the same unwelcome advice is offered to all women, 'Don't go out alone in unfrequented places: never make eye-contact with approaching strangers but look away and lengthen your stride.' Even men are now advised to practise what was known as 'custody of the eyes'.

When I had to leave the convent I was most unhappy but I am now thankful I wasn't there when the changes began, for I could not have coped with such a revolution in the required spirit of Christian forbearance. I was never so carefree in all my life as when I was a postulant, but when I say this now to existing religious or many other Catholics they look away or change the subject. They do not wish to hear because they must believe the old regime was oppressive, harmful, inhumane and outdated; they must believe they have progressed to a more enlightened state of affairs and added to the sum of human happiness. When I point out that the supply of vocations has virtually ceased they agree that it is regrettable but perhaps inevitable and there may be good reasons for it. The likeliest reason, which is that the religious life has been robbed of direction and integrity, is one that they do not care to entertain. There are still some excellent, devoted and hard-working nuns, yet few are joining them because few can see the point. Some claim that the reason for this lamentable dearth is that the promises of Vatican II have not been properly implemented, which is similar to the cry of some in the Labour Party who insist that they would attract more members if they were seen to be more left wing.

Whatever else the Church may or may not have lost in its attempts to march easily with the modern world – cohesion, purpose and credibility all seem in doubt – it has certainly lost style. Style has implications of individuality, of élitism, and is suspect in a climate devoted to the imposition of homogeneity; the proposition that all are not merely equal but the same. Differences of race, class, religion and even sex are seen as threatening and divisive and consequently minimised. The fascistic implications of nominalism, of political correctness, of homogeneity, the pretence that basically we are all the same are evident. If individualism is seen as élitist the individual must be suppressed. The message, decoded, reads: 'If you think about it you will see that you are just like me, so that's all right. Do not refer to yourself as black, female, crippled, homosexual or "different" in any way, for that cannot be tolerated.' It is forbidden to dance alone to a tune inaudible to others.

The old-style nun tended to have a bracing quality about her which could be described as severity, and none the worse for that. Severity is more conducive to an accompanying sense of humour than is sentimentality. Sentimentality has, in many instances, clouded over the Church's once robust and clear-sighted view of flawed human nature, of original sin, and given rise to a pretence that with a few changes such as the abolition of poverty and a proper appreciation of the rights of man – which some would present as the supremacy of woman – all our problems will fade away, and sweetness and light will prevail. I could not understand why some older nuns who now decry the old convent ways had ever joined in the first place if they found the rules so crushing.

It will become apparent that I am no theologian. I am something quite different: a believer in God, a stubborn, simple soul. As the Ba'al Shem Tov, a great Hasidic rabbi, said to a learned man who was wrestling with a rational explanation for the existence of God, 'You are brooding on whether God is: I am a fool and believe.' When I joined the Church it formed, as it were, a suitable framework for my convictions and my aspirations. I was not converted by the Church; I was converted by God, but found, in the Church, an appropriate system of guidance through life. Its tenets made perfect sense in the light of my experience. This experience was as follows and may go some way to explaining why I see God as 'other', as a transcendent Being who exists of Himself, not as immanent, a sort of world spirit.

I once realised that, for me, He was not there – He had gone, had withdrawn – and the desolation was the desolation of Hell. I was alone and powerless in a void. There was no darkness, no merciful shadow, only an all-encompassing relentless light, and I was aware of nothing but my own vileness and powerlessness. I was surrounded by people and was, as I always have been, much loved, but the love of human beings was irrelevant and useless. Nothing could touch or communicate with me. All the comfort in the world, the 'counselling', the psychoanalysis, the reassurance and affirmation could do nothing to help: no probings of my psyche, no pills, potions, drugs or strong drink could do anything to alter the state, nor the glories of nature or the kindness of people.

Sometimes I felt like a blind and limbless creature suspended in that cruel light, and sometimes like a container of evil afloat in a sea of evil. I was asked if I felt suicidal and I said I most certainly did not, for if I deliberately broke the container then that which was within me would merge with that which was outside and I would be eternally lost. There was nothing at all I could do to help myself. I do not even remember that I prayed; for even if God had rejected me I knew that He was aware of and had not forgotten me and there was nothing that I could add. I was unable to live or die, only lost in an unassailable solitude. It was never suggested that I was out of my mind or even clinically depressed. I know all about depression and it is different from being in Hell.

Then, some six months later, it passed and I knew that I was no longer alone. I would say I had been 'saved' but that word has connotations of emotion and hysteria since it is used by evangelists seeking to convert the masses, and I had no sensation of uncontrollable joy, of ecstasy; rather a sense of infinite comfort. It was a gentle, almost imperceptible process as though an arid well were being filled with water from some distant source. Never before or since have I been *aware* of the existence of God in this way but once in a lifetime is enough. I hesitate to describe it as a 'religious experience' because the term can be misused: nevertheless it shook me out of the atheism to which I am temperamentally inclined. I did not see it as a promise of personal salvation but as a dark illustration of a world without God.

2

Farewell to the Bishop

Nature is cunning; it misleads people and tricks and deceives them, and always has its own interest at heart. But grace walks honestly and openly, it avoids all that has a look of evil about it, and it lays no traps; it does everything solely for the sake of God, in whom it find its ultimate rest.

Thomas à Kempis, *Imitation of Christ*

I pursue my quest – Does anyone care about the bishop? – Views of a parish priest – And of an ex-priest – An Anglican priest on the Church of Rome – Of poached chicken – A storm in a teacup

I was no more than a few weeks into my investigations, nose to the ground as I followed up the sometimes startling trails of contemporary Catholicism, when people began looking at me blankly as I mentioned Bishop Casey. 'Who?' they would enquire. 'Oh, *him*.' For a while the subject of Catholic priests and celibacy had held the public interest: several clerics had copied his example and a number of women had appeared on TV, or written in the newspapers about the anguish they had suffered as a result of getting entangled with a priest. They all appeared to believe that their plight was caused by some force beyond their control. No one suggested that it was, to put it no higher, half-witted to enter into so complicated a situation, and very few dared to say it was wicked – on the part of either the priest or the woman. The general consensus in the media was that it was all the fault of the Church for expecting its servants to take, let alone keep, such demanding vows, and the women involved were invariably treated with tender sympathy.

Out on the streets of England the attitude was different. Few people took the matter as seriously as did the newspaper pundits, and few were as astonished at this evidence of human weakness. There have always been women who for one reason or another, usually a sense of insecurity and inadequacy, pursue priests, doctors, other women's husbands and any male who seems out of reach. There have always been men who allow themselves to be caught. Nor do predatory males, certainly not if they have professions, status and position to maintain, present the appalling danger that some claim. A loud, determined announcement to the effect that if the brute does not instantly unhand you you will report him to the Cardinal, the General Medical Council or his wife will often get you, unscathed, out of presbytery, consulting-room or kitchen; but the evasion of seduction does not make news. It doesn't make fiction either: if people never gave in to their baser instincts the airport bookstalls would be greatly depleted.

Mirth is another undervalued protective device: not mockery, for that might get you murdered, but an unaffected laugh has remarkably anaphrodisiac properties, as does the feigning of insanity. In the past when it was not considered positively suicidal to hitch-hike there were always men who assumed that in return for the price of the petrol they could expect sexual favours from their female passenger. When this became apparent, the craftier girls would announce that they had just made their escape from an asylum where they had also been treated for venereal disease. Under certain circumstances these wiles and ruses are more reliable than a hatpin, an aerosol spray or even a black belt in judo. The view that women should fight men on their own terms is foolish and often dangerous. I would never attempt to smack a male in the jaw unless he was very much smaller than me. The confrontational approach is an inevitable consequence of the idea of 'equality', the notion that there is no significant difference between men and women. It lacks that subtlety that has always been one of woman's more useful skills.

Still I could not find anyone to talk to who was as shocked, horrified and profoundly concerned as were the newspapers by the bishop's adventure. Everyone, male and female, made an effort to remember who I was talking about, shrugged and said it didn't bother them and they couldn't really see why it should bother anybody. Perhaps, I thought, I had been talking to the wrong people in the wrong places. So back in London I went, in the company of our local policeman (to whom we are devoted since he is a person of natural goodness), to ask the opinion of another section of our community: the inhabitants of Arlington House and some who sleep in shop doorways. Many of them are Irish Catholics but they didn't care about the bishop's fall either. They were all sorry for him but it was not he who had caused their faith to waver nor could he be held responsible for their non-attendance at Mass. I went to our local church and talked to some parishioners, male and female, and got the same response to my query about the bishop.

Then I went and rang the bell at the presbytery door. I told the technological device that I wished to speak to a priest and after a while there appeared a young man in T-shirt and whiskers at whom I gazed enquiringly. 'I'm a priest,' he said. 'Good heavens,' I responded, adding that I could have taken him for the man who had turned up to mend the electric light. After this unpromising start we got on remarkably well and I took him home for a couple of beers and asked him what he thought about Bishop Casey.

He began, 'I feel terribly sorry for the old boy, to tell the truth. But it does seem to me (not trying to justify anything that he has done) that, if you are going to sin, err on the side of love.'

I remarked that much depended on how you defined 'love'.

'True, very true,' he agreed. 'But without wishing to say good luck to him, it really was understandable – Casey was one of the most human of bishops. If people have warm personalities, this tends to be the area in which they are going to fall. Why condemn him for it?'

'Well, he did break the rules,' I observed. It is this lawless tendency in the bishop that I deplore, rather than his cavalier attitude to his mistress and child which is sadly common among men who have recovered from the initial enthusiasm of an affair. 'But I have heard it said that the woman mistook his ordinary human warmth for something more and it went from there.'

'Well,' said the priest, 'there are some good things to come out of it. Without wishing to criticise too heavily, the Irish hierarchy has been incredibly arrogant in the past – they're never going to be that again. No bad thing. As for the bishop himself, the amount of work he did in the Third World and among the Irish homeless in London was exemplary. I'd like to see any of his critics come out with that kind of CV.'

I considered this view rather too cosy, since I do not find evidence of human weakness in our leaders endearing but worrying, I prefer to believe that we have a few people who are capable not only of kindness but of heroic virtue. Failure is boring and disappointing and if I had to choose I would prefer the hierarchy to be arrogant and well behaved, not comfortably concupiscent like the rest of us. There is a hint of despair in the cry of 'I *told* you so', an element of disappointment in the apparent satisfaction when idols turn out to have clay feet. The human race, when it thinks it has proved that no one is superior, is partly gratified and partly depressed.

*   *   *

One of my friends, Alexander Lucie-Smith, who is a seminarian with the Rosminian Order, gave it as his opinion that Bishop Casey's undoing was the result of curiosity. Alexander is even younger than the bearded priest and evinces a mix of worldly wit and religious conviction which is now unusual.

Janet made a chicken pie and I invited Alexander to lunch; I was tired of travelling for the moment and decided I could continue the quest by luring people to come to me.

'Poor Bishop Casey,' he said. 'Why go on about him when there must be thousands of other clergymen who have done the same thing? When you are seeking God, every now and then you lose that target and think: What are those around me doing? This is fatal. You begin to look for other targets or fall into that fatal solipsism, saying, "Poor little me. I have given up everything and I am not having any fun." In fact, when you say that, the truth is that you *haven't* given up everything, because what makes you miserable is your own selfishness. The Bishop Casey figure looks for companionship and his great emotional experience here on earth. He should be seeking God, but the heart has gone out of that so he turns elsewhere.'

It occurred to me that people who talk about the sacrifices of the celibate never mention the trouble and strife that spouses and families can cause.

Alexander went on, 'This can also happen on a wider horizon – to whole religious orders. A Jesuit I was speaking to recently said he felt the heart had gone out of his Order. The Society was founded for the greater glory of God, but nowadays they are moving out of Mayfair

to live in council flats in Brixton and are being told they must get
involved in liberation theology and so on. This is solipsistic. We
should look at the Scriptures and realise that they tell us what God
can do and that humans are merely tools in the hand of God.'

The French have a saying, 'No one gets married any more except
for a few Jesuits.'

'People fall into thinking, "So-and-so is conjunctive to my life and
soul,"' continued Alexander. 'They snuggle up and feel wonderful
and spend all their time together. They are creating an exclusive
relationship which shuts out first other people, then God, and then
they end up having sexual intercourse. Bishop Casey had probably
idealised sex – most clergymen do. Catholicism tends to idealise sex
a great deal. It is part of God's creation and wonderful and so
on, but there is a great danger of looking through the fence and seeing
greener grass on the other side. The other thing is some religious
people want to have their cake and eat it – I have given up this and
must therefore have compensation – which is logically absurd. Many
people say the giving-up is not material but spiritual. The great snag
with renouncing your will until you're blue in the face is that it may
well be a different story when it actually comes to the crunch.'

All this made sense to me, but by now I was well aware that
other people took a different approach to the question of how
priests should conduct themselves. I resolved to talk to more people,
wondering what I used to talk about before I started on all this. I
thought it would be interesting to get the views of some ex-priests,
since there are quite a few around at the moment.

'What about Bishop Casey?' I demanded of one.

'That was tragic,' he replied sadly. 'I know Bishop Casey very well
and I think that the whole affair was very sad. He must have carried
the most awful burden for years. He was always such a jolly, open,
caring person and now I know that at the back of his head was this
time-bomb waiting to go off. How he managed all the work he did I
don't know. Probably it's fair to say that he hoped to be able to pay
the money back from somewhere else in due course, but that was the
least satisfactory part of the episode – that he took money from the
diocesan account to pay her off. God knows what sort of pressure was
being put on him. I don't know how you answer the dilemma.'

'Would it have been better if he had just owned up?' I asked,
thinking it would have saved him a lot of grief in the long run.

'Yes, although he would have had to give up being a bishop. I suppose in his heart he felt: Well, I'm doing a lot of good I think it would have been better to confess at the time   but throughout my life there have been plenty of errors I should have admitted earlier. I'm sure you have been in the same position: none of us live in glass houses. He made a mistake. If he had confessed then people would have said, "Well, there you are, an honest man, he's owned up." He would have lost no respect and would have been a happier person all his life. It's a tragedy,' he concluded.

On the other hand it might have been worse: he might have found himself stuck with Annie for the rest of his days.

Some time later I was standing by the gate of our house – for we were giving a party and I wished to warn unsuspecting guests not to fall over on the steps which were indescribably slippery with some unction that drips off the tree next door – when, lo and behold, along the street there passed a person in a dog collar. Fired with my obsession and forgetting the party I seized upon him, demanding to know whether he was a Roman Catholic priest. He said he was an Anglican on his way to see his bishop. I was not surprised, since so many of our own priests shamble around in civvies in their eagerness not to appear proud. I thought an Anglican viewpoint would be of interest, so then and there I arranged to see him again at a less stressful moment.

He came to lunch. His name, he told me, was Father Brian Rodford.

'What do *you* make of Bishop Casey?' I asked. 'You being an Anglican priest and all.'

He paused reflectively over his poached chicken. We often serve chicken for lunch since it is a versatile and ecumenical fowl and there are many different sauces which the cook can prepare to preserve herself from boredom. 'He was called to a celibate ministry,' said Father Rodford. 'The Church's discipline at the moment is that all priests should be celibate and he accepted that even though he fell short. I have no doubt that he had and continues to have a vocation. It would be awfully sad if all that he has to offer were not allowed to continue.'

I wondered what the Church should have done.

'The Church has always had a problem about how to deal with its renegade and wayward priests,' he said. 'The Roman Church has found it easier because it has such rigid authority structures. We don't have those facilities within the Church of England.'

He took a bite of his chicken. 'Take the whole business of marriage and divorce, for instance. The Roman Church talks about annulments and it gives people the opportunity to see that what was first of all envisaged as a marriage is not a marriage at all. Philosophically, there is a great deal to be gained from looking at it in that way. In the Church of England, a marriage is a marriage, and if it fails you will never be able to marry before God and His congregation in a church again, because you have made a vow and that vow is once and for all.'

'Is that how you see Bishop Casey?' I asked. 'A man who broke his vows? I find it odd that a largely godless society doesn't express much shock or horror at his adultery – the betrayal of a fellow human being – but goes into fits when a man breaks faith with God.'

'In a sense that is the context in which we should see him. The full weight of the Church comes upon him and the judgement of the world, which is sometimes even worse than the judgement of the Church – "Oh look, there is a bishop: he has set himself up as a good and righteous man and look at what he has done." There is nothing worse than facing the world with that sort of accusation hanging over you. Maybe it is providence that he should have been caught out after all these years. I bet he has squirmed and wrung his hands. That might well be where he needs to be – and might be where we need him to be, not being self-righteous and saying "I am a good Christian" and all the rest of it, but identifying with Christ in his suffering.'

Father Rodford had touched upon something which frequently exercises me. There are few people more repulsive than the consciously virtuous Christian, who despite the current prejudice against authority and clericalism is more usually found in the laity than in the Roman Catholic clergy. If goodness is not unassuming it is not goodness. Some sensitive souls, on accused of being good, find it necessary to swear or get conspicuously drunk. The Ba'al Shem Tov is sound on sin: 'I let sinners come close to me if they are not proud. I keep the scholars and the sinless away from me if they are proud. For the sinner who knows that he is a sinner and therefore considers himself base – God is with him for He "dwelleth with them in the midst of their uncleanliness". But concerning he who prides himself on the fact that he is unburdened by sin, God says: "there is not enough room in the world for myself and him".' Chesterton said that there is no saint who does not know himself to be a sinner.

I continued on my way. Speaking to a nun of the new type, I asked nostalgically whether it was permissible to refer to ex-priests as 'spoiled priests', in the old-fashioned manner. 'Ach, *no*,' she responded, horrified. I wondered why she was so emphatic. I suppose people imagine such priests might feel hurt. 'Hurt' is a popular word among the progressives. Most people use it to describe the sensation when they drop a monkey-wrench on their foot, but in a Church context it means they feel slighted or excluded and their sensibilities have been wounded.

I rang up Peter Hebblethwaite, an ex-Jesuit who is described by the media as Britain's 'foremost Vaticanologist', and asked him to come to lunch. He brought along his little boy, whom I furnished with a plate of sandwiches and a bag of crisps and put in front of the telly. Suppressing an impulse to call Peter 'Father', I said, 'What do you think about poor Bishop Casey?' I was starting to feel like Gary Kasparov beginning with his customary opening. 'Do you think he should have confessed at the time?'

'Well, I hope he did.'

'I mean publicly.'

'Not necessarily. We don't have public confession in the Church. A story: in the progressive circles of the university chaplaincy where I go to church we had a sermon on the idea of reviving public confession. It meant, of course, that we should confess our social sins like ignoring the down-and-out or the famine-stricken in Somalia or whatever. A lady arrives while we are doing this and announces, "I have sinned. I have committed adultery with Father X", pointing dramatically at him sitting over in the choir. She adds, "in the mind".'

I pictured this scene for a moment and continued my questions. 'People were very worried in Ireland that the affair went on while Bishop Casey continued to say Mass and perform his episcopal duties. That worries them much more than the affair itself. Were they justified?'

'This is a classic case in canon law – all his Masses and absolutions or whatever would be valid, but in his case sinful. Valid but illicit.'

I do love the niceties of law: they make everything so much more interesting than simple blame and stone-throwing. Some people get

annoyed with this seeming casuistry but it make an engrossing study
for those who like that sort of thing.

Peter continued, 'My view – but I seem to be the only one who
holds it – is that he should not have resigned. I don't think he was
pressured to do so by the Holy See. It is to do with what you think
a bishop is. Going back to a conciliar document – a bishop, by divine
right and by virtue of his sacrament of ordination, is always a bishop.
He can't be removed unless he is contumacious – another canonical
word. By this time he was not. He had acknowledged his sinfulness
and the child, and tried to make reparation. So I think he should have
stayed. A repentant bishop would be rather a good thing, because his
flock are no doubt equally needful of repentance in different ways.
The fact that bishops are sinners too would be a useful lesson. Casey
talked about going to Latin America, but I have been told that he is
quite incapable of learning Spanish, so he would be no use there. So
some monastery sufficiently remote for the rest of his days? Maybe
after ten years he could resurface as the third curate in a parish.'

'He seems', I said, 'to be contrite and prepared to do penance,
which is unusual these days. No politician ever admits to wrongdoing,
or sees it as a reason for resigning his post.' His contrition, I feel, sets
us a better example than his error.

'It was commonly said of him by everyone who wrote about it
that he lived "in the fast lane",' Peter went on. 'What do you think
that means?'

'He was done for drunk driving,' I suggested.

'Certainly as a driver he did live in the fast lane – he drove
very, very erratically and fast.'

'I think that was the Irishman rather than the bishop,' I said
reflectively, having known several adventurous Irishmen.

'Yes, but it was really a metaphor,' he explained somewhat unnecessarily. 'Some of the Irish tried to say that he was seduced by
this poor little American. That seems to me an absurd idea. You're a
novelist; you know about how seduction happens. It's a fairly mutual
thing.'

'I think it is due to what is called the "occasions of sin",' I
answered modestly.

'Somebody has to take the lead, and in this case it was the bishop.
There was no point in keeping a hideaway on the Atlantic coast
unless he had something in mind. Perhaps it was just the risk. It was

quite common at that time for people to talk about the "spirituality of risk".'

'What did they mean by that?' I asked.

'That you haven't tested yourself unless you have been through temptation,' he explained.

'Like the desert fathers with naked ladies in their caves? I think that's a very silly idea.' I have sometimes been near a packet of fags and vowed not to smoke them. It doesn't work.

'Yes, I think so too,' he agreed.

'I think it far more sensible to avoid the occasions of sin,' I remarked piously.

It was said of the Anglican, Bishop Ball, that he had always chosen to live on the knife edge of spiritual risk and he fell over, making indecent advances to a young monk. He said, as indeed did Bishop Casey, that he was motivated by the desire to comfort and help someone in considerable distress. The human ability to kid oneself is truly extraordinary.

I was beginning to feel that the business of Bishop Casey had indeed been a storm in a teacup and had been drained to the dregs. I hope he can get on peacefully with the rest of his life. By now it was no longer the inadequacies and misfortunes of one man which held my attention, but the variety of preoccupations prevalent among those who are not infrequently described as 'God's people'. There is something about this phrase that I distrust: it has exclusive, cultic connotations and sounds smug. If they're Catholics that's what I call them. Because some of them choose to be celibate they are often considered hung up on the subject of sex. Since this is western society's current favourite subject I thought I'd have a look at that next.

3

The Two-Backed Beast

Sex as a word had not been mentioned in Miss Marple's young days; but there had been plenty of it – not talked about so much – but enjoyed far more than nowadays, or so it seemed to her. Though usually labelled Sin, she couldn't help feeling that that was preferable to what it seemed to be nowadays – a kind of Duty.

Agatha Christie, *A Caribbean Mystery*

The abuse of sex – The evils of psychiatry – Sexuality versus spirituality – The violence of sex – The gruesome twosome – A Vaticanologist speaks – A married couple on sex – Where self-sacrifice comes in – First thoughts on celibacy

I have never had a great interest in or reverence for the topic of sex. On a personal scale it comes somewhere around soccer and sociology. Many of its manifestations are as distasteful as the public expression of gluttony: representations of those 'steaming heaps of flesh' might, as well as inciting the lustful to excess, incline the fastidious to abstention. Neither of these effects is desirable, since those who choose to be celibate should do so for more positive reasons than simple revulsion. It is surely sex, not religion, which is the opium of the people. A cunning tyrant might encourage his subjects to ever greater indulgence, since it clouds the judgement and blunts the sensibilities.

A creature of another species relying on, say, fission as a means of perpetuating its kind, or a being from another planet, might wonder at our human arrangements, at the chaos they cause, the misery, strife, the turbulent emotion, the disease and the violence. He would consider that such a dangerous force as human sexuality required strict control and stringent rules of behaviour. He would be

bewildered at the saying of the old man that sex 'was the loveliest
little thing in the world and they had to go and make a sin of it'. He
would be puzzled by the respect accorded by many churchmen to
this antinomian drive and baffled by the widespread claims that it
was a primary source of fulfilment and joy. The man who speculated
that resurrection might be experienced as a giant orgasm was clearly
not familiar with the saying *post coitum omne animal triste est*, an
intimation of the innate loneliness of each soul, and evocative of the
desolation of Hell rather than the fullness of Heaven.

The same man has also proposed that taking the Eucharist is an
experience as intense as, and similar to, sexual intercourse. As he is
male this is the nearest he can get to imagining a sense of reality,
of tangibility. He neglects the fact that a virgin mother gave birth
to, and with her body fed, a Son who remained a virgin and with
His substance feeds us: our personal experience of God is not so
much that of a lover as that of a child. People once thought that
the mother pelican fed her young from the blood of her breast and
so used the pelican as one image of Christ. Few men seem able to
conceive of love in anything but sexual terms.

Wyndham Lewis wrote that 'very naturally, sensation left to itself
tends to get monopolised by the dominant current of sex'; for
the modern writer 'desires in the deepest way to see everything
converted into terms of sex, to have everything and everybody
on that violent, scented, cloying and unreal plane, where there
is nothing that cannot be handled, the very substance of illusion
sniffed at and tested by everybody, and put to the use of sensation.
In that world most of the values of the intellect are reversed.' It is
no longer just the modern writer but often the modern priest as well.
Our spirituality must be in a sorry state indeed if we now have no
model of love other than sex.

In the search for 'transcendence' sexuality has been as much
abused as drugs but mystical experience is different in kind from
all others and is reached through austerity, not self-indulgence.
Trying to decide why I find the clergy in particular preaching the
beauty of sex so suspect and so depressing, I concluded that they
remind me of Nanny suddenly announcing that jam is good for
you and you're going to have it every day for breakfast, dinner
and tea, and *like* it. The cynical child not only loses its enthusiasm
for jam, it wonders whether it might be Nanny who has the sweet

tooth. It is also possible that Nanny has never tried jam but has heard that it is simply delicious.

As the psychiatric establishment would put it, the decline of religion and the malaise of society at present is over-determined. Much of the blame can be laid at the door of the psychiatric establishment itself. For instance, in the attempt to demystify sex, inhibition became confused with prohibition and taboo was flung aside. That dangerous creature, the Great Thinker or Ideologue, concluded that humanity would be healthier and happier if it was encouraged to do as it pleased. Freud had already sown the seeds of his own disrepute when he denied that some of his patients had actually been abused by their parents and maintained that their disturbance was due to unresolved 'oedipal conflict'. His followers went further. In 1946, in a book called *Sex and the Social Order*, Georgene Seward wrote on the subject of incest: 'the available scientific data tend to underemphasise the importance of prepubertal sex aggressions for later adjustment. Indeed in some cases, far from being the pitiable victim of sexual attack, the child himself has acted as aggressor, apparently deriving positive satisfaction from the experience with no trace of guilt or anxiety.' This could serve as an introduction to a paedophile's charter, and, while few of the general public will have read works of this kind, its views were disseminated like spores on the wind. In the famous case of 'Dora', Freud insisted that it had been 'hysterical' of her to spurn (when she was fourteen) the advances of the paedophile Herr K. Going further, he suggested that she had been in love with him all along.

The idea that the sex drive was of paramount importance in human development reached its logical conclusion in the 1960s when it became widely accepted that sexual activity itself was of paramount importance. Freud, who described religion as 'the enemy', had contrived, albeit unwittingly, to create a new religion (or possibly two, since to its adherents psychoanalysis has the status of religion). This has been insidiously pernicious in its effects, neglectful of the true nature of humanity and offering licence to the expression of selfishness, lust and personal gratification. Freud, as Rudolf Allers pointed out in *The Successful Error*, 'conceives of love only as a particular way of attaining instinctual satisfaction', seeing the other only as a 'sexual object'. There are many who would reject this judgement, but the effects of Freud's theories are undeniable and have influenced even the 'enemy' which he was so concerned to destroy. The 'counselling' and 'therapy' which have in many cases replaced confession and the sacrament of penance are perhaps the most notable proof of this, but the nervous concurrence of much of the clergy in the notion that sexual congress is the most glorious experience available to mankind is more worrying in its implications.

A correspondence in the *Catholic Herald* illuminates – or not, depending on one's ability to grasp the apparent complexities – the divergences of opinion between those who see sexuality as inimical to spiritual development and those who do not. One correspondent stated that 'human beings liberated from sexual instinct can use their energy to grow into "spiritual" things', while another takes issue with her, suggesting that 'to aspire to be liberated from our sexual instinct is to aspire to be liberated from our humanity'. He says, 'we don't achieve wholeness and holiness in spite of our sexuality but because of it', and here he loses me. This sort of remark is frequently made by the liberally inclined but is meaningless. In a recent issue of the *Evening Standard* a letter from a person incensed at the revelation that Islam disapproves of homosexuality stated that this merely went to prove the 'evil of all religion'. The current reverence for sex and sexual expression leads to some curious conclusions. If we are to be liberated from all the old taboos, then sooner or later paedophilia will again try to move out into the open, claiming free expression as its right.

The appalling incidence of child abuse recently revealed as prevalent among the American Catholic clergy does not suggest that a relaxation of the celibacy rule would obviate the problem but rather that the climate of opinion has had a grossly corrupting influence. The Church of England, which does not demand celibacy of its clergy, has long had trouble with those of its vicars who have a penchant for choirboys.

That climate of opinion is not something confined to the pages of the tabloid press or esoteric journals. Dr Jack Dominian is a leading Roman Catholic psychiatrist who appears not to think highly of babies, finding them threatening. 'The arrival of a baby has a serious adverse impact on the life of a couple. Their freedom, intimacy, affection and sexuality suffer and when this is severe it may destroy their marriage.' He thinks very highly of sex. In an approving review of *Childhood and Sexuality: A Radical Christian Approach* by John L. Randall, Dominian writes: 'the author begins by outlining

the pessimistic Christian attitude to sex, which has prevailed until
the middle of this century, and after a brief interruption in the
1960s and 1970s is on the ascendant once again.' We learn that
the author is 'compassionate to paedophile tendencies in which he
takes particular pain to distinguish what he considers the love of
children by men who are gentle and shy and the viciousness of
those who seduce children for sadistic reasons'. This is the sort
of thing that causes the mind to reel. Is the author not aware
that children who have been subjected to sexual attention by their
elders are bitterly unhappy and disturbed? We knew one of these
gentle and shy paedophiles. He also was unhappy and disturbed
and we felt sorry for him – but our children regarded him with
an instinctive mistrust and loathing, invariably referring to him as
Ned the Ped. The Pope has said that priests who abuse children
stand in danger of damnation, which makes very much more sense
than the suggestion that the children enjoy it. I remember my own
childhood horror of men who came too close and the feelings of
freedom and relief when they went away. That anyone can regret the
excesses of the 1960s and 1970s and fail to notice their catastrophic
consequences is beyond my comprehension. The insistence on sex,
on sexual desirability and expression puts the young at risk and
the old in the shadows. The curious assumption that all human
intercourse is somehow related to sexual intercourse has led to
a cheapening, an impoverishment of thought and emotion in social,
religious and artistic terms.

The *Catholic Herald* correspondent writes that 'Sexuality and
spirituality are not and cannot be opposed unless we want to go
back to the dualist philosophy and theology with which Christianity
has been plagued in the past. (I had no sooner digested this when I
came across a passage in a book I had been sent casually observing
that Christianity had ever been concerned with eradicating notions
of duality which had crept in from pagan sources, especially Plato.)
Christianity is now plagued with an attitude which rejects the notion
of sexual sin as being illiberal: the idea arose in American Protestantism but is now respectfully received in some so-called Catholic
circles where it is denied that body and soul are in conflict, and
austerity is perceived as negative.

Lust and sexual greed are still the great nuisance that they
always were, and sex the selfish, lawless force that it always has

been. It was in recognition of this unfortunate fact that rules were first made, and codes of conduct formulated.

It is obvious when it comes to sex that instinct is not to be trusted. For one thing, men and women mean something different by the term and their instincts divide them. For instance, when a woman spends the evening dancing the bacchanalian two-step with a man she may be simply enjoying the music, hoping for a decent meal later or even expecting a proposal. She may, of course, be prepared to end up in bed with the dancer, but she may not, whereas he will almost certainly be considering the possibility as the most satisfactory conclusion to his night out. It was in the attempt to bring the sexes to an understanding and to keep the peace that laws were devised, not some life-denying, puritanical urge to keep them apart. The proposition that women harbour desires and inclinations exactly similar to those of men is largely responsible for the present state of chaos. If men are led to believe that women have the same urges, they will find it difficult to see anything untoward in rape. The bitch, when she says 'No', must be refusing out of sheer cussedness, especially if she is prancing round in vest, peplum and fishnet stockings, tossing her curls. Her 'body language' spells out 'available', what used to be known in less permissive, more cynical times as 'Stop me and buy one'.

I expect that's why nuns used to go round in twos, clad in an unmistakable habit rather than in tangerine jumpers and pearl earrings and make-up.

Yet in the teeth of the evidence there are still those who cheerfully insist that everything is much better now than it was thirty or so years ago, a merry, open, unrepressed climate, free from unhealthy inhibition. They seem not to notice the crime rate nor the divorce statistics, the collapse of family life, the erosion of respect for others, the overall nastiness of society today. And there are still those who persist in regarding unlimited promiscuity as normal, although several pop and film stars have been diagnosed as 'sexaholics' and are undergoing treatment for the condition.

Jeremy Campbell, writing from Washington, begins an article in the *Evening Standard* of 11 August 1993: 'Sexuality, some theologians agree, is beginning to serve the same purpose for American Catholics as the word "soul" did in the Middle Ages.' This was before Columbus stumbled upon that interesting land, but no matter. 'It provides a way of knitting together the various strands of human identity so it makes some kind of sense.' 'Sense' does not seem to me to be the *mot juste* here. He goes on to quote the theologian John Burgess: 'Without our being aware of it, the sexuality debate has become the vehicle for getting at the most basic questions of faith. In many ways the debate about sexuality is not about sexuality at all but about what it means to be human before God. In fact sexuality, so powerful a part of our experience, appears to be real and relevant in a way that theological matters do not. Debating issues of sex distracts us from the nasty suspicion that our faith is empty. . . . Because the Church is no longer sure how to use the language of faith to clarify issues of faith and faithfulness.'

Jeremy Campbell also pointed out that President Clinton had nominated for the post of Surgeon-General a woman who wanted to hand out condoms to nine-year-old primary school children. Perhaps she subscribed to the view that sex is no more than a harmless, friendly recreation, which is curious in the light of certain developments in the States. In an article in *The Times* (15 July 1993) Kate Muir writes: 'The new playground slang in New York for making love is to "hit skins". The phrase cuts out any possibility of affection or commitment: the act is physical, nothing more. Schoolboys use the word "bitch" as a synonym for girl, and schoolgirls use "dog" for boy. Courtship is dead, and in its place is a desire for instant gratification. A popular T-shirt among teenagers says "No more Mr Nice Guy. On your knees, bitch."' Her article deals with the gang rape and murder of two girls aged fourteen and sixteen and the apparent lack of remorse of the teenaged suspects. She tells us that 'in a survey five years ago of 1,700 high school pupils, one in four boys said they believed a man has the right to rape a woman if he spends money on her on a date. What is more, 16 per cent of girls thought that too.' The headline to the article is a quote from one of the boys involved who appeared on a local TV programme before the attack: 'Human life means nothing.' These misguided children have concluded that sex can be separated from love and therefore from all restraint.

Certain theologians, equally unrealistic, are attempting to persuade us that it can be used in the context of the numinous, while certain priests, seeming to imagine that sex needs advertising, witter on about such notions as 'redeemed man and woman walking naked and unashamed in the Garden of God'. They should, one feels, take a closer look at what is already going on in the undergrowth.

*   *   *

Back at my local church I asked my progressive friend whether he did not think that sex was currently overrated, both as recreation and as cosmic force for good.

'Yes, I think it's probably a reaction to the time when it was the last thing you would talk about. Eventually you'll get a kind of balance. At the moment, however, the human family is perhaps just experiencing its adolescence. It's discovered its bits and wants to use them, but hasn't learned how to do so responsibly. But it will in the future.'

I thought this over-optimistic. The evidence seems to point rather to increasing confusion and anarchy in sexual matters. There are women who may be more aware of the positioning and putative purpose of their 'bits' than were previous generations, but who refuse to sleep with their husbands because they regard penetration by the male as an unwarranted intrusion on their privacy. I was going to say 'space', a popular concept, but it sounds indelicate. There are also many women who will not breast-feed their babies because they find it inconvenient, indecent or because it prevents them going out to work. In a saner society they could suckle the child in the intervals between doing deals or pushing dinner trolleys or whatever their jobs involved, but motherhood is not highly esteemed today, and even a page 3 girl would not dare to offer her child a breast in a public place.

Men are similarly confused. The 'sexual revolution' which encouraged women to take the pill and embark on sexual adventure without let or hindrance must have come as a pleasant surprise to them – girls no longer spun round and smacked their faces, explaining they were 'nice' girls and didn't do that sort of thing. But now if they so much as wink at one in the street they can be accused of criminal harassment. They're not allowed to be chivalrous and they're not allowed to be beasts. This has led to deplorable misunderstandings and a loss of male confidence. There is a group of young men in the north of England who would once have raced whippets or competed to see who could drink the most pints of ale, but who now spend

their leisure time sleeping with as many females as they possibly
can. Somebody keeps the score. This apparently gives them a sense
of masculine worth and solidarity.

One of my friends, Stuart Mason, was briefly convinced that
the freedoms of the sixties were a sign of the progress of humanity.
He has changed his mind and is now a seminarian at Ushaw. I
turned to him for a little common sense, and invited him to lunch.
He too had chicken. I worry about seminarians in case they are
not being properly fed. I once had a conversation with Stuart in
which he told me that no waste was permitted in the seminary. I
said I entirely approved and had many ingenious ways of utilising
leftovers. A moody expression clouded his face as he asked whether
I had ever considered quiche soup. (Al the driver often reminds
me that I once put some redundant sausage rolls in his lentil
soup.)

'Very few people dare say anything that's not adulatory about
sex,' I began. 'They do now admit that you have to be careful,
but they're terrified of suggesting that anyone should refrain from
doing it.'

Stuart was eating his chicken appreciatively. It was lemon-
flavoured. We add the juice to the stock in which it is cooked
and then scrape a little zest into the cream or yoghurt which finishes
the dish. I find food a more interesting topic than sex but dragged
my mind back to the subject under discussion.

He looked up. 'The Church could have said something quite
sharply to that effect,' he observed, 'instead of seeming to spend
all its time saying how wonderful sex is. It does seem now rather
vieux jeux to hear Catholic pundits, often bishops, saying "The
Church is not against sex, you know. The Church is in favour of
sex. Intercourse is the matter of the sacrament of matrimony." All
of which is true and, in the 1990s at least, deeply unremarkable,
but if that is *all* the Church seems to be saying then it seems to
be assenting to the world's claim (world used as in "the world,
the flesh and the devil") that a fulfilled life is a *sexually* fulfilled life. I speak of the English Church as it has been reported
in the press and on television. I would scarcely be being fair to
the Pope, who has spoken most intelligently about married sexual
love, but who has been either ignored or quoted out of context
to make him look ridiculous.'

I found this fair comment. There was much more that Stuart said, but more on the subject of celibacy than sex *per se* – and which I shall quote later when I have left sex behind.

After Stuart had gone I recalled an Irish priest who told me that his mother had said to him, 'The thing is, you'll never want for a loaf of bread or a jug of water', meaning that on the whole he was going to have a good life. She herself had had a hard life with dozens of children and not enough money and she certainly didn't idealise sex. People with dozens of children seldom do. She'd been with her husband long enough to get over any illusions about men, even that another man might be an improvement on him. Poverty doesn't leave time for romantic illusions. You have to get on with living. Apart from the fact that it's wonderful to give a son to the Church, I think she was simply delighted to think her beloved child would have enough to eat and was not at all concerned that he would have no sex life. Unbridled sexuality has ever been a sign of heathenism and decadence and does not recommend itself to harassed and hard-working mothers. I don't think women ever do idealise sex in the way men do (or at least they never used to). Not like D. H. Lawrence, who had 'a positive belief that the phallus is a great and sacred image: it represents a deep, deep life which has been denied us and is still denied'. To give Lawrence his due, although I have never liked him, finding him humourless, hysterical and deplorably unsympathetic to Frieda's grief for the children he had persuaded her to abandon, he did do the cooking and the washing-up when he wasn't fussing about the phallus, Aztec blood sacrifices, mystical and savage abandonments of the self, abstract sex rage, etc.

It is a well-known masculine ploy, tried and trusted, to tell the unwilling female, not that she is ungenerous for refusing to submit to the wishes of the male, for that might be indicative merely of his lust and selfishness, but that she is sadly repressed and doing herself psychological damage by resisting him: this gives an impression of altruism. Ever since, and doubtless long before, Andrew Marvell tried to alarm his coy mistress by going on about the grave, men have tried to persuade women that unlimited sexual congress is entirely beneficial and eminently *natural* and all that really matters in the overall scheme of things – especially men who move in artistic and intellectual circles. As Stella Gibbons put it in *Cold Comfort Farm* in 1932:

It cannot be said that Flora really enjoyed taking walks with Mr Mybug. To begin with, he was not really interested in anything but sex. This was understandable, if deplorable. After all, many of our best minds have had the same weakness. The trouble about Mr Mybug was that ordinary subjects, which are not usually associated with sex even by our best minds, did suggest sex to Mr Mybug, and he pointed them out and made comparisons and asked Flora what she thought about it all. Flora found it difficult to reply because she was not interested. She was therefore obliged merely to be polite, and Mr Mybug mistook her lack of enthusiasm and thought it was due to inhibitions. He remarked how curious it was that most Englishwomen (most young Englishwomen, that was, Englishwomen of about nineteen to twenty-four) were inhibited. Cold, that was what young Englishwomen from nineteen to twenty-four were.

When I was at the art school the place hummed to the sound of men of all ages, shapes and sizes broadcasting this intelligence to the females. The twentieth century is obsessed with sex as was the nineteenth with death. George Orwell wrote, 'I really think that this modern habit of describing love-making in detail is something that future generations will look back on as we do on things like the death of Little Nell' (*Collected Essays, Journalism and Letters*, vol. 4).

Living in the world, I find frequent cause to deplore the emphasis put on relationships. The kitchen is thronged with people I often hardly know, worrying away about their loves and loathings and the neuroses they engender. 'Be still and know that I am God' is a phrase that I constantly invoke, and 'it'll all be the same in a hundred years'. I cease to wonder that there are so many millions of therapists and counsellors about. I yearn for the calm, remote benevolence that I have found in convents (the old-fashioned sort, that is; I am told that many now are hotbeds of strife and dissatisfaction) where scrupulous courtesy was once the order of the day, no one bothered you to 'share with them' any psychological unrest you might be experiencing, or reproached you for keeping yourself to yourself. If you were miserable for whatever cause, there was always someone you could go to, but there was none of the hysterical emotionalism now so prevalent. No one ever said 'Get out of my space', because there was no need to. Besides, then, if you spoke at all you spoke in English, not jargon. If your mind is concentrated on God you have no time for the sore distraction of jealousies, squabbles and wounded feelings, or even singing and dancing and staying up late. Stable relationships are doubtless necessary to human development and comfort but are not of continuing overriding importance.

How many people, when they get better, look back on their passion with bewilderment wondering: what on earth was all that about? A friend, just the other day, lay on her sofa idly smoking a cigarette and listening to her answerphone. Twenty-eight years ago, she said, she'd have killed to possess the speaker exclusively; his infidelity had caused her unspeakable torment, she had loved him to the point of desperation and now she couldn't be bothered to pick up the phone. 'Funny, that,' she said.

*   *   *

I decided to talk to my friend Stoddard Martin, an American professor and Harvard scholar who can be relied on to take a historical perspective and not mince his words. What, I asked, did he think about sex?

He began, 'Any man who has gone through periods of both sexual activity and inactivity will recognise the effect on one's personality is substantial. In periods of great sexual activity one is more passionate, more liable to emotional outbursts, more liable to fights; in periods of celibacy one begins to realise that the sexual issue is able to fall away. It's not entirely a pat matter – in young men periods of sexual inactivity can lead to a kind of frustration and violence. But if you sustain non-sexual activity for long enough you will become calmer – a less biologically fertile personality might be the way to express it. Your sperm is not ejaculating as often: the whole business of your body creating sperm begins to abate, and the metabolic effects that come with the creation of sperm and its ejaculation are altered as well. When you look at phenomena like the Charles Manson cult, in which sexual activity was very rampant, you find an association between excessive sexual activity and physical violence, leading to murder. It was the same with the Marquis de Sade – his sex fantasies were continuous and developed greater and greater aspects of violence until they became fantasies of mutilation.'

I was gratified to find some confirmation of my view that sex is
not necessarily the calming and benevolent influence it is frequently
claimed to be. The exponents of 'flower power' with their rallying
cry of 'Make love not war' had neglected to take into account the
fact that the two are often synonymous. I sometimes think that
all strife has its roots in the strife between the sexes beginning
with the contretemps in the Garden of Eden. Perhaps it is in
unconscious acknowledgement of this that many people now seek
to claim that if there is any difference between male and female it is
only minimal and can be overcome by encouraging them to behave
similarly in all circumstances.

'But, if one looks at society more broadly,' Stoddard continued,
'simple logic will tell you that the dedication to any enterprise
requires sexual discipline – perhaps even abstinence, or "no fucking
around" to put it in the vernacular of our day. Think of athletes in
training – they simply don't screw when they're working up towards
a big event. The scandal of David Mellor and his actress friend is
really that he was too knackered to do his job as Heritage Secretary
after staying up all night to screw five times at the age of forty-six.
I can't understand why he didn't resign immediately after the affair
became public knowledge, nor why the Prime Minister and the people
seem to have turned a blind eye to such obvious dereliction of duty
in favour of self-gratification. It doesn't matter a bean what you or
I may get up to; but, with a person in a position of public trust
and power, a bit of good, old-fashioned self-control seems to me
something we all have a right to demand.

I observed that five times a night sounded to me like boasting, but
Stoddard resumed: 'There is one more issue here. That's the question
of what sex is all about. What is semen after all if not the most
obvious component of the Life Force? Perhaps most men can produce
an infinite amount of it. Nevertheless, I wonder if it doesn't have a
kind of sacred, if not sacramental, quality. I suspect D. H. Lawrence
thought so. I know the so-called wickedest man in the world, Aleister
Crowley, did. He believed that every sexual act, even masturbation,
should be undertaken in a serious ritualistic manner with a spiritual
goal in mind. With every act, he demanded concentration on a god
(he believed in the existence of many very weird gods) and invocation
of the god's power to affect matters here on earth that went well
beyond sex itself. Crowley, of course, is no model. But the idea that

each sexual act should be undertaken consciously and significantly seems to me to have more merit than regarding sex to be, in T. S. Eliot's phrase, the more "cheery automatism of the modern world". The constant shooting of sperm into the neutered womb – stopped up by the pill or some horrible spermicide – seems to me a form of onanism or worse – the outright making of love to infertility, symbolically very little different to the act of buggery.'

I reflected that I knew of few religious lay people, and fewer churchmen, who would have the nerve to express themselves on the subject of sex in such terms, and remembered a correspondence in a Catholic paper in the course of which a priest gave the impression that many of his parishioners had sobbed themselves to sleep at the suggestion that celibacy might have the edge over sexual expression in the life of the spirit.

Another old idea has recently re-emerged; the notion that 'for every man there's a woman', that either God or nature has designed for each of us the perfect mate who needs only to be discovered to be recognised. Many of the clergy who take a Mills & Boon view of life would doubtless find the argument convincing, but the inherent possibilities of confusion and disappointment are discouraging.

Here I realised that I had not yet asked a married person about his view on sex and marriage. I don't know too many married people, and those I do know tend not to be as decided in their attitudes as the single person who does not need to refer to anyone else before stating his or her position on matters of moment. Many divorces come about because people get tired of being told by their spouses what to think – especially at present when there are so many opportunities for differences of opinion.

I asked Peter Hebblethwaite why he had left the priesthood.

'Love,' he said.

'Ah,' said I, wondering if he had felt much happier when he married.

'Not immediately,' he said. 'For me it was a question of doing the honest thing.'

'So now', I said, 'we get down to this problem of humanity and sexuality. Freud said that sexual relationships were essential to a whole person. Would you agree with that?'

'Some Catholics', he answered, 'used to believe in the possibility of sublimation – that it was possible to gather up those energies available for sexual activity into something else, perhaps for humanity or the revolution. Revolutionaries were often recommended to be celibate. I wouldn't want to say that celibacy is impossible, because I know it's not, but I would also have to add that its successes are pretty rare.'

'You mean that most priests are breaking their vows?' I asked, leaving aside the implicit suggestion that no Catholics any longer thought this way.

'I don't mean in that sense.'

'You mean that most priests are unhappy?' I suggested.

'For me,' he said, 'a successful celibate would have to be a fulfilled one, not just one who had avoided sin, because that would be a negative success. Somebody for whom it is true that the denial of a particular relationship with one woman has not meant a punishment or turned him into a crusty bachelor, but has actually been a fulfilment that opened him to a lot of people.'

'What', I asked, 'do you think about allowing priests to marry?'

'It would be perfectly possible', he replied, 'for the Pope to say that those priests who were laicised and duly married, if they can give proof of sobriety and Christian virtues in their marriages, could be useful as auxiliary priests, especially if there is a shortage. The reason why this won't happen in the present pontificate is it might seem like an incentive to priests to get married.'

'Do you agree with the idea that a married priest couldn't give as much time to the parish as the celibate one, simply because he has to worry about the little woman and the kiddies?' I asked.

'Not at all. Perfectly compatible. Celibate priests do not devote themselves to their parish all the time. You should talk to my wife, Margaret,' said Peter.

So I did.

Margaret Hebblethwaite is a writer and journalist as well as a wife and mother. I sat her down at the kitchen table, for by now the dining table had disappeared under a mass of documents and cuttings about Church affairs and the cat had muddled them further by nesting in them.

'Margaret,' I said, 'your husband left the priesthood to marry you.'

'Let's be precise,' said Margaret. 'He left the priesthood for personal reasons and he married me. This means I have a stake in this question and therefore feel it's not appropriate to be a very outspoken advocate of the position. It's much more important that people who are not married to priests should say what they need for the Kingdom of God. I think as a rule enforced cellbuoy is bad, wrong and counter-productive, but it is the rule; therefore you leave if you want to get married. If they changed it it would be great, wonderful, but I don't think it is appropriate for me to make a song and dance about it.'

'Do you like married people?' I asked, because on the whole I tend not to. A generalisation, but I have a weakness for highly flavoured individuals and there is something in marriage which blurs and dilutes personality. Not to put too fine a point on it, I find couples, married or not, hard to understand and a little boring. Too often it is a case of 'loved him, hated her', or vice versa, of course. I believe that marriage and family are the basis of society and offer the best possible structure for the rearing of children, but I would not voluntarily go out to dinner with a number of married people. I agree with the lady in Somerset Maugham who 'made it a point to ask wives without their husbands, because she said each cramped the other's style and if they didn't like to come separately they needn't come at all.' But perhaps the very blurring of the outlines of personality in the parents is of use in providing an unthreatening environment for the child trying to forge an independent, individual form and existence for himself: an example of the unselfishness and self-sacrifice necessary for the continuation of the species. I have known children of florid and extraordinary parents and they have seldom been happy or contented human beings.

'What an interesting question,' she replied. 'Yes, I think I like married people a lot. There is something quite different about marriage. I used to notice this when I went baby-sitting as a teenager. For instance, with body language – married women didn't give out the same signals as me and my friends. They were not available but still attractive, with a sense of fulfilment and satisfaction beyond the question of whether their marriage was happy or successful. There was a certain amount of experience that they had lived through.'

'They'd caught their man?' I suggested. I know quite a number of married ladies who are dying to prove they can still catch other men. This is truer now than it was in my childhood, although there were always women with a roving eye. Marriage was regarded with more respect, as a final goal rather than a staging post. Married men and women were more interesting when they felt secure in their roles and free to talk of their varied interests. There was not then the feeling that you had to do everything together on terms of 'equality'.

'I think I feel safe with married people,' said Margaret.

'I did some au-pairing too,' I interrupted, 'and I never felt that safe with the husbands. I think they felt they had *droit de seigneur*.'

'You said that,' noted Margaret; 'I'm the one who's meant to be the feminist.'

I continued, 'Why is marriage still regarded as a sacrament? Most people now see it as a secular contract – with added frills if they marry in church.'

'I think it is a sacrament,' said Margaret, 'because when we love someone we see them with the eyes of God, a window into their lovability. We share in God's nature when we love, and an important part of love is fidelity. There is love without fidelity, falling in love or out of love – but we share much more in God's nature when we love faithfully. So I think to love and swear fidelity in ignorance of the future is a sacred thing and rightly called a sacrament.'

'This cuts across certain aspects of feminism,' I observed. 'Lots of women say that women have been denied full sexual experience, by which I think they mean promiscuity, but you don't have to be a feminist to realise that a great many men will try it on if they think they have a chance. Now it's "affirm yourself" – if you want to have a fling, go ahead and do so, you mustn't be bound by these patriarchal rules of fidelity which are all to do with my ox and my ass and my wife. I think a lot of women now feel the marriage bond is very restricting – you are still like a possession.'

'It's a different thing to have an affair if you're not married,' she answered. 'Pre-marital sex is very different from extra-marital sex.'

'But there's a lot of it going on,' I pointed out. 'Some years ago there was a report from the north-east where they did blood tests on a number of families, trying to track down some virus or something. They found they couldn't publish the figures because so many of the children weren't those of the putative fathers, and it would have led to trouble.'

'How awful,' said Margaret.

I agreed. The uncertainty inseparable from paternity is one of the reasons I feel sorry for men. 'I think it must be very difficult to be a feminist Christian,' I said, restrainedly, since I actually think it impossible. I had in mind the ladies who decry marriage as 'legalised prostitution'. Shaw said it first but they've revived the phrase.

'I wouldn't want to identify that with feminism,' said Margaret. 'I've never heard it argued thus. I wouldn't have thought it more common among feminists than those who aren't.'

'Then who are these women who recommend sexual experience so highly,' I asked, 'who advise women to sleep with anyone they fancy?'

'Well, that maybe was the result of the 1960s.'

'It's still going on.'

'There's a good and bad side to it. The rediscovery of sex has had a positive side – I'm very doubtful whether the good boys and girls of the 1930s and 1940s who didn't have sex before marriage had really good sex lives.'

I am constantly amazed at talk of the 'rediscovery of sex'. Where does everyone think it was? But I only said, 'Sexual intercourse wasn't invented in 1963 – a lot of people must have got something right before then. And at least they stayed married on the whole. Now if your sex life isn't up to par you get divorced and try someone else.'

'Yes,' she agreed, 'there *is* too much divorce – but maybe there are too many people getting married. I'm quite keen on discouraging people from getting married.'

'So am I,' I said. Janet and I are given, when we see people approaching churches in bridal attire, to saying *Don't do it*, but only, of course, from the safe seclusion of the car. 'People have been led into unrealistic expectations. We're living in an era of enormous confusion and they'd do better to wait for more settled times.'

'Not as confused as the 1960s – my generation,' said Margaret.

I look back with horror to the 1960s. 'A lot of my friends,' I said, 'took to wearing medallions and flowers in their hair and tearing their shirts down to their navel – both men and women – and were usually vaguely cross-eyed on pot. They all seemed more or less crazy and you could never remember who was having an affair with whom. It was a terrible time to bring up children.'

'Perhaps it was,' she said, remembering it somewhat fondly, 'but I was of the generation of the children. We felt sorry for our parents.'

'As well you might,' I said, thinking that I had been deserving of pity not because I had missed out on the 'swinging', but because feeling like one of the few sane people in a lunatic asylum leads you to wonder if it might not be yourself who's gone potty. People keep telling me not to denigrate the decade because it had its points but I can't see any. 'It seems to me', I went on, 'that both the Church and the world are in confusion. What can the Church do to improve the situation?'

'Well, the Church can only go on being faithful to Jesus and proclaiming what He stood for – forgiveness, justice and sacrifice. Some people are against sacrifice, but I think it is a good thing.'

'That's very unusual today,' I said. 'Certainly self-sacrifice seems to be out of style. I suppose that's part of the problem with marriage. Now that women have been told it's oppressive they see themselves as self-sacrificial if they stay at home. And other people encourage them to go to self-assertiveness classes or whatever, because only idiots sacrifice themselves for others and it all leads to trouble. Marriage is difficult to get right, not merely in the relationship but in society. A happily married couple – when you find one – can seem exclusive and rather offensive to the lonely.'

Margaret agreed with me. 'It is a power-base being married. People sense that with a couple.'

I don't. 'But the world does not seem conducive to contented marriage,' I said.

'The Church must just breach it, not only in words but in action. The martyrs of our age are a treasure to all of us.'

I like the idea of marriage as the only contemporary source of martyrdom. Once it was seen as the happy ending.

Both Peter and Margaret Hebblethwaite had proved interesting, for I had not previously met people with their particular views. After Margaret had left, I thought for a while about the proposition that marriage is to do with seeing people with the eyes of God, through windows into their lovability – and found it unconvincing. It *sounds* all right, but it doesn't bear close examination. Some people marry for romantic and some for practical reasons, and on the whole it seems that the practical stand a better chance of making a success of it. The romantic get so disillusioned and cross when the scales fall from their eyes and it becomes evident that matrimony is, after all, a sadly mundane matter of endless adjustment, hard work and making allowances. Arranged marriages often work better than the spontaneous sort, since those who fix them are not blinded by passion; but in an age obsessed by self-expression and fulfilment and the cult of the individual, people are looking for and expecting happiness. Poor saps.

My doubt about the sacramental character of matrimony is my own pet heresy. I believe, again purely for practical reasons, that you should do it once and stay with it until death intervenes. This is only common sense when you consider the cost, in monetary and emotional terms, of divorce, but has little to do with religion. The concept of the 'soul-mate' was never Catholic and the idea of the couple who are all-in-all to each other is yet another offshoot of Protestantism. Catholicism places an emphasis on the family and on motherhood, not on the relationship of the pair. It is as much a matriarchal as a patriarchal religion and the bride and groom are of less significance than their purpose – the procreation of children. I just have to remind myself that Christ chose the marriage at Cana as the occasion for his first miracle and 'whom God hath joined together let no man put asunder'. George Eliot wrote in *Middlemarch*, 'But the door-sill of marriage once crossed, expectation is concentrated on the present. Having once embarked on your marital voyage, it is impossible not to be aware that you make no way and that the sea is not within sight – that, in fact, you are exploring an enclosed basin.'

I have known a few happy, successful marriages (I apply this term to those which have lasted thirty or forty years or so, other-wise it's too soon to judge), and they have had in common that sense of mutual regard, more usual in friendship, whereby neither merely tolerates the other: they greatly rely on each other for support and esteem and each seems to have for the other the depth of concern and affection which is usually given only to children. When death does intervene they are lost, having invested everything in that one relationship.

*   *   *

I next spoke to John Wilkins, who is the editor of the Catholic journal *The Tablet*. He emphasised the need for women to have more say. 'Most of us are married. Most of us have to try to direct our lives, by being married, towards some sort of holiness, and yet there are hardly any married saints.'

'I'm not surprised,' I said. 'The mere institution makes the pursuit of sanctity virtually impossible.'

'I would be sorry to think that marriage was regarded as a second-class institution,' he said. 'It certainly didn't make the Lord think that St Peter wouldn't do.'

I made a mental note to re-read the Gospels. I seemed to recall that Jesus required his followers to leave their families and follow Him, but knew there was a long-running argument about this.

'Another problem is that lay people have been excluded from the Magisterium on sexual matters,' John went on. 'The congregation for the Doctrine of Faith makes these definitive statements about IVF and so on, and the entire commission that decides these things is male. I don't think women are even consulted. Something is lacking from the input into the Magisterium – the organ which forms the teachings of the Church. It's no good telling me that if you have married priests in the Church those statements would be exactly the same, because I don't believe they would. Feed in the information and then people won't talk about contraception in this idealistic and unrealistic way which ignores the psychological facts that married couples have to face.'

I have often heard this argument put forward, that if the Magisterium would listen to women (and married people) then things would change. Just because a voice is loud doesn't mean it's right. Anyway, I refuse to believe the Magisterium is ignoring the views of women because it hasn't heard them: the more extreme utter their demands in tones of such shrillness you could hear them on the moon. But more of feminism shortly. And I was tired of talking to people about sex and marriage. There seemed to be more interesting things to say about the positive side of celibacy.

4

Wedded to Christ

Thou hast made us for thyself and the heart of man is restless until it finds its rest in thee.

St Augustine

The call of Christ – Playing for high stakes – The nun's life – Assessing the sex drive – What the Church should say – A lack of statistics – Being a vessel for God – The Mrs Proudie problem – Holding back from intimacy – Limitations of a married clergy – The views of Bishop Spong

Protestantism has always ridiculed celibacy. I don't know why, unless it is because Protestantism is deeply rooted in humanism and cannot see God alone as sufficient to a humanly fulfilled life. Dean Inge said somewhere that it was the height of vulgarity to deride the monastic vocation. Someone else said marriage was like a little winter warmth in a dark corner. Sometimes in the spring when you have a fire glowing in the grate the sun will suddenly come pouring in through the window and you can no longer see the brightness of the flames. You turn from the fire to the sun. There was once a saint who refused to marry because she held that no man on earth was good enough for her. She had a vocation if also a possibly overblown sense of herself. I asked Stuart Mason for his opinions on celibacy.

'When it works, which it seems to do in a far higher proportion of cases than, for example, marital fidelity, it is the most powerful sign there could be that the call of Christ – that we should forsake all and follow Him – is not empty rhetoric. For a man to suppress his desire for sexual intimacy for no reason is neither good nor wise. To do so for a purpose – whether to live a life of prayer and community in a monastery, or to dedicate himself to the unconditional service of Christ's people in the active ministry – is to show that to follow Christ is more important than any of the good, God-given things of life. The Church is saying that what some see as the highest good on earth, which is sexual love in marriage, is not essential for a happy and fulfilled life in Christ, and that, if it gets in the way of what you are called to do or to be, it must be forgone.'

'Bishop Spong', I said, 'says that one of the things that is wrong with Christianity is the cult of Mary, that it's responsible for the low esteem in which women are held. He doesn't seem to notice that a lot of non-Christian cultures treat their women rather roughly. He appears to believe that if Our Lady were held not to be a virgin but a victim of rape or possibly an adulteress then this would give women a more positive image of themselves and their own sexuality, and they'd have no problems. He seems to take the view that sex is of supreme importance. I don't think Bishop Spong believes celibacy is desirable for anyone, no matter what his sexual orientation.'

'Celibacy becomes harder in a world where priesthood is not valued,' said Stuart, 'where celibacy is regarded as ridiculous and where the Church (that is in England, not Rome) is feeble at speaking back to the world about that.'

'They daren't,' said I morosely. 'Being dismissive of sex is secular blasphemy.'

Stuart went on, 'When you count up the children, adolescents and unmarried people in most of the world – widows and widowers, those whose orientations are, even in the most liberal society, ruled out of bounds, married couples whose sexual life is, for good or ill, stilled – you must be accounting for half the human race. The Church should also be speaking for those people, assuring them that their lives are not wasted or, in the case of the young in most of the world, to be invested only in the future. One way to do this is through a celibate priesthood where a priest can show "I have voluntarily chosen not to satisfy this very good human appetite and I am a recognisably contented, useful human being".'

'And perfectly cheerful and not climbing up the curtains,' I added.

'Of course. But only if you love and value your priesthood and invest yourself in it – saying Mass, preaching, instructing, hearing confession with care, being closely involved in the lives of the people. You are playing life for very high stakes by becoming a celibate Catholic priest. It makes no sense to make such an ostensibly crazy choice and then to live a comfortable, lazy life.'

I agreed. 'The insistence on sexual fulfilment seems rather less than compassionate or sensible because not only is it going to make the celibate clergy miserable, it's going to make millions of people miserable – the ones who aren't getting any.'

I felt it was time to speak to a woman about celibacy and in particular a nun. Sister Anne Murphy (no relation) is a teacher at Heythrop College. I asked her to lunch, and cleared a space at the dining-room table.

In all the uproar about the celibacy of the clergy there is little talk of female chastity, of nuns, perhaps because there are so few left. With all the talk of equality the underlying assumption remains – that woman's principal purpose is to be available for the sexual needs of the male. There is little acknowledgement of the fact that women too might want to devote their lives exclusively to the love of God. The nun's life has often been described as 'selfish', presumably because she isn't washing socks or cooking chops for a man. The devotion they give to many more people than they would have encountered in a worldly context is quite passed over, as though it were of no consequence.

Sister Anne arrived not in a habit but in a navy skirt and jumper so that I could almost tell she was a nun by looking at her. I can sometimes tell by looking at their feet, as they have a tendency towards thick stockings and sandals, but Sister Anne had sensible shoes on.

She turned out to be a pleasure to be with, warm and kindly and as sensible as her shoes, but she too was inclined to idealise 'interpersonal relationships', even though she recognised the inherent 'dangers'.

'What', I demanded, having served the lunch, 'do you make of the celibacy of the priesthood?' A quest does strange things to one's social graces. Under normal circumstances I would not initiate a conversation with a nun in this way. Well, I wouldn't have done once.

She said she thought priests should have the option of being celibate or married. 'Vocations are now coming later in life – young people are tending to not commit themselves. However, people who have lived their professional lives and whose families have grown up could be a source. If would-be priests have to wait until their wives are dead, how do you think their wives feel?'

Better, I reflected, than if there was a mistress waiting in the wings; but I said I thought you could only love one person at a time; and if you loved God so much that you thought of Him constantly then living with someone else would only get in the way.

Sister Anne differentiated between the monastic and the secular vocation. 'Traditionally, the priest who wanted to live a contemplative, mystical and celibate life would have done so in a religious order. In the past, most of the secular priests dotted around in the parishes lived very faithfully with one woman. They worked in the fields, came home for their meals, and she was the housekeeper/wife. The sort of steady relationship was allowed because it was understood how hard it is for men to live alone. Traditionally, the monastic was the religious life. Priests were of two kinds: one was just able to read and write in order to say Mass, and the other studied some theology in order to preach.'

'So you're saying that celibate priesthood has always been a problem?' I said, thinking in a positively feminist fashion that men were pathetic. It is true that most men when divorced, widowed or simply dumped find living alone intolerable and go seeking a replacement more usually than do women, who are sometimes only too pleased to be free. This is why I admire adult, celibate men who do not cling to women's apron strings.

'Indeed,' said Sister Anne. 'Why do you think there was this rush of priests getting married after the Reformation? Because they were in those sort of relationships anyway, and not for any great, thought-out reasons. So your idea of the ideal priest, which is certainly shared by a great number of Catholics, is relatively new. What we're trying to handle today is how can a priest or nun relate to a mixed group in a parish – does it put strains on them or is the alternative a kind of unhealthy isolation?'

I wondered why isolation should be seen as unhealthy. Reciprocity is not necessary to love or generosity. My ideal of a religious is someone scoured of self, a vessel for God, an intermediary. Not a chum. I can also understand, without any trouble at all, the appeal of the eremetic life, since I am subject to occasional attacks of people-poisoning and feel I never want to see another one. There is also an idea that the celibate priest leads a sad and lonely life. I have known many who found it difficult to get any time to themselves since they were in demand, not only at parish activities but at social gatherings where it was felt they added a certain tone.

'But we all have to relate to each other from our different positions,' I countered. 'In fact, I don't find that married people relate to anybody else at all very much. They relate to each other, at least for a while if they're lucky, and they worry about the children. I would never go to a married couple for advice or help. If they're on speaking terms they'd talk about you when you'd gone.'

Sister Anne let this slanderous remark pass. 'You have married couples and single people; and then you have priests and nuns who have lived separately and managed to remain celibate, partly because of the barriers that have been put up. Now they are in the world again. The question is, how do you live a celibate life at all? Married people say they have to handle their relationships too, but it is slightly different if you are in the Church situation because being on a pedestal isolates you from the dangers of all interpersonal relationships.'

'What annoys me', I said, 'is the cant talked about sex. Sexual relationships can often be a nightmare. I don't know all that many people who are happy with theirs. The appetite is sometimes so strong it cannot be denied, but this is clearly often quite separate from love. Everybody's encouraged to do *it* all the time for fear something disastrous will happen to their psyches if they don't. "If you don't want to lose it, use it." All the women's magazines now have articles on orgasm or impotence or some outré aspect of sexual behaviour tucked in between the recipes and the knitting patterns.'

I think Sister Anne was eating cheese pudding. This is another useful dish to offer religious persons of all persuasions as it avoids offence.

'Somebody said recently', she remarked, 'that no one would admit to being a virgin – it's like saying you've never been abroad on your summer holidays. People sometimes ask if we would accept somebody who is sexually experienced in our convent. We have to, really – most young people are nowadays.'

'It was always regarded as manly to take a keen interest in sex,' I noted. 'Now I keep meeting women who insist on telling you how important their sex drive is to them. Once they might have announced they were regular church-goers; now they tell you they're sexually active. It's a sort of claim to credibility.'

*   *   *

I asked John Wilkins to tell me more about his views.

'The celibacy of the clergy is a discipline that could be changed tomorrow,' he said. 'It's a heroic thing and does give great spiritual power if you can do it, but the Lord did not choose celibate disciples – Peter had a wife and took her with him when he went around preaching' (probably to wash his socks, I thought sourly) 'and presumably this was true of at least some of the other disciples. There is no doubt you could make a change if you felt it was the right thing to do, whereas women priests and feminist issues raise fundamental questions about the doctrine of the Church.'

'What do you think about contraception and abortion?' I asked, by way of a change. 'I'm baffled by the way the pro-abortionists consider the anti-abortionists to be inhumane. We're always being told that Catholicism is a negative "death" religion, then when it speaks out against killing – abortion or euthanasia – everyone roars.'

'Abortion is something that every Catholic, with that central icon of mother and child, should feel temperamentally and psychologically against. If they don't I would question it.'

'Do you think contraception should be the concern of the Church?' I asked, since most progressives do not. 'I often wonder when I hear people blaming the Pope for the over-population of the world. The population of Egypt, for example, where I don't think his influence is great, is increasing at the rate of a million a year.'

I also wonder about the motives of the west when it grieves about ecology and over-population and tells other people about the value of condoms. Surely if people were left to grow the crops they needed to sustain themselves, rather than items for export, they would have more autonomy and be able to keep their families instead of submitting to market pressures and the profit demands of the multinational superstores. But then I know no more of economics than I do of theology. I hauled myself back from this tangential preoccupation and listened to John.

'I think couples have to decide these things themselves,' he continued. 'On the other hand, any sexual act is a moral one – it has morality in it of its very nature. There isn't such a thing as a neutral sex act, since it involves the couple and the creation of a possible third person. In that sense it is impossible for the Church to say anything goes. But I do think that the sexual doctrine of the Church is causing great problems and is partly responsible for the haemorrhage of young people. The doctrine needs, at the very least, strong updating with the help of social sciences. Wherever you look – divorce, homosexuality, contraception or whatever – the Church's position appears to be outdated and harmful if it creates guilt where perhaps there shouldn't be any.'

'I sometimes get the feeling that a constant awareness of guilt should be the condition proper to mankind,' I observed. 'It isn't pleasant but it often seems entirely appropriate.' Nor do I have the remotest faith in the 'social sciences'. Human nature hasn't changed since Adam and Eve and Cain and Abel first all fell out with each other; since David lusted after Bathsheba, Lot repulsed the Sodomites or Onan spilled his seed. I also know that my own 'young people' refuse to go to church because it's lost its elastic. They prefer rules to being patronised and are aware only of the liberal movement, not of the hard core which does remain, if often seemingly silent. The sophisticated young are even less tolerant of the Church's attempts to offer them what they imagine they will find inviting than I am. The sneer on the face of the street-wise young person who witnesses a Rave in the Nave is enough to freeze the blood.

Stephen Pile wrote in a review of a TV programme in February 1994 about the mothers of murderers and rapists: 'The fashionable wisdom here is that social factors explain such behaviour but we found sweet, kindly, upright, baffled women whose other children were lovely. No-one in this moving, there-but-for-the-grace-of-God programme confronted the chilling conclusion of this idea. Such behaviour can now only be explained by our long-lost chum, Evil. Goodbye, psychologists and sociologists; your redundancy money is at the door. Hello, conservative theologians.'

'But people are not going to go and confess to sins that they don't think are sins,' John continued. 'I can't see the problem: don't confess them; confess what is on your conscience. I don't know how most people view celibacy now, but to both of us it is an heroic, positive thing – if it can be done. Nobody knows what the situation is about celibacy; there are no statistics or facts, and "what is freely asserted is freely denied". If it is the case that one-third of priests can live their celibacy and get power from it, that another third make a heroic sacrifice which some find burns them out in the end so they have to leave, and the final third take celibacy not as chastity but as a commitment to not marry, this is not a satisfactory position. In the days when celibacy was a sort of caste-mark for priests (which was not very long ago) the priesthood was seen as the important thing, not the person. That was the doctrine – the ideal.'

'That makes sense to me,' I replied. 'I'm bored with the cult of personality, of "personhood".' I have a number of friends who are priests but that means nothing when they're at the altar. When they stand *in persona Christi* it doesn't matter if they're Joe or Jimmy. People will not keep themselves to themselves but attempt to impress you with their personalities. I'm going to say it again – holiness consists in keeping the basic structure of one's own humanity while trying to be a vessel for God.

'In Africa', continued John, 'there is a major problem about celibacy but the bishops will never say so in Rome. There are two reasons for this. One is African courtesy – you must never make someone lose face, so must never say anything that will embarrass him or her in public. The other reason is that if they took the lead on this it might imply that they were less good at keeping the celibacy rule than the ex-colonial western powers. The Africans might be pleased if westerners brought in an adaptation of the rule, but they are never going to take the lead themselves. This is quite important in this whole debate. Personally I think that if you have the ordination of married men, which is what I would favour – mature men in stable marriages – I don't see that there would be any threat to the discipline of celibacy.'

But how, I wondered, could you ensure that they were mature and their marriages stable? This happy state is most unusual in western society.

'There is another point about celibacy,' John went on. 'It's a gift, but there are others. St Paul lists them: preaching, creating communities, the charismatic gifts and speaking in tongues. Now celibacy has somehow become the gift that excludes all the others. You may be a very good preacher or wonderful at creating a community, but if you don't have the gift of celibacy you're out – you can't be a priest. The reaction to the Casey affair is in part a manifestation of a feeling amongst a certain number of Catholics (but there are others who are very strongly opposed) that the time has come to enrich the priesthood by this other sort of priest.'

'Enrich' is another favourite buzz word among the progressives. I'm reminded of a friend who maddened his mother by adding curry powder to the turkey gravy one Christmas. It certainly made a wealth of difference but completely disordered her dish.

'But', I answered, 'the trouble here is wives – the Mrs Proudie problem. It's very difficult to get along with wives – doctors' wives, politicians' wives can all be terribly irritating. They tend to throw their weight about and put on airs. And what would happen if a married priest wanted to get divorced?'

'It's quite sad', agreed John, 'to listen to priests in the Church speaking as though marriage would remove all the problems of the world. The naivety of such views is staggering. You're quite right that one problem would be the women. In the Orthodox Church the woman is sort of vetted by the congregation in a way you couldn't have here.'

'Also, in the Eastern tradition women know their place?' I asked craftily.

He did not answer that directly. 'We all know that it can be a huge problem. A bishop who has an atheist wife is in a terrible dilemma, and as for choirboys and so on – it's a sort of stock Anglican joke. The view that all this would be solved by matrimony is quite wrong. How many married saints do we have?'

'Not a lot,' I answered. 'They are trying to canonise the parents of St Thérèse of Liseux at the moment, however.' I can't think why. Her poor papa was mad. I suppose madness is not necessarily a bar to holiness but it does cloud the issue.

*   *   *

I asked Father Rodford about the celibacy of the priesthood. What were his feelings on the matter?

'I stand in the Anglican tradition,' he replied, 'but there is a place for celibate priesthood. It is difficult for a man who is married not to share all aspects of his life with the person he chooses to be his partner: this is just part of the human predicament as it were. As a priest you have to hold back from sharing intimate details of peoples' lives; indeed, your wife should not really know what you have been up to in these respects, because to actually say where you have been is almost to give away the game. I'm not married but I share a house where there are a lot of people in and out all the time, and just out of sheer interest they often want to know what I have been about. Because I have no intimate relationship with these people I can hold back and nobody is offended. But I can see a situation where, if one was close to another person, there would be some offence if one constantly had to say, "No, I cannot talk to you about that, I can't tell you what I have been doing here, I can't tell you where I have been this afternoon or am going tomorrow or why that call came from the hospital."'

Here I remembered something that Barbara Cartland had said about lady priests – to the effect that if you confessed to a woman it would be all round the village in five minutes flat. This is unfair but amusing. Barbara Cartland shares with Monsignor Gilbey the opinion that women do not like each other and cannot be friends. I mention this only because it is another illustration of the power of the *Zeitgeist* – they are both very old and were brought up in an age when that opinion was received wisdom. It was fashionable to think thus for a time, and it is against such absurdities that militant feminism is now overreacting. But back to our muttons.

'All the same,' I said, 'you do believe there is a place for married priests?'

'Yes,' he replied, 'but we have to understand their limitations. The celibate priesthood is effectively married to nothing less than the Church itself.'

'There is another aspect of the celibacy of the clergy,' I went on. 'Because, God forbid, if any clergyman should be called upon to be martyred in the old-fashioned way, rather than being held up to public ridicule and opprobrium, he would have to think twice if he was going to leave a wife and children behind.' I have since wondered how a priest with children in – say – a siege would feel called upon to behave. If he had access to a tiny amount of food would he succour his own children or others? If he could save one child who would he choose? I have wasted time agitating over this problem as a lay person. It must be very difficult to be a good priest and a good father in a dangerous world.

'We should be prepared to be martyred in a number of ways,' Father Rodford replied. 'It is not just the physical death. Baptism talks about death in a very positive way. It is dying to all sorts of things, to the many facets of humanity which it is healthy to deny and get rid of. Yes, I think you are right there. I would not be good at it, even as a celibate priest, nor would I be very willing.'

Here is another knotty problem. The views of Father Rodford are more orthodox than those of many of the Roman Catholic clergy. High Anglicans think of themselves as Catholic but the Roman Church sees them as Protestant. I shall think about it later.

*   *   *

I end this chapter with one last interview. Bruce Kent is an ex-priest now married who, as everybody knows, was a leader of the movement for nuclear disarmament. Having a regrettable tendency to pessimism, I sympathise with his aims but think he was wasting his time. If humanity is determined to blast itself to bits some-body somewhere will provide the means to ensure that it does so. So I asked him about celibacy.

'It's quite clear now,' he replied, 'over this issue, that the official Church is completely out of step with the actual thinking of the great majority of the people – clerical as well as lay; but the Pope has just snapped a lid on it. It's ridiculous. There was a period in the Church when it was quite usual to have married clergy. It took hundreds of years before celibacy from the monastic orders was imposed on the secular orders. No one can say this is a divine source that cannot be changed, but the Pope's trying to make it so: he's just not listening to the rest of the Church. I'm not saying that what the majority think is always right: most would lie in bed on a Sunday morning or spend their lives watching television – the lazy way out is often the easy way out. But I think that when concerned Christians and prayerful people have actually thought about things their voices should be heard.'

Vox populi, vox Dei? I don't think the *majority* of Catholics want married priests, and people who call themselves 'con-cerned Christians' are usually concerned because some aspect of Christianity doesn't fit in with their own views, desires, aspirations or inclinations.

'What about the question of homosexual priests?' I asked, with the ideas of Bishop Spong in mind. One of the bishop's claims to fame (I believe he is an Episcopalian) is that he ordained a practising homosexual who held that Christ had a gay lover and maintained that the 'best thing Mother Teresa could do was get laid'. Bishop Spong said it proved how 'our Anglican community is more honest, open, loving, inclusive and Christ-like'. He must have changed his mind since he eventually sacked this vicar, who later died of AIDS. God rest his soul.

'It's a dilemma for homosexuals and the Church,' Bruce replied. 'The Church has not come near to understanding that problem or knowing what to do about it and indeed I don't know either. But it's not celibacy in the normal sense of celibacy. Men and women normally get together and marry and produce children and have homes and so on, and that's what I'm talking about when I mention a married clergy.'

I am puzzled by more than one aspect of homosexuality and I preferred not knowing in too much detail what they *do*. When the gay community revealed the practices indulged in in cottages, tea-rooms and bath-houses I found myself regarding them askance. One such practice involves the presumably unwilling co-operation of a gerbil. It sounds cruel to animals and not beautiful. Nor do I understand why so many people seem determined to define themselves by their sexual orientation. It seems unnecessarily limiting. When a person fixes you with a glance and says 'I'm gay/lesbian, you know', you think: So what, darling? Just don't eat with your mouth open.

There is a pious pretence among the *bien-pensant* that homosexuals wish only to be permitted to 'marry' in the way of the heterosexual and make a 'lifelong commitment' to each other, but such liaisons are comparatively rare. I was told by a well-known homosexual who does not wish to be identified that many initially close relationships last on average six months, whereupon it's back to the bath-house, for male homosexuality is often characterised by a demented promiscuity. I have close male friends and a relation who would have lived long and faithfully with other men, but they have had to make allowances for their lovers' determined and frenetic infidelity.

'You have married since you left, haven't you?' I asked Bruce, not caring to follow up this line of thought. 'Do you like it?'

'Yes. I think I would have been a very miserable person if I hadn't married. I'd have probably turned into an alcoholic or something. Marriage has been quite an eye-opener in terms of personal living; to actually share your life and know that you have to consult somebody else on your diary and wonder where they want to go on holiday, which a priest has no need to do at all.'

I know several alcoholics who took to the bottle because they were married, and two who got divorced because their husbands interfered with their drinking. But still . . .

Thinking of women I turned my attention to feminism.

5

Here Be Dragons

*The reason women are more attracted to church-going than
men may well be that they are more attracted to the
idea of Jesus Christ than men, especially if he is taken
to symbolise maleness broken and victimised, reduced to
powerlessness.*

Clifford Longley, *The Times*

On being unequal – Some militant feminists – The
insistence on happiness – Generals and foot-soldiers –
Who clears the drains? – Why Christ had to be a man
– The 'me' thing – The generosity of women – Ritual
and biological roles – Women in history

These days once you start moving around in the world at all, whether
you're on a quest or a trip to the supermarket or out to dinner, sooner
or later you will encounter feminists. You do not need to seek them
out. You may not encounter too much strident feminism in the
secular context but in the field of religion you will find it hard to
avoid. Like all subversives and revolutionaries, feminists recognise
a soft underbelly when they see it, and much of the clergy is over-
concerned about seeming intolerant of anything, from women to sin.

Many years ago, towards the end of the 1960s, I found myself
at a 'consciousness-raising' meeting with five or six middle-class
white women who were all in a rage about something or other.
The strangest complaint on the agenda was that unless you were
attractive men seldom wanted to sleep with you. I could see no way
of overcoming this inherent unfairness and therefore no point in
talking about it. The idea was that men were culturally conditioned
to prefer pretty women to ugly ones but I found this argument flawed.
I sat through the evening without contributing much, for I did not

recognise the world these women were describing with such resent-
ment. I could perfectly well see the point of expecting equal pay for
equal work, but their other grievances appeared imaginary, bloated
out of all proportion or incapable of satisfactory resolution, and I
could not see myself as the tragic victim of patriarchal oppression
that they had in mind. I'm not mad about men, which is one of the
reasons why I do not wish to resemble them, but I've never found
much difficulty in standing up for myself when they show signs of
becoming over-domineering. On the contrary I know many women
who are careful to pull their punches when it comes to a battle, for
men are painfully vulnerable and their fragile self-esteem is easily
damaged. They are often all outward show and bluster. Sensible
females, being aware that they constitute the stronger sex, do not
suffer the same impulse to cut a figure and make a mark but quietly
get on with the business of progressing from the cradle to the grave
without too much fuss or demanding to be 'visible' – a dangerous
condition, inviting brickbats. Some of them used to be acutely aware
that their first purpose was to seek God.

Edith Stein was jewish, born in 1891 in Breslau. She became a
Catholic and eleven years later joined the Carmelite Order, taking
the name Sister Teresa Benedicta of the Cross; she died in Auschwitz
in 1942. She wrote, 'the total gift of one's being and of one's whole
life is the will to live and work with Christ, which also means to
suffer and die with Him that terrible death from which the life
of grace issues forth for humanity, and it matters not whether
it is she herself who works directly for the salvation of souls or
whether it is only her sacrifice which yields fruits of grace of which
neither she herself nor perhaps any other human being is conscious.'

This contrasts with many current views about what the human
being is *for*. Princess Diana once made a speech to a conference of
women on mental health; she said that women should not be required
to sacrifice themselves for their loved ones and live shadowed by
others at 'the cost of their health, their inner strength and their
own self-worth'. She has a particular axe to grind and doubtless
much to complain about, but is far from being untypical, seeming
to epitomise the self-seeking, vengeful qualities which distinguish
much of the women's movement.

Militant feminism is yet another movement which sees its own
aims, survival and eventual triumph as of more significance than

almost anything else. Where it is concerned with Christianity at all it is dedicated to the overthrow of 'patriarchy', the denigration of all that can be perceived as masculine and the imposition of a female 'priesthood'. At its most ludicrous it speaks not of God but of the 'Goddess'. It is perhaps the most harmful current element in the Church in its sometimes covert, often overt, contempt for men, its relentless insistence on female self-affirmation and 'empowerment' and its refusal to recognise any inherent value in masculinity or the essentially self-sacrificial nature of motherhood. That it makes woman appear ridiculous does nothing to further the cause of justice, peace and reconciliation either between the sexes or in a wider context. Looked at with a cold eye, what strikes the observer most forcibly about the wilder aspects of feminism, particularly when it goes into paganism and witchcraft, is that it is so flaming *silly*.

Rosemary Radford Ruether, an American feminist theologian with a professed fondness for Isis, Artemis and Athena, has advised Catholic feminists to give the appearance of adhering to legitimate 'Catholicity' as a useful camouflage while revolutionising from within. This is the maggot syndrome. A parasite invades a body and proceeds to kill it, unaware – this being the blind nature of the parasite – that when the body is dead it will have no more sustenance and will be unable to live autonomously. The parasite has no relevance to and feels no concern for anything other than itself.

The then plain Barbara Castle was employing the same means when on taking up her seat in the House of Lords she said, 'I want to be there to plan its destruction. You have to permeate the centre and manipulate from the inside. You have to understand your enemy.' The women's movement and the Left have much in common. Communism, in its effort to take over society, has left chaos in its wake, much as the Movement for the Ordination of Women has divided the Church of England. I think of these lady priests as having wrought what could be called 'the queens' revenge', for they are destroying the church instituted by Henry VIII, who so cruelly mistreated so many royal wives.

An article in *The Times* on 17 October 1992 described how an organisation dedicated to the ordination of women and known as Uppity sent out a newsletter calling on women to wear a white flower and demonstrate outside Church House for the decisive debate on women priests on 11 November. It recommended: 'Go sick, resign your job, cancel your holidays, neglect the kids, sell the antiques to pay your fare if you live abroad, but be there.' A woman who resigned as executive secretary of the Movement for the Ordination of Women because 'there was too much prayer and not enough action' said, 'The issue of women priests concerns women everywhere. It goes beyond the Church.' Quite. This is a good example of the Trotskyist tactic of entryism and does little to back up the claims of those who insist that a female ministry will offer the community a glorious example of tender care and compassion as well as added insight into a profound aspect of spirituality.

When our second-born son died, a number of women attempted to console me by enveloping me in an embrace. I find being hugged by strange women a peculiarly distasteful form of sexual harassment, rather worse than being hugged by strange men. These women meant well but their attentions were unwelcome. They suggested I should cry, should 'let it all out'. Some tried to 'counsel' me, speaking of the 'stages of grief' and intimating that I would eventually 'get over it'. They were not telling the truth. They lied, I am sure, unwittingly, seduced by the notion that happiness should be the normal state of mankind or, as they would say, womankind, implying that if I were myself in good health and had a proper awareness of my own 'self-worth' then I would gradually settle back into a state of contentment. Some also claimed that a greater trust in Jesus would restore me to equanimity. The Jesus of whom they spoke, however, was a marshmallow figure I did not recognise.

This unthinking insistence on happiness most probably springs from the absurdity enshrined in the American Constitution that man has a right to 'the pursuit of happiness': an empty promise which has conspired with later doctrines to mislead people into selfishness and greed. Combined with religiosity as exemplified by many Bible Belt preachers, it leads to all manner of scandalous aberrations. Freud, despite being the originator of the 'talking cure' which has degenerated into the ubiquitous 'counselling', cannot be held to blame here, since he acknowledged that the normal state of man was one of mild depression, not all that far from Thoreau's opinion that 'the mass of men lead lives of quiet desperation'. It is futile to make happiness a goal: it is always and only a by-product.

I have retained enough of my early Catholic teaching to know that the only way through suffering is to 'offer it up', to believe that we

Sun Worship: a ritual is performed by a member of the Dragon
Group on Oratory Hill.

Brompton Oratory:
exterior.

The face of present-
day Catholicism:
modern church
exterior.

Brompton
Oratory: interior.

'Scooped out' look
of modern
Catholic church
interior.

(*Above left*) Annie Murphy holds a press conference, 1992.

(*Above right*) Bishop Casey: before

and after . . .

A group of
new style nuns
sitting round a
table.

A novice is
prepared for
the taking of
her vows.

(*Above left*) Two women priests.

(*Above right*) Father John and Bishop Clement are founders of the Church of the Beloved Disciple, in support of New York's gay community.

Traditional nuns getting down to work.

A French street priest: not immediately recognizable as a man of the cloth.

Armagh Cathedral: explanations for the presence of this sculpture would be welcome.

'Christa' by Edwina Sandys.

can share in Christ's work of redemption by accepting suffering and loss and assimilating it, not by rejecting it as an unfair imposition on our innocent selves. Grief is a salutary reminder of what love is, of its power and its eternal nature. Love exists beyond happiness, beyond tranquillity, beyond reason and, in this life, is inseparable from pain. Talk of Christ 'reduced to powerlessness' is meaningless if you believe that by His death and resurrection He overcame death. 'If Christ be not risen, then is our preaching vain, and your faith is also vain', as St Paul very sensibly observed.

*   *   *

Josephine Robinson is Chairman of the Association of Catholic Women. I asked her what influence she thought feminists had in the Church.

'I don't think there are many radical feminists in the Catholic Church in Britain, but those that exist are dedicated and work hard for their cause. They are characterised, it seems to me, by feelings of dissatisfaction and bitterness. They seek power and influence in the Church and are very unsympathetic to the ordinary work that goes on in parishes. I was told a story recently about someone who offered her help to the parish priest on moving to a new parish. When he said, "Oh good, we're a bit short on the church cleaning rota," she drew herself up to her full height and said grandly, "I do not do cleaning". They all want to be generals and not foot-soldiers, but both roles are for the greater glory of God. After all, Jesus said that He came "not to be served but to serve". Of course, the word "feminist" covers a variety of positions from mild irritation with the parish priest to anxiety that we are still waiting for Pope Joan.'

We were having mutton broth for lunch and I have just realised an interesting truth: if you are lunching with someone whose conversation you enjoy you should try and persuade them to have the soup. The reason is obvious if you think about it. Soup does not need much dissection, cutting or chewing and so will not congeal while the speaker explains a point. A mouthful is quickly swallowed and the conversation can continue while the speaker's lunch stays warm. I wish I'd thought of that before.

'The image of the Church I like best', continued Josephine, 'is that of an inverted pyramid, with the Pope at the bottom – the servant of the servants of God. The Church should be free of ambition. The bishops are in a difficult position because their first concern is the faith of the flock. They don't want to propel feminists out of the Church. Even so, radical feminists are always telling the press how beastly the Catholic Church is to women.'

I thought of a fat, sleek, indignant female who on hearing that I had no time for lady priests said, 'Ooh, that such a woman could speak so after all our struggles.' She wasn't even a Christian, being yet another nature-worshipper, but she was very cross with the Church.

'One sometimes hears of women who are said to have been "hurt" by the Church,' I remarked to Josephine. I was thinking now of a new-style 'nun' who, finding herself at dinner sitting between two Jesuits, burst into tears because they spoke only to each other. She felt ignored and therefore diminished – and fled, weeping. As a married woman I am entirely accustomed to this kind of experience and do not mind it in the least. It gives you time to think your own thoughts, which are often more diverting than the conversation of men. Perhaps she would have felt more at ease in an old-fashioned convent where she would not have had to cope with the complexities of social intercourse between the sexes.

Josephine was thinking on less trivial lines. 'Well, if you are divorced, can't get an annulment and wish to marry again and your parish priest says no, sorry, you can't, you might feel pretty miserable. It can't be easy to be in that position. But if he were to say OK, go ahead, don't worry, he would be doing away with the sanctity of marriage. Without the Church to stand up for it, marriage would be lost. Who else would support it?'

Almost nobody now, I reflected. I was brought up in an extended family. The institution of marriage itself was well protected under the old system, since many family members saw themselves as guardians of morality and family honour and it was difficult to conduct clandestine affairs without drawing down well-expressed opprobrium. It's hard for a younger generation to realise the scathing contempt levelled at the adulterous, the promiscuous or the neglectful mother.

'I remember', I said wistfully, 'when you knew where you were and what you had to do. Women did some things and men did others – like clearing the drains.'

'Try saying to one's husband, "That's man's work", and the chances are he'll get rather cross about it,' said Josephine.

'That's because it's still usually something like carrying out the garbage or burying the cat,' I said with a certain satisfaction. Then I relented, for I believe many men lead far nastier, more boring lives than many women do. 'When I was a child I used to feel sorry for the men who had to go off to work every day dressed in their stifling work garments while the women and children could go off for a picnic if they felt like it. Most of the women I knew preferred house to office or factory work. This was one of the reasons why they got married as soon as the chance offered itself. "Let hubby bring home the bacon" was the attitude. It seemed to work quite well. I knew a lot of contented women. To hear people talk now you'd think they'd all been kept in dungeons, working the treadmill in the intervals of being fiendishly raped.' I suppose part of the trouble is that contented people seldom make history, since they're too content to bother making a song and dance about it. Life is now harder for women who are trying to raise a family as well as having a job. Very soon (according to statistics) there will be more women than men in paid employment; this might, one report concluded, free a great many men to follow their criminal inclinations.

Josephine went on, 'It seems to me the mutuality of the sexes is essential for bringing up children, who need to know how both men and women behave. They keep the whole thing going and are always there and children have the security of knowing that their family life isn't about to fly out of the window. The husband and wife have to serve and respect each other in every possible way. Of course, there may be cases where the parents have to separate.'

'This is where women can prove their Christian principles,' I observed, for it seems that in most cases it is women who initiate divorce proceedings. 'A great deal of forgiveness is required in marriage. I think it's true to say that what women do at home is very often not seen as work; even if you have twenty-five children it's not the same as being in the bar with your chums because that *is* work.'

'Absolutely right. Men can be extremely unfair. In a letter of the Pope's he says that man's need to dominate is a result of the Fall. This is so true, and something which they have to fight against – it is their besetting sin, and I don't think that can be denied.'

I agreed, although I have been told by men that they have to keep up the testosterone level and assert themselves in order to function as males. Bless them.

'There is a tendency to pretend we're all the same,' I said. 'People don't make allowances for differences in culture and faith, of sex, even of attitude. They say if we are all as one then we will be very happy. When my children were small they had terrapins that had to be fed little worms called Tubifex which used to cling together. Even if you had to throw them away they still clung together – not one would escape. They hung together madly while I bunged them down the plug-hole. What I mean to say is that "togetherness" can be fatal.'

'It's almost like the heresy of nominalism,' said Josephine, 'that there is no significant difference between men and women and therefore Christ could have been a woman. I think both you and I would agree it was inevitable that Christ was a man.'

'But there is now the feminist cry of "anything you can do I can do better",' I said. 'Nothing would have persuaded me to get on that Cross. I have a feeling that women, because they bear children, tend to be careful with their bodies and avoid putting themselves into positions of danger. I believe it was a man's role to die for us, and that women mostly are called upon to endure the things that men do and the things that happen to the people you love – Our Lady stood at the foot of the Cross and she watched her son die and I can think of no worse torture. Now I come to think of it, I'd have died for any one of my children if for no better reason that that I'd rather be dead than live with the grief. Once you have children, whatever happens to you is largely immaterial except in so far as it affects them.'

'Feminists argue that Christ was only a man because of the social climate of the time,' said Josephine warmly. 'Rubbish! If God had wanted to send a woman, the social climate wouldn't have bothered Him. Women are receptive, which is not the same as passive, while men are active. This doesn't mean that women cannot do the jobs of men or vice versa.'

'Your instincts guide you in certain directions and to do certain jobs and tasks?' I suggested. It was delightfully restful to talk to someone who did not regard the word 'instinct' as either politically incorrect or evidence that one was deeply in accord with the Earth Mother.

'Yes. Certainly it is not – as it's fashionable to say – just a question of conditioning. It is inbuilt. In a letter in *The Times* recently a woman wrote that she had given her granddaughter a set of bricks to improve her creativity (it was obviously that sort of household) and the child had placed a brick flat, put another one on top and said, "Shush, gone to bed, sleep well, baby." That is just natural instinct. A boy wouldn't have done that. Not long ago I watched some children at play in our local school and the boys were in gangs going "bang, bang" and the girls were skipping and sitting at the side and talking.'

I sighed. 'It seems ungrateful to God to try to alter the arrangements when He ordered things that way.' But even as I spoke I remembered that militant feminists do not approve of God.

'It certainly sits awkwardly on religious perceptions,' said Josephine. 'I think it comes from secular feminism – anything which prevents women from being like men is unfair and a bad thing. It's actually a good thing – not only would the world be rather boring, it would come to a full stop.'

It's a great mystery that women so despise men yet want to copy them in every possible way, I reflected, then added, for since we were talking about a form of selfishness it seemed to follow: 'Do you think it's possible to figure out where this *me* thing started?'

'I don't know,' said Josephine, looking baffled. 'Perhaps when they began to say, "I don't pray to the God out there any more; it's the God within me that I pray to." That gives me a practical problem – I don't know how one does that. Do you say "Dear *me*"? There are similar ideas in Gnosticism and pantheism, and now it's been taken up by the New Age – everything has God in it. The tree is God, God is the tree.'

There are New Age males but on the whole the movement seems to appeal more to females. I said I found it irritating that western woman could be so daft.

Josephine went on: 'Of course, conditions for women in parts of India, the Middle East and South America are dreadful, even today, but men suffer from the poor conditions as well. One of my daughters said the other day, "How awful, women didn't get the vote until 1918." The first parliament was held in England in 1275 and only consisted of bishops, nobles and soldiers. It was 1884 before there was almost universal suffrage for men and the landless rural workers were included. When you think of that span of six hundred years and then the final few decades for women to get the vote, it looks rather different. The idea of democracy developed and when it had gone sufficiently far women were included in it.'

'Besides, men had to go off and fight in futile battles getting their arms and legs chopped off, shot full of holes, enduring all manner of horrors,' I said, thinking of "famous victories" I had read of, and acknowledging that I would have preferred to be third kitchen-maid in a boarding house overrun by cockroaches rather than valiant in some rat-infested trench in the Somme. 'You'd think, listening to some people, that only women ever suffered pain and injustice. It's really rather remarkable when you consider military history. Are feminists rewriting history in the way the Marxists did?' I asked.

'Absolutely,' replied Josephine, and went on to talk about a book she had read some years before by the sociologist Ann Oakley which dealt with the history of the English housewife. 'In an agricultural society, women have their children and work at home – for example, in Elizabethan times women made the beer. Then, during the Industrial Revolution, some women went to work in mills while others stayed at home because they couldn't have children and look after them *and* work in factories. The author deduced from it all that we had to get rid of the nuclear family, as she chose to call it, and must all muscle in, rather like in a kibbutz. I believe, however, that it's better for a woman to be at home with her children than working in a factory. That doesn't mean that there is some kind of general intention to keep women down. Christianity has always held women in esteem. Catholic reverence for Our Lady, the greatest of all purely human beings, provided an aura for all women until the Reformation.'

She continued, 'Chaucer's *The Nun's Priest's Tale*, about a cock and hen, is a wonderful satire on a bourgeois marriage. There is great parity and humour, and it contains the popular medieval quotation "woman is the cause of men's downfall". Chaucer, who was a man of his time, makes a great joke of it, and knows that although some people believed that about women the idea wasn't universally accepted.'

'People can never believe that those in a previous age were either intelligent or had a sense of humour.' I forgot to add that they can't believe they ever had sex lives either.

'They tend to see things in terms of slogans,' Josephine observed. 'If you don't have much knowledge of the past, you may think you see the total oppression of women. But in the Church in the Middle Ages there were monasteries run by abbesses. In Anglo-Saxon times

St Hilda ran a mixed monastery, monks one side and nuns the other. There were very powerful women like Teresa of Avila and Catherine of Siena; not many, perhaps, but there weren't very many men either who were in a position to speak to the Pope.'

'Even now, although there are few women in obvious positions of authority, there are a lot of powerful women who are never heard about. Men have a greater need to be visible, to be seen and heard, or they develop a sense of failure. I don't think most women have the same urge to be perceived as successful in worldly terms.' Then I wondered why on earth I'd said that.

Josephine went on to remark that women are the prime educators of their children. 'They may reject your ideas as they grow up or you may make a hash of it, but nevertheless your children have got something from you as their mother that they won't have got from anyone else.'

'The maternal influence is very powerful even if children don't do exactly as you tell them,' said I somewhat ruefully. 'But they do tend to grow up in the way you mean them to.' It may take some time and in the years from twelve to twenty it may seem like eternity, but if you've done your best, be it ever so feeble, in the end you find you've reared some perfectly acceptable people. 'If you have a baby there is no question about what needs to be done. If the children have to be picked up from school or the baby fed or taken out or changed, that's it. Babies and children impose a time discipline and you don't need to make decisions about whether to go to the pub or sit down and write a book. You know what you're *for*.' I have always found this reassuring and have never minded any sort of menial work if I knew that it had to be done. Anyway it always makes a change from writing and is a good excuse when you don't want to go out.

'I agree,' said Josephine. 'People might say we were defining women by motherhood; I don't think it is that, but the qualities you need for being a mother are basic female qualities. Nuns are spiritual mothers and unmarried women can be mothers to those around them. Somewhere Freud said that having a child was the most generous act you can perform.'

'That's unlike him.' I idly spat out a mutton bone – one of the little ones.

'Yes, I almost wonder if it's a misquote . . . Of course women can be selfish, but simply because of the demands of a small child women have been given the responses and instincts that enable them to deal with that.'

'And I *don't* think men have those instincts,' I said, possibly thumping the table. 'There was an argument recently about male au pairs and sex discrimination. There was much indignation at the suggestion that males were unfitted to the care of small children. Obviously some men are fine with them, but they don't have the same instincts. Scandals keep emerging about abuses perpetrated – usually by men – on children in homes and institutions. Female nurses who murder those in their care are still comparatively rare and usually recognisably strange.'

'That instinct and generosity is common to almost all women,' said Josephine, 'married or not, mothers or not mothers. Men can be generous, but they also have to have qualities like strength and courage – the transcendent, benevolent things going out from themselves – whereas women are accepting, receiving, living within themselves.'

'In the Gulf War,' I said, thinking of an item of news which I had found inexplicable, 'some American women insisted on going to the front, in the firing line, even though they had small children. That seems perverse beyond belief. Apart from anything else, the soldiery is hyped up already with fear and aggression and if women appear on the scene they tend to feel: Aha, that's a woman and I shall do what I like with her. It's impolite and far from correct, but instinctive.'

'There is a wonderful image in Cardinal Newman's *Apologia*,' said Josephine, 'where the Church is full of people with passions and angers and instincts for good and they were all ground together, not as if they were pushed into a hospital or prison or sent to bed, but as if in a huge factory for the melting and refining of human nature – "so terrible, so dangerous, so capable of divine purposes".'

* * *

While it still seems to me that the members of the Church of Humanity were wrong in most of their assumptions – their belief in the perfectibility of man, their conviction that if only various warring factions would sit down round a table and talk then all their differences could be ironed out, their dismissal of the concept of original sin, their faith in the innate niceness of humanity, and so on – yet they were right in one important respect. The Church of Humanity recognised that the relationship between mother and child was the most significant of all. I was once asked by a newspaper to write down a thought for Valentine's Day. I wrote, 'Men love women, women love children, children love hamsters and hamsters don't love anybody.' I wanted, for the sake of neatness, to begin, 'God loves men', but I couldn't because that would have implied He loved women less and, as we all know, He loved His mother best of all. In *Paradise Lost* Milton wrote, 'He for God only, she for God in him', a typical piece of male arrogance aggravated by a tendency to wish-fulfilment. D. H. Lawrence suffered similarly. He was troubled by the suspicion that women did not dote on him sufficiently, that they failed to venerate the unique glory of the male and probably gave way to bawdy giggling when out of earshot. He was right of course. Milton and Lawrence belong to the same Puritan tradition. The Romantic tradition too, pessimistic and despairing, springs from the dim awareness that sexual love is never fully reciprocal, that there is 'one who kisses and one who is kissed'. Once a child is conceived, the male, in a very basic sense, is redundant. The Troubadour went wailing round the castle walls because his lady was either a virgin or all sewed up in a chastity belt and not for him. In real life she would probably have been too busy minding the baby to hear his plaints.

There is a rude song which begins, 'Once aboard the lugger and the girl is mine'. The insolent pride inherent in this ditty falls into perspective if you picture the aforesaid lugger foundering. The most unregenerate pirate would lose face and all credibility if he were perceived to be treading over the girls to get into the lifeboat. Women and children first. There are men who would ignore the precept, but they bring shame on themselves and are beneath our consideration. And no true mother would save herself at the expense of the life of her child.

The theologian Don Cupitt has written, 'The cult of virgin motherhood is linked with morally repellent attitudes to sex and, even more, to women.' It is men who don't like the idea because it makes them seem unimportant. The truth is, there are many women who want a child more than they want a mate. They spend a great deal of time and money subjecting themselves to uncomfortable and dubiously successful medical procedures in the effort to give birth. Many would be content to be virgins if they could also be mothers.

One day my friend Ruth Rees went to listen to a talk given by a nun who was keen on lady priests and the further 'empowerment' of females. 'But', demanded somebody, 'what about Christian humility?' 'So what's so great about "humble"?' riposted the nun, her choice of phrase revealing both the American influence on her style and the distance she had travelled from traditional Christianity. She had failed to gain the sympathy of her audience, which must have been an unpleasant surprise, since she was used to addressing feminist groups who greeted her militant utterances with applause. My friend, seeing the speaker's hands tremble in the face of hostility, was moved by an entirely proper Christian compassion but could think of nothing to say by way of reassurance since she was in total opposition to the woman's sentiments. I am familiar with this problem. Most people are lovable and vulnerable even when they let loose some crazy bee in their bonnet, and I have often revealed a lack of honest intellectual rigour by attempting to change the subject or smooth over any little differences of opinion that arise over the luncheon table. The words 'Lady, you're a perfect fool' are consonant neither with Christian courtesy nor with ordinary human hospitality. However, as I have never entertained the Archbishop of Canterbury to lunch, I feel free to describe him as a chump. It was he who stated it was a great heresy to deny that women could be priests.

I once heard an ex-nun say on the radio that when she wore the habit people would edge away from her. As I had always felt comfortable and unthreatened in the presence of nuns dressed in the old style I wrote an article suggesting that if people were keeping downwind of her it might well be due to some other cause. This thoughtless remark prompted the poor woman to write to me, not in a spirit of complaint but desirous of explaining her position, and I have seldom been so mortified in my life. I did not agree with her views, and the way of life she described held no appeal for me at all, but one must not be spiteful.

Fighting for the Faith while trying to maintain your status as a Christian gentlewoman can present almost insuperable difficulties. However, so devious is human nature that you can gain great satisfaction simply by *stating* in the presence of feminists that you aspire to be a Christian gentlewoman, a handmaid to the Lord and to mankind. These words cannot be construed as manifestly offensive yet can be relied on to madden people. You can also claim that you get up early in order to make breakfast for your husband and family before they go out to work, and that you like to rest in the afternoons so that you feel fresh and able to entertain them in the evening. Still, this may be going too far, and may well not be true.

*   *   *

Sister Anne Murphy subscribes to the view that the Church would benefit from a greater degree of democracy and that women should play a larger part in what is popularly known as 'the decision-making process'.

'I think that the Church could be really transformed by coming out with these differences. So many structures have been male dominated, rule dominated, canon-law dominated, that, quite apart from the ordination of women, if you have women around in the seminaries and schools you would at least get another point of view, both in professional life and at home. If we can actually work together and say that men and women do things differently and have different contributions to make to the team, then you can network and problem-solve. I think there could be a different kind of Church at the local level.'

'But there's something unnatural about men and women working together,' I said. 'When they're in committee now the men tend to get wimpish, the women strident. It used to work the other way. I've never seen them working together with any great ease. Men tend to do all the talking – contrary to accepted wisdom – and the women have to jump up and down to get a word in edgeways until they get really furious, whereupon the men start pretending to be "New Men" and apologise for existing. I saw a Church of England clergyman on TV the day they decided to ordain women. He was surrounded by beaming ladies clutching candles and he was apologising to the whole of femalekind for centuries of Church oppression. If it wasn't mad it would be funny. Damn it, it *is* funny.'

'Well,' said Sister Anne, 'we'll just have to work at it, because basically that's what the Church is all about. It's been a Church for the men, and the women have sat to one side.'

Then why, I wondered, has it always been women who were the most regular and devoted church-goers? I spoke. 'Not literally we haven't, and I for one wouldn't have cared if we did. I have Jewish

women friends who don't mind where they sit in the synagogue.'
(Although, of course, I know others who do. Judaism is not immune
to feminism.) 'A male Jewish friend of mine went recently to a
liberal synagogue and was rather taken aback. There was a woman
in front of him wearing yarmulka and tallis. He's a liberal, gentle
man but he didn't feel easy with it. It's not her role, just as it
isn't the rabbi's role to have babies. I believe the Chief Rabbi
and I are in accord on this one.'

'You are confusing the ritual and biological roles,' said Sister
Anne, 'and I don't think they are necessarily juxtaposed. It's just that
you are used to that. I think in time the idea of a female priesthood
might be acceptable, but we have to work through various stages.'

There was a suggestion a few years ago that with some surgical
readjustment men could bear children. I find this not much odder
than the idea that women can be priests.

'One of the moments when I changed my perception at an
emotional level', continued Sister Anne, 'was at Easter vigil at
the cathedral, which always gave me a great liturgical uplift. On
this particular occasion I saw, as usual, choirboys followed by
choirmen, followed by clergy, followed by altar boys, followed by the
cardinal. I became aware for the first time that the whole liturgy was
something active on the altar for all those men, while the women were
almost silent participators. I felt excluded, even though I loved the
liturgy and music and ceremony.'

This was incomprehensible to me – you might just as well want
to rush on the field and join in the rugger – so I said, 'I find
something infinitely touching in the sight of males serving at the
altar. A seriousness, a dignity and a humility which are not readily
apparent in most of the other things they do. Women don't give
the same impression. I saw some round the altar in New Zealand.
They looked incongruous and bossy, very much as though they
felt only they knew how to wash up properly, and I've never felt
excluded. By the time I've got everything ready for Sunday lunch
I'm glad to sit in church and watch someone else doing the work.
Men, that is. This is probably completely beside the point, but it's
to do with separate roles: with the whole unfashionable concept
of separateness, exclusivity. There was a time when men weren't
around when their wives were giving birth; then it was accepted
that they should be, and some of them liked it and some of them

didn't and passed out. Now there are two views – that the woman has a right to do this on her own, except for the medical team if she chooses to have one, or the dolphins if she fancies giving birth in a dolphinarium; or that she has the right to have her man around. It seems to me a matter of personal preference, but the tendency is to politicise everything and make it a question of principle. I think I'm trying to say that we don't *have* to share everything: I don't think we should be forced into togetherness.'

'I met a Hindu woman recently,' said Sister Anne, 'and we spoke about her experience and I realised we were both asking the same questions. The burning concern that justice still isn't being done remains. Actually, women in the four major religions are raising roughly similar issues and they aren't radical or aggressive or way-out. This brings me to the emancipatory model, where women want to catch up, join and be as good as men. It won't work. It's a stage.'

The word 'burning' caused me to reflect that if I was a Hindu woman I'd still be asking myself why, at one time, I'd have been expected to immolate myself on my husband's funeral pyre. Compared with that I don't see that Christian females have had too much to complain about. Nor have Christian females regularly been exposed in infancy or 'accidentally' incinerated by their mothers-in-law. The pretence that women everywhere have suffered in similar ways and to the same degree is exaggerated. Justice, whatever that really means, seldom is done. Life is inherently unfair. Each generation gets worked up about different 'injustices' as it perceives them and exhausts itself trying to remedy the situation. Sometimes they succeed in doing away with the more blatant inequalities but it should be evident by now that we are never going to have a perfect world.

'I could never understand', I said, 'why women wanted to emulate men. A lot of them wanted to do the sort of jobs men invented for themselves. On the one hand they were maintaining that men were the source of all the trouble in the world, and on the other they were trying to copy them. At one point, I seem to remember, there was a suggestion that sperm could be collected in banks and the male sex could then be annihilated.'

'I'm embarrassed by the emancipatory model,' said Sister Anne. 'There are differences and therefore we have different contributions to make, but when we are in dialogue and see each other's gifts to the Church it could be a richer place of ministry. Why, for example,

are women only allowed as observers at Church Councils? We live in
a world where women have political rights, for what that's worth.'

'There again we have fallen into that male model,' said I. 'Simply
wanting the vote, in a way, is accepting that men are running the
world in the only possible fashion and so we are going to join them.
I don't know what on earth we could have done rather than insisting
on having the vote, but I think we should have done something more
radical; we should have said much more clearly what sort of world
we want. The political mode, social engineering, is no way to run
a society. The urge to over-control is disastrous. Women are better
than men at coping with the way things are rather than trying to
bring about vast change with no awareness of what the possible
consequences might be. What's happened is that women have tried to
emulate men. It's the way the *Mary Rose* fell over; all the sailors flew
to one side to say hello to Henry VIII and the ship fell down.'

'I think the emancipatory stage is something that we have to go
through as we take our place in society,' said Sister Anne.

Here I remembered those of my Muslim friends who are content
to go round covered since it relieves them of unwanted attentions.
I also remembered the saying of the old Turk who, after the reforms
of Kemal Atatürk, remarked that the unveiling of women had been a
great shock to the menfolk, who had lost many of their illusions.

'I've been coming across quite a number of young women who
are very bitter,' said I to Sister Anne, 'and I can't quite work out
what they're cross about. We met several in California, all very
successful, and all they could talk about was the latest hairdresser
in town and whether he was gay or not. There seems to be a
shortage of heterosexual men in California and I think women
are beginning to blame themselves or the women's movement or
something.'

'Most of the movements in America are stronger and what annoys
me is the feeling that eventually they will come over here. I discovered
last year at the European Theology Women's Meeting that we have
our own brand of feminism. Rosemary Radford Ruether and some
of the biggies from the States were over and were very interested
in the fact that European women theologians were making such a
contribution. First of all we let the eastern voices speak and women
were telling horrendous stories from Czechoslovakia and Hungary
and so on.'

And here I recalled a Romanian friend, a poet and politician. We had met in New Zealand at a Writers' Week and feminists were out in force at each and every event. She was asked how the movement for the equality of women was progressing in her country and responded that she'd had more than enough of equality and now wanted nothing so much as to be looked after. In the light of the known course of her life and career she could not be accused of laziness, cowardice or complacency, and a grim uneasy silence settled over the sisterhood.

'Very few women represented the south,' continued Sister Anne, 'because Italian and Spanish women are not in that position, full stop. Women are in lots of academic posts in Germany. The Americans are socio-political and therefore very much into the political issues – one side of feminism but the rather aggressive side. The French made you think that Europe takes its time and comes up with its own ideas – a much more philosophical and radically thought-through form of feminism. I got a sense last year, thank God, that we are beginning to hear our own voices and coming up with our own form. I'm not saying that it's the same throughout Europe, but it has deep cultural roots. We're able to pick up our history and say what contribution women made to the Renaissance, and so on. It's called "retrieval".

'You're saying that women have always had an enormous contribution to make but it's been ignored?' I asked. It seems to me just another question of priorities. You can get quietly on with the business of living until you die or you can leap on the stage, strike an attitude and demand recognition.

'Yes,' said Sister Anne. 'I'm now committed to a course in which I study what happened to women in various stages of the Church's history. Were they segregated in congregations and what was the pastoral practice towards them throughout the centuries? With the help of women historians I'm learning about what women actually experienced.'

'I've discovered something about the scold's bridle and the ducking stool,' I said, remembering something interesting. 'I'd always thought they were for what the police call "domestics" – rows in the home and women nagging their husbands. Not at all. There were groups and gangs of unruly women who terrorised the neighbourhood. And in Liverpool years and years ago there were women who were very frightening. They were street fighters. The Victorians persuaded us that women were meek and mild little things. I think they were probably terrified of the women out in the street – rather like football yobbos now – beyond reasonable appeal. Kipling wrote a story about women brawling in the East End. Women have not always seen themselves as utterly powerless sweet wee things. Even when I was a child we had "role models" in the *Dandy* and *Beano*: Pansy Potter, the Strong Man's daughter, and Beryl the Peril. Girls now like to imagine my generation was brought up on *Rebecca of Sunnybrook Farm* and we all had to curl our hair and wear pinnies.'

'In general I'm very sympathetic to what women are trying to do to become visible,' said Sister Anne, 'and I think that some of the biblical and doctrinal studies are revealing in new dimensions. After all, that work has previously been done by men, and it's quite clear that when women engage in it something different is going to emerge and that's very exciting. On the other hand, I'm ambivalent because at the end of the day you could get a whole group of contrary positions, and I'm wary about where we're heading. It is perfectly all right to call God "Mother" if you realise this is a metaphor. Sometimes it might be helpful to use expressions like "God is Mother" because it jolts your presumptions that there is something wrong about that.'

'We've always talked of Mother Church, haven't we?' I demanded.

'Yes, and that is also a metaphor. The danger is that if you can get into a position where you say that Jesus, as a man, can't represent women, you're really in great danger with the whole Christian doctrine of salvation. For example, Daphne Hampson says that you cannot be a Christian and a feminist and she now calls herself a post-Christian. A lot of feminists in the US are Christians who have gone out.'

'Well, at least Daphne Hampson tells the truth,' I said approvingly.

'The feminist movement, at its most extreme, says we can do without men altogether. Women have always had a tendency to hold men in slight contempt – "Oh, they're just little boys" etc. – but now a lot of women seem to hate men passionately.'

I once heard a woman deacon saying that *she* did all the work in the parish and then when it came to Holy Communion she had to step aside and let some *man* take over. She said it made her angry when people dressed up their misogyny with theological frills. Her voice trembled with rage, and her words were not those of a rational woman.

6

Jesa Christa

There were also certain folk of Pedasus, dwelling inland of Helicarnassus; when any misfortune was coming on them or their neighbours, the priestess of Athene grew a great beard.

Herodotus, Book I

On women priests – Everyone starts out female – Blood-thirsty ladies – Religion 'à la carte' – A crucified woman – Nuns in anoraks – Balls of red yarn – Priestesses – The 'en-male-ment' of women

'Disruptive and utterly futile as are the efforts of those who seek women's ordination, it was singularly inept of Dr Janet van der Does de Willebois to invoke the name of Mother Teresa as a possible ally in that particular cause,' commented a correspondent in the *Catholic Herald* on 11 February 1994.

Mother Teresa, when interviewed on Scottish television during her visit in 1982, was asked if she felt hurt by being barred from the priesthood. Her answer was: 'No, I would never like to become a priest because I would stop being a woman then, and I have a great power of living and putting my love into a living action . . . no one . . . could have become a better priest than the Mother of Jesus, yet she remained only the handmaid of the Lord and she in all sincerity could have said even better than a priest, "This is my body", because the body of Jesus was made only of her body. So we have to be like her.'

There is a great deal of talk, even among those who don't think there is any significant difference between the sexes, about the 'gifts' that women would bring to the priesthood. It has escaped their notice

that when women take up positions of power in traditionally masculine roles the differences do indeed become minimised. It seems that
the feminine qualities of tenderness, compassion and understanding
make themselves apparent only in women in conventional female
roles. People of both sexes have been brought to tears and the verge
of a nervous breakdown by ruthless women bosses who often seem
astonished at being called unkind. And a woman is overseeing the
crumbling of the National Health Service.

I asked Father Rodford for his views about the whole debate on
women priests.

'There are theological debates,' he replied, 'and the proponents
of women's ordination have said that we do not put forward any
theological objection – they are all sociological and gut reactions.
They cannot see that Jesus did not actually choose women to be the
special ones among His disciples in so far as He chose men to be
His apostles whom He sent out with special authority. We know He
had disciples who were women – Mary Magdalene, his own Mother
and Mary and Martha – but, as far as ministry is concerned, theirs
seems to have been of a different order. It is easy to say that Jesus
was working within a particular social and theological setting as a
Jew and consequently He would not have wanted to upset people
more. To that there is the counter-argument that He upset people
anyway, so why wouldn't He have upset them by choosing women
even though it was socially unacceptable?'

Father Rodford told me he took those arguments seriously. 'I
have seen some excellent women deacons who I thought could be
excellent priests. On the other hand, I have seen others who leave me
absolutely cold, and I think, with their family set-ups and particular
feminist views, they really ought not to be priests. In this whirl of not
knowing, I am certainly dead against the idea of women priests at
the moment. One of these arguments is ontological. I think we need
to take seriously the argument that women have their own role which
is independent of that of a man and essentially and substantially is
different. At the most basic level we are talking about reproduction
and motherhood. In this age we often assume that men have the
same sort of responsibilities, but often a woman is the only thing
a child needs. If a child is left with only a father and he assumes
as far as he can a woman's role, to what extent he is successful is
open to debate. It is the same with the priesthood; we may not be

able to discern at this time that it is a simple truth, a simple fact of being, that the priesthood should be open to men only.'

'Can you imagine changing your mind on this?' I asked. The feminists take the hopeful line that in the end we'll all agree with them in the cause of 'progress' or give in out of sheer exhaustion.

'Not really. I would hate to say that I have got a closed mind, because I think that the Holy Spirit moves within historical settings just as he moved within Jesus, and just as Jesus influenced people of His own day in a particular way. I can envisage a time when, perhaps, there will be a new revelation, that women should be in the priesthood. However, I think we need to have matured far more than we have as a Church. Clearly it would be destructive at the moment and, in consequence, it cannot be within the influence of the Holy Spirit. Perhaps we are not listening enough to the Holy Spirit.'

Having been somewhat reassured by the views of an Anglican, I returned to my young friend, the bearded priest. I have grown fond of him, for he is well-meaning and eminently likeable.

'What do you think about women priests in the Anglican Church?' I asked.

'This is a good story which sums up the whole thing, I think. One of the deaneries in the area has an ecumenical day every now and then, when people come across – Baptists, Methodists, and so on. The Anglican priests were saying that they would leave if they ordained women, and one of our priests asked why. One Anglican said, "Because we don't have the authority to do it; so we would become Catholics." And the Catholic then asked, "Well, what if *we* ordain women priests?" The Anglican replied, "You have the authority to do it." I can't see the reason why we shouldn't have women priests. A lot of it is based on what Aristotle said; it's nothing to do with Jesus. Aristotle felt, erroneously, but in accordance with his time, that a woman was simply a deformed man.'

'He got that wrong: everyone starts out in the womb as a female,' I said, annoyed with Aristotle and letting pass for the moment the hint that it was mere absent-mindedness on Jesus' part that led to His choosing male disciples.

'That's right. He was completely wrong. But if you start from the premise that a woman is human but less than a man, then how could such a person possibly embody all people?'

'I don't start from that premise,' I said, running my fingers through my hair, for how do you talk to a person who assumes you hold views which you do not? 'I take a simple view. I'm not alarmed by the concept of patriarchy. Seems to me that a male priesthood is a corrective to the aggressive, destructive image of the male – gives them something positive and, if it's done properly, something loving and creative to do. Women, by nature, are already supreme creators. They *utter* human beings. Maybe if men were encouraged rather than denigrated they wouldn't be so bad-tempered.'

'That's a very good point. I'll say something else on that: if the Church wasn't run by male celibates, the emphasis would not be placed upon such issues as contraception, abortion and sexual continence. If it was run by women the emphasis would be on war: how wrong it is to fight and things like that.'

'I can't think where you got that idea,' I said, thinking of the bellicose lady prime ministers our century has known. 'It's only quite recently that war ceased to be regarded as the normal state and peace as a sort of aberration. I expect you'd say we've evolved, but in the First World War a lot of women went round handing out white feathers – "What, still alive at twenty-two, a fine upstanding chap like you?" And a lady wrote to the papers, signing herself "A Little Mother", saying she'd given all her sons to the war effort and she wished she had more so she could give them too. You take an idealised view of the female. And the song "We Don't Want to Lose You but We Think You Ought to Go" was written by a woman. And how about Mrs Thatcher and Boudicca and Elizabeth I and Catherine the Great? And the Chinese empress who cut the arms and legs off her rival and kept her in a jar to amuse the courtiers, and Countess Elizabeth Bathory who bathed in virgin's blood to retain her complexion? Women in power can become quite as bloodthirsty as men.' In fact they can be worse. Who said a woman can be a man but she can never be a gentleman? Quite a few women are now taking up boxing. I should have asked what he thought about lady soldiers.

'But what is warfare if it's not wrong?' asked the priest, trying to stick to his point. 'It seems to me one of the reasons we emphasise these things is not so much that it is an ethical priority, but *who* is making the ethical pronouncements. If you are going to be male and celibate then neither abortion nor contraception is going to affect you.'

'Except that with the abortion issue and the idea of the right to choose', I pointed out, 'it is always assumed that it's the woman's choice, whereas very often the woman wants the child but the man involved doesn't want the embarrassment or the inconvenience or whatever. The priesthood should perhaps address itself to the male sex on the subject of responsibility. Then perhaps we could move on from the extreme feminist notion that all men are pretty hopeless and women are never, ever, under any circumstances, at any fault whatever.'

'I got very upset with one feminist commune which decided to vote for Mrs Thatcher on the grounds that she was a woman,' remarked the priest. 'That says it all, really. But you are always going to get extremes. On the other hand, theologically there is simply no objection to women priests. Or, if there is, it's something to do with ... well ... Jesus didn't ordain women. On the other hand, there is no evidence that he ordained anybody.

'Isn't there?' (I recalled the words 'Do this in memory of Me' and 'Thou art Peter and upon this rock I will build my church'.) I also thought it was a theological impossibility for a woman to be a priest because a woman cannot stand *in persona Christi*. 'I have an instinctive feeling against it,' I said. 'Priestesses make me think of pagans and women racing round in the woods, flown with wine. They have no place in Christianity.' I expect I had in mind Agave who, with a number of other women, tore her son Pentheus to pieces and ate him raw while under the influence of a Dionysiac frenzy. At the time she mistook him for a mountain lion. She later realised her error but it was too late for regrets. I should have mentioned the Ethiopian woman who explained that one of the reasons her Church would never countenance women priests on the altar was because of Christ's words to Mary Magdalene after the Resurrection: *Noli me tangere*. The Ethiopian lady said that was perfectly clear and unequivocal – 'Touch me not.' I have told other people of this and they mostly go a little pale with horror and say they'd have to go back and look at the Aramaic. He probably meant, they insist, that the Magdalene shouldn't *cling* to Him because He had further things to attend to. This reading does not reflect well on her. It makes her appear fussy, over-reliant and female in the worst possible way.

Thomas the Doubter, a less loving friend of the Lord, was permitted to put his hand in His side. God was born of a woman. What more of God's love and trust and tangibility does the female sex require?

The priest went on, 'Again, harking back to the New Age thing, one of the great insights is that intuition is important. Listen to intuition rather than try to be too analytical. There is a lot of wisdom there. Rationally there is no reason why women can't be ordained. There is no theologian in the world who doesn't accept that, unless they are going to argue there were no women present at the Last Supper.'

'I believe there are some theologians who don't accept that. And were there any women at the Last Supper? If so, nobody bothered to tell Leonardo da Vinci,' I observed. There is a move to introduce women retrospectively into the Last Supper. It is probably led by those who insist that women should be allowed into all-male clubs.

'You get the stories', said the priest, 'about how women can reach into places that sometimes men can't, particularly when it comes to things like absolution. I've always found it easier to talk to a woman rather than a man unless I know him very well.'

'Everybody says this,' I said. It's probably because they don't interrupt as much. I went on, 'But you have to be careful. You mustn't give them too much credit. Both men and women gain a sense of power from hearing secrets and few can resist passing them on or dining out on them. This is why so much is made of the seal of the confessional, or hadn't you noticed?'

'It seems silly in a baring-of-soul type of thing', said the priest, 'that a person couldn't give absolution afterwards. And the men that I would go to somehow have a motherly, anima, side to their nature, so I don't know.'

I am suspicious of indulgent people, of people who say 'Tell me all about it' and 'You mustn't blame yourself'. How do *they* know? You get the feeling with keen listeners that hearing a recital of your shortcomings or anxieties makes them feel more at ease with their own. It makes them feel good. I also have a particular loathing of both patronage and pity.

'I believe that only God through a priest can absolve sins,' I said, in my old-fashioned way, 'but I always go to Our Lady and ask for her kindly and powerful intervention.'

'That is, of course, how the cult of Mary began,' said the priest:

'the archetype deep within ourselves. Fair enough. It's also a relation to the earth itself – the earth mother – that which brings forth all life. This is locked deep in evolutionary history.'

Sometimes one's co-religionists can be as exasperating as evangelisers from other faiths. I once had a particularly taxing drive across the Sahara with a man who lectured me on the Crucifixion. It was absurd of me to imagine – he said – that God would permit Jesus (who my friend conceded was a great *prophet*) to die on the Cross in that ignominious fashion. What happened – he continued, warming to his theme – was that Judas was substituted for Him. I didn't argue, since there was no point. Nor did there seem much point in explaining to the priest that I did not agree with his theory about archetypes and was totally unmoved by the concept of the 'earth mother'. Male feminists make me uneasy. I am less struck by their broad-mindedness and generosity than reminded of Uriah Heep and Quisling. They are not, I feel, to be trusted. If they are sincere then they are gullible.

*   *   *

I made my way to St Etheldreda's, Ely Place, in London to talk to Father Kit Cunningham. Father Kit is the sort of priest I am or used to be accustomed to: he is large, wise and benevolent and you feel you can get mildly plastered in his presence without the need to apologise too extravagantly. I asked him if he shared my impression that men were unsure of themselves at the moment and felt themselves to be in disrepute. 'There seems to be a feeling that women can do no wrong,' I said, 'but men are a bit of a dead loss.'

'Well, I've read some articles', said Father Kit, 'that have astonished me with the vehemence of the language that we men are just not good at anything. I'm sure that it's perfectly true that lots of men are inadequate, poor lovers, etc., or that they are domineering and insensitive, but it's not true of every one. It's just one of these feminist attitudes, making sweeping remarks of that nature.'

'What do you think about calling God "Her"?'

'It's a basic misunderstanding of language, apart from theology. I wrote to the Conference of Bishops when they took the words "men" and "man" out of the Mass. I pointed out that the bishops were never properly instructed in English grammar, because "man" here doesn't refer to individuals but to mankind, and that includes women as well.'

'Christ was the Word. And when you start misunderstanding and misusing words you lose your way,' I suggested.

'The manoeuvring of language is certainly something that goes on,' said Father Kit. 'We're now deprived of that wonderful word "gay" in the language because it's been purloined by these gentlemen in Los Angeles and elsewhere. What do we make of the word "democrat" now? Nothing. I'm sure the feminist thing will all pass. I don't think there will be any feminists in thirty years' time. It's just a phase and it will have been got over by then.'

I hope Father Kit is right. It has all been a terrible waste of time and energy when atrocities are being committed on human beings all over the world. There is no sign that the overall condition of humanity has been improved one iota by the feminist movement.

'The movement seems a bit insulting to the whole of humankind,' I observed inadequately. 'If one half is no good, it doesn't say much for the other.'

'Again, this is taking something from America and translating it, twenty years later, into religion, and getting some nuns who have become feminine conscious and started attacking bishops. If you talked to some of the nuns twenty or thirty years ago it was a tough life for them, sure, but there was a justification for it, because they were seeking holiness, and I think they led useful lives. I can understand that some possibly were broken by the system, but also that some of those great Reverend Mothers and heads of teacher training colleges were women of power. They'd have some of these feminists for breakfast before they started on the outside world. They were "liberated" to love God. I'm sure that their devotion to Our Lord hadn't actually inhibited them in any way. It gave them a sense of well-being and a sense of worth, knowing that they were doing the right and the good thing.'

'I also think that the existence of such people is of great benefit to the rest of us,' I said. 'People used to talk about powerhouses of prayer, but they don't any more.'

'I suppose that's why saints are there,' mused Father Kit, 'to give us some sort of reason. I'm aware that there were things that went on which were obviously unjust for individuals, but this is where any system which has high ideals shows that some are going to fail – not everyone can be perfect and totally up with the system in every way.'

'I was reading about someone who refers to Our Lord as Jesa Christa. It seems mind-bogglingly ungrateful and hair-raisingly insolent and, in the end, quite pointless,' I said.

'It's total sadness that people could become so twisted and confused. They mean well, try to adapt to the latest fashion and lose all sense of reality. My father used to say that once we took our religion *table d'hôte*, where the younger generation wants it *à la carte*. A rather good summary of it all. We used to take the package, and the young ones are all picking and choosing the bits that they like.'

*   *   *

'What do you think of feminism?' I asked Peter Hebblethwaite.

'The feminist reading of the Bible can be totally absurd, but there is evidence that part of it is convincing and also that there has been a kind of writing out of women. The supper at Bethany and the Last Supper can be considered as two parabolic and symbolic events very similar in meaning. There is a reference at the beginning of Luke 8 about the women who follow Jesus around "ministering" to Him – that sounds like them doing the washing-up, but it wasn't. One of them was the wife of Herod's steward; more like a patron than a domestic help.

'That reminds me to say something about the ministry which I should have said earlier. Timothy Radcliffe, who is now Master of the Dominicans, has recently drawn attention to it. We think that servant, the word *diaconus*, means something like a waiter at a table. (Imagine a bishop introducing himself to his congregation – "Hi, I'm Ken and I'm your waiter.")'

The way things are going this does not strike me as so outrageously unlikely. I was recently at a motorway café where the waitresses are now called 'servers', which is pretty mad since I imagine they were first called waitresses in order to do away with the servile connotations of 'servant'. Anyway I entertained the possibility in *The Sin Eater*.

'It does mean "waiter",' continued Peter, 'but in the sense of a go-between, between the table and the kitchen, just as an ambassador is a go-between. The essence of the ministry of Jesus, who comes not to be served but to serve, is as a go-between of the things of God and human reality. That changes the whole nature of ministry.

'I told this to a retired Scottish Episcopalian bishop and he replied, "I shall have to tear up half the sermons I have written." So I do think the place of women in the Church needs a lot of attention; but the promotion of women in the Church doesn't necessarily entail ordination. Ordination means status and the humblest place in the Church is the laity: they have to be made aware of their ministry and their status in the Church. So it is a slightly paradoxical thing.'

Shortly after this I heard with my own ears a woman stating that women should 'fast from the Sacraments' until they got their own way and were allowed into the priesthood, which reminded me of Lucifer's 'I will not serve.'

I asked Margaret Hebblethwaite what she thought about it. 'What about feminism in the Church specifically? Where do you stand on women priests, if you see what I mean?' I can no sooner imagine a woman as a priest than I can imagine one as a husband.

'I'm very firmly committed to women priests. It's an issue of urgency and justice. Having said that, I don't wish to be one. I've always felt that I wanted particularly to work for the vocation of the laity; to build up the dignity of being a lay person and to build up the number of areas in a ministry that lay people could do. I came round to the idea of women priests as an afterthought to that. I began to realise how compelling it was, and how it was important to work for that as well as the lay thing. The two have to work in tandem. If you just work for women priests you end up with clericalism – the idea that you can't do anything in the Church unless you are a priest. This is bad because it doesn't make full use of the laity, the variety of things they can do and the levels at which they can work. I think it's to do with a real sense of salvation and being redeemed. If a woman can't represent Christ, how can Christ represent women?'

Without any trouble at all, I'd have thought. Sounds to me like a fallacy of the undistributed middle. Wine is stored in barrels. Diogenes lives in a barrel. Therefore Diogenes is a bottle of plonk.

'The theological way of looking at it', Margaret went on, 'is to ask to what extent Christ identifies with women and to what extent we are taken up by Him into the divine nature and the possibility of sharing grace. The sex of the priest is a symbol, a very negative symbol.'

I enquired, 'You wouldn't go along with the lady who now calls Our Lord Jesa Christa?'

'It depends on what you really mean by that. Obviously, as a matter of historical fact, Jesus was a male human being. He was Jewish and lived at a particular place at a particular time – all clear and simple. But there is something universal about Christ, in which Gentiles are saved as well as Jews – women are saved by Christ just as much as men.'

'Was it ever in any doubt?' I asked, because if it was it's news to me.

'I think there is doubt if people say it is illegitimate to represent Him artistically or whatever in one of those other forms. It's generally acceptable to have a black Christ so by the same token it's OK to have a female Christ. It doesn't mean that historically you thought Christ was a woman, but it is to say that womanhood is redeemed.'

'It would surely be a remarkably dense woman who imagined that it wasn't,' I said, wondering where in the name of all that's wonderful this peculiar idea had arisen. Surely it was discarded centuries ago.

'A woman had the very distressing experience of being raped,' said Margaret. 'She had a sort of vision of Christ as a crucified woman and that was profoundly healing to her. I think that is the sort of sense in which there is that Christa statue. We know historically that Jesus Christ was not a woman, but to portray Him so sometimes can say something very powerful and important about the truths of our faith.'

'Except that it's false and misrepresentative. I remember a lesson in the convent when the Mistress of Novices was talking about the various heresies. I think she must have got to Gnosticism when she pointed out that you couldn't circumcise a non-corporeal body, that the circumcision was yet another proof that Christ was truly human, truly male. I don't imagine the most ardent feminist would want to circumcise a female. Once you start thinking on those lines you think you're going mad. I can't get my mind round Christ in drag and anyway wouldn't that lead on to sometimes thinking of Our Lady as a man?'

'I've never heard of anyone doing that but I wouldn't find it offensive. I think it's quite important that men should find her as helpful as women do.'

'Many men are devoted to her,' I said, briefly imagining a Nativity play in which the infant Jesus was represented by a girl and a man was dressed up as the Blessed Virgin.

'Yes, she becomes very much their mother.'

'Well, she couldn't if she was a man, and as for thinking of Christ as a woman it seems extremely denigrating to men – an alarming element of feminism. I think women have always had the feeling, "Oh, poor stupid things, they can make war and money but they are otherwise impractical and useless", and this feeling seems to be getting stronger.'

'Yes, it is. There *is* a feeling that we can do without men.'

'Why do you think there is such a terror of patriarchy and even a deep horror and loathing of men – of men *per se*?'

'I don't see it quite like that. There is a great deal of anger among women and there is quite a lot of inverted sexism around at the moment. But women-against-men sexism is just as bad as men-against-women.'

'What about the view that women do many good things,' I asked, 'loving people and looking after them, exemplifying gentleness and generosity, and that one of the few ways men can also do this is in the priesthood? At its most extreme, the view is that men are little use for anything else and it would be unfair for women, who have so much power already, to muscle in on the one area where men can be seen to be useful.'

'I have heard this said and I don't agree with it. I value the priesthood more than that. A lot of men don't see it that way either and want women in the priesthood. It's a bit like men keeping out of the kitchen and the women wanting them out because they can't have jobs and careers and so they want control in some area. If it was something like the army it wouldn't matter but the priesthood does matter.'

The reason I don't want women in the priesthood is because it matters so much and should not be seen as merely another area for equal opportunity. Then I thought of how much I disliked having men in the kitchen: they cook quite well but they don't wash up as they go along. But I said, 'There was a problem with women in the army. They insisted on being allowed to go to the front line and everybody said, "Oh, you'll be raped by the enemy", and then they got raped by their own comrades.'

'Did they? British?'

'No, Americans.' My husband, when I discussed this with him, said that it was probably described as 'friendly fire'.

'That's what worries me about this idea,' I said. 'It's the kind of homogenisation that's very dangerous. I think it is essential that we should be able to make allowances for the differences between people – colour, sex, everything – and not try and pretend that we have the same potential, skills, genes, anything. This pretence that we are all alike is sinister, because we are not.'

'I agree with the underlying point, but with women priests one of the most exciting things when you see them in other denominations is that they aren't actually aping the men. They are very feminine women and have a style that's quite refreshing. I think the women's liturgical movement is a very creative thing – it enriches it and adds variety. What one wants to avoid is women doing what were the men's jobs in a male kind of way.'

'I met one liberal and progressive person who said she didn't like the Anglican lady priests because they look so dykeish with their dog collars, as though they *were* aping the men. It had made her think again about the whole issue.' Quite a few women wear dangling earrings with their dog collars, which gives a confusing impression.

'That's interesting,' said Margaret. 'I did a piece in *The Tablet* about this firm which makes women's clerical dress. Apparently it's completely out of the question for women to wear the clerical shirt – that sort of square shape designed for men. Instead, they have got a lot of new garments, principally cassocks, all designed for the bosom, I was amazed by it, but basically the idea is right. One does go back to one's prejudices. I've always detested the dog collar because it speaks to me about clerical power over the laity; so I thought I would hate to see women in it. In fact, I've come to like it because the whole message it's giving out is a different one. I still hate it on a man, but the symbolic sense of a woman in a dog collar is different. Still, I think she's got to get away from the clerical shirt.'

I never believed in Freud's concept of penis envy until I saw a woman in a dog collar.

I had also discussed with Margaret the question of the habit, how in some places it has been modified and in others abolished. She said she much preferred the new mode, since the sisters looked more feminine: the old habit had made them look hard and sexless, she said. I was surprised at this, as most nuns now remind me of plucked chickens robbed of their natural covering and on the whole look like hell. Nor could I think that such films as *The Sound of Music* and those starring Audrey Hepburn as a religious would have had the same impact if the wardrobe mistress had been constrained to clothe the actresses in ill-cut skirts and anoraks and little scarves revealing hair which would be better concealed. Margaret said that the sisters who had taught her now looked more human in the new mode and were more easily approachable.

This just goes to show you can never win. I was talking to a schoolgirl at a convent run by new-style nuns – who, I must say, when I met them seemed nice enough. She said they were a load of cruel, drunken, sybaritic lesbians. This eventually translated into the fact that they made her do her homework, had central heating in the rooms, partook of the occasional sherry and could be heard laughing and talking behind closed doors after lights out. What's more, she said in tones of indignant disgust, they didn't even *look* like proper nuns.

I forgot to ask Margaret about the suggestion that if God is a woman then the devil might be one as well. Madam Lucy Fur. Since the sisterhood persist in regarding God as female, it seems only fair to offer the same advantage to the Prince of Darkness.

A report in *The Times* quoted from a feminist pamphlet: 'The term "clergy person" should be preferred to "clergyman". "God" should never be "He" and Jesus should be "He" as little as possible. Even the devil should be sexless, according to a campaigning pamphlet . . . which declares war on sexist language in the Church. But Jesus Christ was male "and we must necessarily use some male nouns and pronouns when referring to Christ". Several of these "can certainly be reduced without approaching heresy", the pamphlet states. It is important not to emphasise his maleness, it says.'

One 'nun' wrote to ask me whether I had never realised that the BVM was an incest victim, having been abused by God the Father. Some people when I pass on this *aperçu* refuse to believe that I ever received such a letter: these are the people who insist on regarding all forms of feminism as beyond criticism. When you give them evidence – and I mean the evidence of the movement's own words and actions – they say you must be exaggerating and laugh lightly. A Frenchman, on hearing that someone had made a statue of 'Jesa Christa', at first accused me of joking and then, having seen a photograph of it, observed that it added yet another dimension to sexual perversion. It reminds one of nothing so much as a Madonna video. The Dean of the Cathedral of St John the Divine in New York, where this statue resides, said on its installation, 'I think God was making a feminist and political statement when he made man and woman.'

A lady called Vicky Cosstick wrote in *The Tablet* of 6 March 1993: '*The Catechism of the Catholic Church* defines a lie as a "profanation of language". According to this definition *The Enemy Within* is certainly a lie.' She says indignantly of this revealing and amusing book which deals with feminism in the Church, Its first chapter named names, dates and places and purported to be an exposé of a feminist conspiracy to infiltrate the structures of the Catholic Church.' Yes, well, it does: it gives names, dates and places, and chapter and verse, and exposes a feminist conspiracy (although not using that alarming word) to infiltrate the structures of the Catholic Church. Ms Cosstick doesn't actually deny this, and I don't see how she could, since the documentation appears perfectly sound, but she seems to think it mean of people to point it out, and claims that her opponents are the conspirators. 'This vigilante campaign targets any progressive tendency in the Church, including feminism in general and feminists in particular.' 'Feminists', she continues later, 'in general are too various to agree on enough to constitute a conspiracy.'

Turn to the next page in the same issue of *The Tablet* and you find the following. 'It is deeply disheartening when some Catholic women show themselves prepared to insult their sisters by, for example, referring always to women priests as "priestesses"' (I find this remark touching in its glum innocence and am loath to admit the terms in which Janet and I refer to them; we picked up the phrase from Al the driver) 'as though there were some pagan link and ontological bar, which neither Paul VI nor John Paul II nor the college of bishops has ever alleged.' No? Well, far be it from me to accuse the hierarchy of inattention, but I do suggest they take a look at *The Enemy Within*. On page 20 it states, 'Alternative liturgies are a particular speciality of the women's movement, having strong pagan overtones. They cultivate symbolic activities, such as "apple blessing" and "green ribbon liturgy" used at joint CWN and Catholic Lesbian Sisterhood sexual orientation workshops, with its symbolic "bonding". While Sr Myra Pool, Contact Secretary for the CWN, and the St Joan's

International Alliance representative on the NBCW, reported on a Women in Ministry day at the Jesuits' Heythrop College, saying: "All participants were anointed with symbolic oil and Suzanne Fageol (an American priestess) led us in a Circle Dance".'

This is where the mirth starts, and I should be reluctant to believe it all untrue for the worldly and unworthy reason that many a long winter night has been enlivened by the revelations of pure daffiness here portrayed. 'Reclaiming Menstruation', for instance, a suggested ritual. Women gather in a circle (they seem to be mad about circles) clutching red and green candles and bowls and balls of red yarn; then they swap anecdotes about their monthly cycles (a tiresome female preoccupation), then they're meant to jump in a pool and climb out and get into clean frocks – 'bright robes of new cloth'. At some point they incant, 'We are the circle of the mothers, the lifebearers. This yarn is the stream of power that unites us with each other, with all women and with all the powers of the universe.' As Josephine Robinson, the author of the essay illuminating these practices, remarks, 'What powers, one wonders, does she have in mind?' – 'she' being R. R. Ruether again. We read of a 'Rite of Mind-Cleansing from the Pollution of Sexism' and a 'Coming Out Rite for a Lesbian', and none of it sounds remotely Christian or even sane. I defy anyone to keep a straight face on reading the description by one Brid Fitzpatrick of a 'roly-poly session' during Holy Week in which women gave each other 'bear hugs', rolling over and over with much wild shrieking and giggling. 'Women on their hands and knees side by side with another woman lying on their gently swaying backs. Women swaying backward, caught and tenderly held, then lifted high and lowered again – learning letting go and trust.'

Is it really not true, despite the sources quoted at the end of each chapter? Did the contributors to *The Enemy Within* make it all up out of whole (bright new) cloth? I do hope not. The author of the piece in *The Tablet* complains that people keep sending her letters and telephoning her in order to take issue with her views. She says a sense of humour helps, but, since the article ends by suggesting that 'perhaps all the writers of the letters could get together and try a bit of circle dancing. You never know, they might enjoy it', you have to conclude that she wouldn't recognise a sense of humour if it leapt up and strangled her with a ball of red yarn.

*   *   *

'And what are your views of feminism?' I asked Stoddard.

'I'm sure that most of what we need to know about feminism has already been said many times over. I would just add that this aspect of the so-called sexual revolution has not only been the empowerment (i.e. en-male-ment) of women, but also about the depowerment (or en-female-ment) of men. Nor should it be assumed that in the New Age this process is driven only by ambitious women. I suspect that there are any number of men who either covertly or overtly welcome a more passive, domestic, unheroic, easy life.'

Not I, I was sure he said in his soul. And if I were a man I would say so as well.

Since meekness, compassion and humility have always been regarded as Christian virtues, I find it hard to reconcile this with the feminist view that the Church has, in the past, been overwhelmingly patriarchal and masculine. The sisterhood is scornful of the aforementioned virtues which could be seen as pertaining to what was once known as the gentle sex, preferring self-affirmation and empowerment. It is very confusing. Christ Himself exemplified the gentler human traits, so if women now are contemptuous of them why do they want to be priests? It seems they want not to follow in Christ's footsteps but to usurp His position and restate the case. It grows increasingly clear that feminism and Christianity are incompatible. Not only do feminists find God the Father unappealing, they despise self-sacrifice and must therefore consider the Saviour of Mankind to be something of a wimp. Women are constantly being told to put themselves first. Even mothers are offered this advice. Happily not all of them take it, or the human race would grind swiftly to a halt.

One curious aspect of the debate is the secrecy surrounding it. I have spoken to other people who have written to various Catholic journals quoting, verbatim, the words of feminists, and have been refused publication. No, no – the editors seem to say – this is unfair. People should not be expected to fall into the pits they have dug for themselves. In the effort to appear liberal they deny the evidence, utterly disregard the wilder aspects of the movement and endeavour to keep up the pretence that what we are dealing with is 'progress' rather than distortion and heresy. They employ that censorship which they claim to deplore and evince not only bias but cowardice. Many male editors, and indeed many bishops, are terrified, not only of appearing 'chauvinistic', but of women. This is, admittedly, not unreasonable. I have known several women who have frightened the life out of me. An especially aggressive 'nun' – the one who tells bishops who disagree with the ordination of women to 'go away, little boy, and come back when you've grown up' – did not welcome the influx of disaffected Anglicans into the Roman Church because she claimed they were all misogynists and would interrupt the inevitable progression towards female RC clergy. Her own view of men makes misogyny look mild by comparison.

I have long been puzzled by the Protestant position which avers, on the one hand, that Catholics 'worship' the Virgin Mary and are suffocated by 'Mariolatry' and, on the other, that the Roman Church is overwhelmingly patriarchal and has no time for women.

The Roman Church permitted and encouraged women to form communities of their own, to live autonomously in convents and beguinages. They were allowed to reject men and marriage and the constraints of family life; to take a name other than their patronym and escape from the limitations and irritations of wedlock and a male-dominated society. They had freedom in its true sense, not anarchical but ordered. Now many have abandoned the simplicity of conventual discipline and emerged to demand the spurious freedom of the world. One is tempted to echo Freud and ask 'What *do* women want?'

7

Speaking in Tongues

!#!*! !@*&#!! !#*&! !*&#@#*! !&#@#!

To the Holy Land – Israeli breakfasts – The Jerusalem
syndrome – The Plain of Armageddon – Home to Wales
– In search of Charismatics – A carpenter and a crucifix – On being raptured – The 'Forgiveness Prayer'
and the 'Prayer of Inner Healing'

I am obviously not the best person to go on a quest, having no
sense of direction and being easily diverted. if a tangent offers
itself I will go off at it. People have to recall me to the task
in hand and frequently find I have forgotten what it was. When
I began this search I was looking for some discernible theme in
religious, specifically Christian, matters today, but there isn't one;
rather there are dozens. Happily, human life is conducted on many
levels and when one proves too much you can emerge on another
and worry about something else for a change. You can travel in
fact and reality on an aeroplane and *go* somewhere else. When, in
the spring of 1993, a large lump appeared under my ear and the
doctor observed that since I smoked so much there were probably
other lumps where I couldn't see them, I told him not to be ridiculous,
tore up the forms which would have admitted me to the hospital to be
X-rayed and went to Jerusalem under the wing of my friend Shelley.
Looking back, I do not understand why I behaved like this except
that I have always felt that since it is my body I would be the first
to know when anything was badly wrong with it. I also felt that I
had too much to do to be bothered with being ill, for apart from
this book, which was now mostly referred to as the Bloody Thing
(because whenever I thought I was getting near the end I would

come across some hitherto unsuspected development which usually
turned out to be some old-hat heresy), we were being threatened
with bankruptcy, my husband was far from well, our daughter was
going to Los Angeles to join our fourth son just as the riots were
breaking out, while our fifth son was exploring Africa. There were
several other sources of anxiety, trivial and serious, and I was also
much concerned about the welfare of Basil the cat, since he belongs
to my daughter and is a responsibility. (I fear this may sound winsome,
but people who have the care of an animal will know what I mean.)
I am a gifted and comprehensive worrier but there are limits.

Our trip did not begin auspiciously: Shelley, who frequently flies
to and from Israel, passed through the initial interrogation at London
airport without trouble, but I was questioned for nearly an hour. I
was asked if anyone had given me anything to take to anyone and I
said – for I had grown exasperated – that, yes, one of my chums had
given me a packet of Liquorice Allsorts to take to one of her chums
in the Old City. It was true, but I should not have mentioned it. Their
eyes narrowed suspiciously and the grilling grew in intensity. Shelley,
watching the proceedings with increasing agitation, was approached
by a Pentecostalist who wanted to know what I had done. She was
going to Israel, it transpired, to walk around its borders, praying
for it. When we finally made it to the plane Shelley found herself
sitting beside her new friend, who spent the journey questioning her
in order to ascertain why I had been grilled for so long. I apologised
on behalf of Christendom but Shelley said it didn't matter.

It was raining when we landed and chilly and dark, but we hailed
a *sherut* (a shared taxi) and said we wanted to go to Jerusalem. To be
precise it would have been a shared taxi but when the driver learned
of our destination he expelled from its interior a large family –
mother, father and a number of children – and ushered us in in
their stead. Presumably they wished to take a shorter journey in the
opposite direction. We felt very bad about this and worried all the
way to the Holy City as we bounced around in privileged seclusion.
When we arrived we had an Israeli breakfast – fruit, cheese, olives,
yoghurt, tomatoes, cucumber, flat bread and jam and boiled eggs.
Then we went on a tour of the city.

Now, one of the purposes of our trip was a questing one: we had
some idea of finding traces of our common heritage, Jewish and
Christian, and we also had the notion of talking to Jewish and

Palestinian women to see if what they had in common was not more powerful than what divided them. (This was before I started taking a closer look at militant feminism and thus before I had gone off women.) We had an idealistic hope, as many have had before us, that we would find the female preoccupations with the lives and futures of the children – with life itself – stronger than hatred, stronger than death. It may well be, but we didn't have the chance to find out, for we only had ten days and we only met one aspect of Israeli society: kind and thoughtful people who deplored the violence and enmity but could see no way out of it. We were taken by a rash young fellow with a gun to the City of David, where, we were told afterwards in a horrified chorus, the stranger takes his life in his hands. No one came to talk to us, only to glare at us from inside a closed car, the windows opaque with dust. In Nazareth we went to sit in on a Palestinian women's group which seemed promising – until we realised that we had happened on a consciousness-raising session which could have been going on in California – or north-west London come to that. The women were kind and hospitable and delightful, but women's issues seem of relatively minor importance when you have the sense that all hell could break loose at any moment, and more appalling suffering be unleased on humankind. Saddam Hussein was again making ominous noises at the time.

One day after breakfast of fruit, cheese, olives, yoghurt, tomatoes, cucumbers, flat bread and jam and boiled eggs – but I must not grow tedious; though I do wonder why all the Peoples of the World are so set in their ways when they get out of bed – we went on a more detailed tour of Jerusalem, to visit the holy sites. There was a snag here: no one seemed to have the remotest idea of where they really were. Titus had flattened the place in the year 70 A.D. and since then Crusaders, Muslims and Lord knows who else had trampled all over it, while the Israelis have now made most of it very clean and tidy.

Queen Helena, a notorious bossy-boots, had decided on various places as the principal locations for the important events in the life of Our Lord, while General Gordon, for whom I have a soft spot but who himself had a weakness for brandy and soda, had decided on others. Between them these two characters had succeeded in muddying the waters beyond redemption. In the Church of the Holy Sepulchre – as in the Church of the Nativity in Bethlehem – the various Christian factions had contrived to create a strangely sordid atmosphere. In the darkness I had an impression of decay combined with commerce and the feeling that religion had disappeared in a suffocating fog of religiosity.

One of our guides, an English Jew called Joe, who was born in the East End practically in the same street as Al, said he was sometimes required to take charge of groups of born-again Christians or of an organisation calling itself 'Jews for Jesus', both of which were prone to pester him with the insistence that if he would only see the light and join them he would find true happiness. Some caused him embarrassment by attempting to cross themselves at the Western Wall, while others jumped in the Jordan, clad in tallis and yarmulka bearing the legend 'Jesus the Messiah Has Come'. His worst experience, however, was in the Upper Room with a group of 500 Charismatics who spoke in tongues. They began by muttering and proceeded to a threatening cacophony which, he said, was the most frightening thing he had ever heard in his life. He and his three fellow guides made a hasty exit until the hysteria had subsided. There is a phenomenon known as the 'Jerusalem syndrome' which afflicts people of previously sound mind when they enter the Holy City: they go into high mania, supposing themselves variously to be the Angel Gabriel, the Virgin Mary, the prophet Elijah or, in extreme cases, God. They are treated and sent home, whereupon, I am told, they almost invariably regain their sanity. The Church used to be adept at recognising religious mania for what it was, but now seems less sure and more inclined to tolerate the excesses of the enthusiast. It is the Israeli psychiatric establishment which is left to cope with the temporary lunatics of whatever religious flavour.

'I have seen', said Joe bemusedly, 'ladies in their forties and fifties weeping and shaking in the churches, embracing each other like lovers. It wasn't religion – there was something wrong with them.'

We came across a group of young people singing a hymn which they seemed to have made up themselves, all wearing expressions of piety. That was nothing, said our guide: you should see them getting baptised in the Jordan while one of their number videos the scene. They leapt about, he said, with much carolling and splashing. While I yearned to explain that persons of the Catholic persuasion did not carry on in this unrestrained fashion I could not, for frequently they do. Joe said he knew that: he had once had a group from Ireland, including two priests – one of the traditional and one of the modern sort – and the nuns in the party had had to keep them under control and separate since they could not agree. One was given to arm-waving and tree-kissing, while the other, with whom my sympathies lie, was against it.

Shelley rebuked me for intolerance. Did I not realise, she enquired, that these people were afraid and alienated in the world and were looking for a sense of community, of 'togetherness', that they needed emotional expression? I said I couldn't see it myself, and that it all looked to me like yet another search for excitement, for a 'high', and if they couldn't get it from drugs they'd get it some other way.

We drove across the Plain of Armageddon agreeing that it seemed sufficiently capacious to accommodate the Last Battle although it was peaceful enough at the moment. 'The horses will welter in blood up to their fetlocks,' Joe reminded us cheerfully, handing round fresh dates. I had a feeling of oppression which I couldn't trace to its source until, casting about in my memory, I realised that, by the time I was old enough a child to understand, the end of the Second World War was in sight. People were already talking of the 'duration' in the sense that they could see the war ending; whereas here, while the Israelis we had met were brave and resolute, few of them could see any near end to the tension in the Holy Land. I said it must be hellish to live in constant apprehension and Joe said you got used to it.

We came to Capernaum and Joe pointed out with an air of apology the new church which has been built there. His attitude was that of a man who, while he does not in the least hold you personally responsible, cannot conceal from you a vulgarity perpetrated by your relations. This church appears to have been inspired by ideas of what a flying saucer might look like, compounded by knowledge of what a hamburger does look like. I had learned from another guide a useful means of expression when confronted with the unexpected: with your forefinger you push back your hat while simultaneously running your other fingers in succession down your face, remarking, 'Oy, oy, oy, oy, oy.' 'Never mind,' said Joe consolingly, and went on to take us to another church built on more traditional lines. We all relaxed. I wondered why, when I could contemplate with equanimity the dolls on sale in Nazareth which represented the child Jesus with blond nylon hair and gold-star-spangled nappies, I was so repelled by this church. We concluded that since it had been constructed to appear 'modern' it was already hopelessly dated: that it had not been built with the glory of God in mind, but as an illustration of what man could do with his new technology and materials and a fluffy notion of the 'future'. Ideas of magic and science, close cousins, were clear in its lineaments: the urge to change, control and impose human will on the world. I suppose it was Le dratted Corbusier who started the trend towards designing buildings that people couldn't live in, and by a natural progression we now have churches which have no room for God. We agreed that social engineers and designers were devil's spawn. Modernism according to the *Oxford English Dictionary* is 'a tendency or movement towards modifying traditional beliefs and doctrines in accordance with the findings of modern criticism and research'. Spilling over into the physical world, it found expression in materials such as pre-stressed concrete and formica which are as life-enhancing as a religion constructed on a few shards of reason and a partial grasp of physics.

There are several new 'religions' masquerading as Christianity but I decided to think about these later. I had gained from Joe the impression that the Charismatic movement was the most prevalent among the fashions so I thought I'd better address myself to that.

After Vatican II it is plain that many people felt deprived of a previously existing spiritual element in the Church and began to search for it elsewhere. Some claim to have discovered it in Pentecostalism, particular enthusiasm for which arose, I am told, in the 1920s in the American Deep South. The writer Tom Hedley dates it earlier: 'The first American charismatic experience can be traced to Cane Ridge, Kentucky. In 1801 about twenty-five thousand Protestants of all denominations came out of the backwoods for a week-long revival meeting. An astounding number of people for those times; it was our first Woodstock. After long, hypnotic worship and heavy drinking, people started to fall to the ground, jerking, shouting, singing rapt in ecstasy. Spiritual conversions took place next to couples having the wildest possible sex. Sexual ecstasy and intoxication, taboo in daily life, can become sacred if seen as a sign of possession by the spirit in a Pentecostal service: a kind of redemption through sin.' (As a matter of interest, the Muslims hold that when Christ promised His people that He would send a Comforter He was speaking not of the Holy Spirit but of Mohammed. This is an example of the variety of interpretations available to the People of the Book.)

The Charismatics insist that we must all be baptised in the Holy

Spirit, but the emphasis seems to be less on the spiritual awakening than on emotional fervour (although I am sure that few now carry on like the people of Cane Ridge). This is hard on the unimpressionable who although devout are repelled by physical manifestations of piety. To confuse things further it seems that the Methodists have decided that the Holy Spirit is female. In a publication called *Partners in Learning* which is used in Sunday schools of all denominations we read: 'In this material we will use the personal pronoun She for the Holy Spirit.' For example, 'One of our beliefs about the Spirit is that she helps us to discover more of the truths about God' and 'Jesus said . . . when I go away another helper will come from God, called the Holy Spirit. You won't be able to see her, but she will be there . . . she will help you understand what God the Father is like: she will help you say your prayers and she will help you to live in God's way.' If I were a Sunday school child I would instantly assume that the Holy Spirit was Mrs God, sent round by God to keep an eye on things when He was engaged elsewhere.

We flew back from Israel and I went home to Wales, a land once so fervently Catholic that it was dedicated to Our Lady. It is a great puzzle that a people who were described by contemporary observers as joyful and much given to singing, dancing, drinking and the pleasures of the flesh should have turned with apparent enthusiasm to Calvinism. Perhaps it was when the climate went through a change and it began to rain all the time. Still, looking on the bright side, the last century saw some splendid preachers who utilised the old oral tradition to bring the Bible stories alive, and identified their own with the Holy Land. I did myself even in my irreligious days: the hills and the valleys, the barren uplands and the soft meadows, the herds and flocks and the lakes and sea. There are holy places in Wales, harbouring the bones of ancient saints, where the awareness of the existence of God forces itself upon you. I am not given to seeing the face of God in the geographical or weather conditions but it is sometimes easier to think about Him when you're sitting on a lonely hillside rather than when you're in a re-ordered church having your hand wrung by the community.

*   *   *

In search of Charismatics, I spoke to Richard, who had spent ten years in a Charismatic community in a remote area of the British Isles. He is a skilled carpenter, and had restored the rood screen in the local church, and mended my seventeenth-century crucifix. He is quiet and competent – the sort of man to whom you instinctively trust your broken crucifix. He had gone to this distant place with high ideals and been delighted to find others of similar mind. For some years he and his girlfriend, who had been instrumental in persuading him to join, were content. So I began by asking him why they'd left.

Richard said that Susie – for that is the name of his girlfriend – was the first to feel uneasy: she became conscious of being increasingly submitted to subtle pressures and grew restive. What sort of pressures, I demanded, imagining perhaps an insistence that they should work harder or give greater evidence of heroic virtue. No, it was simply that they found themselves being forced into roles. If you were perceived as a giver you were expected to give more and more, and if you were seen as a receiver you were prevailed upon to accept more and more, and a strange polarisation took over. I wondered how this had demonstrated itself and Richard gave me an example. There was one woman who was constantly having demons cast out of her and seemed to have grown positively addicted to the practice, while those who did the casting out also thoroughly enjoyed it. It had grown tedious for the onlooker. The 'ministry of healing' played a great part in everyday life. Those with sore throats and streaming noses refused to admit that they were suffering from colds, while, more seriously, a woman with cancer who had been prayed over and 'healed' felt guilty for not getting better and for feeling desperately ill. A man with back pain was 'healed' on stage. Richard said that something very peculiar had taken place: he had seen the man, who had been diagnosed by the healer as having one leg shorter than the other, put both legs on a chair and had seen one leg grow in length under his very eyes. But how amazing, I remarked. Yes, said Richard, but two days later he was in agony again. Richard and Susie are unable to have children: they were prayed and prayed over until they got thoroughly fed up with it.

The community had started out with only four people. It was lovely, said Richard. It had been open and innocent and full of good will with no outside influences. They had worked happily together until they decided they needed new input and were joined by other groups. Here it gets confusing. The Plymouth Brethren appeared, but apparently in two sorts, one described as 'open' and the other as 'closed'. The closed despised alcohol, the cinema and Catholicism. They loathed Catholicism most and were devoted to the views of Ian Paisley. They evinced a paranoiac, siege mentality and Richard avoided them. Another group was called the Restoration Charismatic Movement and they spoke in tongues as well as healing people. You were not absolutely expected to speak in tongues, said Richard, but you were regarded as 'much better' if you did.

In the beginning each person had attempted to work out his own approach to the 'priesthood of man' but over the years this faded as hierarchical ambitions became apparent. Richard and Susie, being personable and bright, were invited to go on a leadership course since it was felt their 'faces fitted'. Richard said he was terrified by this concept: he had eschewed all ideas of leadership and was now being asked to go around giving a good impression so that the unregenerate would recognise him as being among the happiest people on earth and be converted. He said that, while it was held that other Christians were right, they were the rightest and the best.

Other influences had then begun to emerge, most originating in America and Canada and having strong 'end-time' connotations incorporating the views of such as David Wilkinson, an 'end-time preacher', and Jerry Fallwell, who is waiting for the final cosmic cataclysm whereupon he and the righteous will be 'raptured' bodily into Heaven – or something like that. I'm not altogether clear about the precise process whereby this separating of the sheep from the goats will be achieved. I said that I and some friends had spent time discussing the probable scenario. Would we be strolling round the supermarket when suddenly the elect among us would disappear through the roof? Yes, said Richard simply. The fundamentalists had made films portraying this very happening. Great confusion is forecast on the freeways as elect drivers are parted from their vehicles, which will zoom along by themselves, adding to the disruptive nature of this eschatological event.

Richard then explained that for him the final straw had been the overall acceptance of the view that personal prosperity was an inevitable concomitant of Christian belief and practice: it was linked to the Charismatic movement as well as to the fundamentalists and upset him greatly. He and Susie left when they realised that the ideas of Ronald Reagan and the American 'moral majority' had permeated the group. Islam was regarded as the arch-enemy, while in the last days Israel would somehow be subsumed into the Church. In the meantime they were all eagerly looking forward to Armageddon. I believe in the Second Coming but cannot share the relish of the fundamentalists who seem to delight even more in the prospect of the damnation of those who don't agree with them than in the salvation of those who do.

I had a few more questions. What, for instance, did these people think of – say – Teresa of Avila and Mother Teresa of Calcutta, to mention but two Christians not notable for their prosperous lifestyle? Richard said that on the one hand they respected them for giving Christian witness but on the other they despised them because they were poor. Oh, I said. After a while I asked what, in that case, they thought of Christ? Richard said that the movement was much more Bible-based than Christ-centred and that he himself had spent years trying to prove to other people that Christ was a *person* and had never succeeded in proving it to himself. He said he was no longer even a Christian and the ten years he had spent with the Charismatics and the rest now seemed like a dream. There were intelligent people still there and he couldn't imagine why. Sometimes, though, he woke in the small hours with that terrible four-o'clock-in-the-morning feeling of *Oh God, I'm damned*. I said a lot of us felt like that at four in the morning and it was an excellent reason for not allowing one's emotions to rule one's rational faculties. He said sadly that when he first had that sense of conversion it had been wonderful; no doubts, no fears. We agreed that it would be nice to feel like that all the time but not if it meant abandoning one's common sense in favour of false signs and portents. The price is too high.

There have always been saints who had visions, went into trances and sometimes, like St Joseph Cupertino, flew in the air, but when the system of canonisation came in they were carefully investigated and had to give evidence of great holiness and be proved free of prestidigitation. With the present proliferation of charlatanism there are fewer safeguards. Anyone suffering a fit of what I believe used to be known as gross conversion hysteria can now claim to have been 'slain in the spirit'. They lose consciousness and fall down. The great saints who suffered strange manifestations, from stigmata to levitation, always made light of them as being of no real importance. Now many things which are merely odd are claimed to be miraculous. The word 'holiness' is seldom employed these days; instead people talk about 'charisma'.

I then went to a Charismatic meeting in Westminster and found it simultaneously depressing and comical. Perhaps it is a matter of personality: many doubtless good and worthy people enjoy these occasions. It began with a nun leading us in a desultory saying of the Rosary while most people wandered around, then a few participants 'shared' their experience of being 'saved'; some waved their arms in the air and some began to 'speak in tongues'. The friend I was with said it sounded demonic to her and anyway it was giving her a headache, so we left while it was warming up. We took away with us two documents. One is called 'The Forgiveness Prayer' and has all the marks of having been written by a social worker. The second is called 'Prayer of Inner Healing' and has the appearance of having been written by a mad social worker.

The Forgiveness Prayer

Lord Jesus Christ, I ask today to forgive everyone in my life. I know that You will give me strength to forgive and I thank You that You love me more than I love myself and want my happiness more than I desire it for myself.

Lord, I forgive MYSELF for my sins, faults and failings. For all that is truly bad in myself or all that I think is bad, I do forgive myself.

For any delvings in the occult, ouija boards, horoscopes, seances, fortune telling, lucky charms.

For taking Your name in vain; for not worshipping You.

For hurting my parents; for getting drunk; for taking drugs; for sins against my purity; for adultery; for abortion; for stealing; for lying, I am truly forgiving myself today. Thank You Lord for Your grace at this moment.

I truly forgive MY MOTHER. I forgive her for all the times she hurt me, she resented me, she was angry with me and for all the times she punished me. I forgive her for the times she preferred my brothers and sisters to me. I forgive her for the times she told me I was clumsy, ugly, stupid, the worst of the children or that I cost the family a lot of money. For the times she told me I was unwanted, an accident, a mistake or not what she expected I forgive her.

I forgive MY FATHER. I forgive him for any non-support, any lack
of love, affection or attention. I forgive him for any lack of time,
for not giving me his companionship, for his drinking or arguing
and fighting with my mother or the other children. For his severe
punishments, for desertion, for being away from home, for divorcing
my mother or for any adultery, I do forgive him.

Lord, I extend forgiveness to my SISTERS and BROTHERS. I forgive
those who rejected me, lied about me, hated me, resented me,
competed for my parents' love, those who hurt me, who physically
harmed me. For those who were too severe on me, punished me or
made my life unpleasant in any way, I do forgive them.

Lord, I forgive MY SPOUSE for lack of love, affection, consideration,
support, attention, communication, for faults, failings, weaknesses,
and those other acts or words that hurt or disturb me.

Jesus, I forgive my CHILDREN for their lack of respect, obedience,
love, attention, support, warmth, understanding; their bad habits,
falling away from the church, any bad actions which disturb me.

My God, I forgive my SON/DAUGHTER-IN-LAW and other relatives
by marriage, who treat my child with a lack of love. For all words,
thoughts, actions, or omissions which injure and cause pain, I forgive
them.

Please help me to forgive my RELATIVES, my grandmother and
grandfather who may have interfered in our family, been possessive
of my parents, who may have caused confusion or turned one parent
against the other.

Jesus, help me to forgive my CO-WORKERS who are disagreeable
or make life miserable for me. For those who push their work
off on me, gossip about me, won't co-operate with me, try to
take my job, I do forgive them.

My NEIGHBOURS need to be forgiven, Lord. For all their noise,
letting their property run down, their pets who are a nuisance, for
ignoring or hurting me, I do forgive them.

I now forgive my CLERGYMAN, MY CONGREGATION AND MY
CHURCH for all their lack of support, pettiness, lack of friendliness,
not affirming me as they should, not providing me with inspiration,
for not inviting me to serve in a minor capacity and for any other
hurt they have inflicted, I do forgive them.

Lord, I forgive all PROFESSIONAL PEOPLE who have hurt me in any
way, doctors, nurses, lawyers, policemen, hospital workers. For anything that they did to me, or my family, I truly forgive them today.

Lord, I forgive my EMPLOYER for not paying me enough money,
for not appreciating my work, for being unkind and unreasonable
with me, for not promoting me, and for not complimenting me on
my work.

Lord, I forgive my SCHOOL TEACHERS and INSTRUCTORS of the
past as well as the present. For those who punished me, humiliated
me, insulted me, treated me unjustly, made fun of me, called me
dumb or stupid, made me stay after school.

Lord, I forgive my FRIENDS who have let me down, lost contact
with me, do not support me, were not available when I needed help,
borrowed money and did not return it, gossiped about me.

Lord Jesus, I especially pray for the grace of forgiveness for that
ONE PERSON in life who has HURT ME THE MOST. I ask to forgive
anyone whom I consider my greatest enemy, the one who is the
hardest to forgive or the one whom I said I will never forgive.

Thank You Jesus that I am free of the evil of unforgiveness. Let
Your Holy Spirit fill me with light and let every dark area of my
mind be enlightened.

AMEN

At this point the typist went into hysterics. Sometimes when my
friends are unhappy I show them this document and it invariably
lightens their spirits: not, sadly, because of its original intentions but
because of the irresistible image it evokes of a hopelessly ill-done-by
and cross-grained human being. Most people find the sections on
clergymen and employers particularly choice, but everyone has his
own favourite. It reads like a litany of spite, the mode of the
embittered spinster, well represented in literature, who approaches
the vicar with the words 'I don't want to make trouble but . . .' and
proceeds to reveal the misdemeanours of every single dweller in the
parish under the pretence of Christian magnanimity. It is very far
from the modest simplicity of 'Forgive us our trespasses as we forgive
those who trespass against us' and can only serve to encourage the
neurotic into increasingly obsessive self-centredness. Its author would
probably claim that it is intended as an *aide-mémoire* but it reads
like a rather wicked little incitement to grievance. I was warned
in saner times about the dangers of 'scrupulosity', the constant,
fevered rehearsing of one's own minor shortcomings, but I don't
think it even occurred to my spiritual directors to advise me against
the meticulous recitation of the failings of others. Nor was I ever led
to believe that forgiving myself without benefit of the Sacrament of
Penance would avail me much. This 'prayer' is another example of
the blurring of distinction between confession and wild analysis, a
further result of the widely disseminated idea that the individual and
his or (more commonly) her happiness are of prime importance.

I have never seen any reason to believe that my temporal happiness, rather than the salvation of my soul, was of any particular interest to God. Teresa of Avila was once overheard telling Him that the reason He had so few friends was because He treated them so badly.

The 'Prayer of Inner Healing' is chiefly remarkable for suggesting that the Lord is prepared to dismiss the arrangements of Time and go back to sort out any little local difficulties which may have arisen at the moment of conception or birth.

Prayer of Inner Healing

(Find a place where you can be quiet and uninterrupted. Choose a physical position which is comfortable. Come before the Lord in an attitude of humility and trust. Enter into this prayer in whatever way that you feel led to enter into it. Since healing is an ever ongoing process, this prayer will not solve all your problems. We will never get to the point of saying, 'Now all my problems are gone, all my memories have been healed,' but we can get big barriers that are keeping us from health and wholeness, out of the way. Inner healing has been accomplished when a past event no longer has the power to hurt – when it can be recalled without sadness, shame or guilt. Come into the presence of God.)

Lord Jesus, thank you for being here, for the privilege of feeling your strength and your presence.

Lord, you can walk back through my life, all the way back to the very moment I was conceived.

Help me, Lord, even then: cleanse my bloodlines and free me of all those things that may have caused me difficulty at the moment of conception. When I was formed, within my mother's womb, you were there; free me and heal me of any bonds upon my spirit which may have entered me through my mother or the circumstances of my parents' lives even as I was being formed. For this, I give you thanks.

I praise you too, Jesus, that you are healing me also of the trauma of being born. I pray, Jesus, that you would heal me of the pain of birth and all I went through being born. I thank you, Lord, that you were there to receive me into your arms as I was born. Consecrate me in that very moment to the service of God. I thank you, Jesus, for this has been done.

Lord Jesus, I praise you in those early months of my infancy, you were there with me when I needed you. There were times when I needed my mother to hold me close, and to rock me, and tell me the little stories that only a mother can. Lord, do this in the very depths of my being. Let me feel such an overwhelming sense of maternal, comforting, nourishing love that nothing will ever separate me from that love again. I thank you and praise you, Lord, because I know it is being done.

For whatever reason I may feel neglected, Lord, fill in that part of my being now with that strong fatherly love that comes only from a father. Even if I am not aware of having needed to have strong arms around me and a 'daddy' to love me and give me security and strength, do that for me now. I thank you, Lord, that this too is being done.

I have come to understand and accept it, but a part of me never really felt complete, never really felt wanted. I ask today for a healing of that, Lord, let me know that I am your child, an important person in your family, a unique individual that you love in a very special way.

Heal me, Lord, of the hurt that came because of the relationships in my family, the brother or the sister that did not quite understand, or didn't show me love and kindness as he should have. Part of me never felt loved because of it. Let me now reach out in forgiveness to that brother or sister. Perhaps, over the years, I have never quite been able to accept them, because they have not accepted me: give me a measure of love for them so that the next time I see them, there will be such an overwhelming love that all the old things will have passed away . You will have made me new. I thank you for that, Lord.

I pray, Lord, for a healing of those years I spent in the classroom, that you would take from me any pain or suffering that was inflicted upon me at that time. I withdrew within myself then, Lord. I began to be afraid to speak out in groups because I had been ridiculed, or chastised, or criticised in classroom situations. I stopped speaking out because it was too painful. Lord, I ask that the door within my heart be opened up. Let me relate in groups in a more open, more free way than I have ever been able to do before. As this healing takes place, I will have the confidence and courage to do what you call me to do in every situation. I thank you, Lord, because I believe this is being healed now.

Lord, as I went into adolescence, I began to experience things that frightened me, embarrassed me, and caused me pain. I have never quite got over some of the experiences I had as I was learning about myself and what it means to be a person. I pray, Lord Jesus, a healing upon all the experiences I had as a teenager, for the things that I did and for the things that were done to me that have never quite been healed. Enter my heart and take from me now all of the experiences that have caused me suffering, embarrassment, or shame. I am not asking you, Jesus, to erase these things from my mind, but to so transform them so that I can remember them no longer with shame, but with thanksgiving.

Let me understand what young people are going through today, because I have been through it myself – that time of searching and seeking and conflict. As I am being healed, let me help others to find this healing.

Lord Jesus, as I emerged from that period of my life and began to grow into the vocation that you called me into, I had difficulties. I ask you, Jesus, to heal me in the state of life that I am in today, and all that that has meant to the world around me.

(FOR MARRIED PEOPLE)

Lord, heal these things. Let my marriage begin again to be what God has called it to be. Let all of the old hurts and sorrows be put into your hands, so that from this moment, this marriage can be cleansed, and begun anew, as free and as healed as it can possibly be. Thank you, Father, that through this healing we can become the kind of husband and wife that you have asked us to be.

Lord, help me feel such warmth and such strength of love pouring into me that I will never again doubt the path I'm travelling is the one that you have called me to be upon. Give me courage and confidence in the work that you have called me to do. Carry me forward with newness of purpose and goals. I thank you, Father, because I know this is being done.

I have felt lonely and sometimes abandoned and totally rejected by the rest of humanity. Lord Jesus, instill in me today a new sense of strength and purpose. Let me understand what you have put upon my heart. Let me be a living witness for Jesus Christ. I thank you, Father, that this is being done.

As the anointing of your love flows over me, I give you glory, Lord, because I know it is done. Lord, there is no power in heaven and earth that can stop it. I praise you, Lord, because I know that the more I give to you, thanking and praising you for it, the more you can give to me the strength of your presence, the power of your spirit, the love of your divine Son. I praise you, Jesus, for this healing, and I give you the glory. Thank you. Amen.

(Now take ten minutes of quiet. Let the Spirit of God do His healing work in you, emptying your heart of things that are not of God. Let God refill it with His love.)

This curiously greedy petition, self-pitying and demanding, seems to end with a quaint type of bribe: the more I give to you, the more you can give to me. Have people always prayed 'you scratch my back and I'll scratch yours'? It is the first time I have read this sort of thing.

8

Charismatic Renewal

Turning and turning in the widening gyre
The falcon cannot hear the falconer;
Things fall apart; the centre cannot hold;
Mere anarchy is loosed upon the world . . .
The best lack all conviction, while the worst
Are full of passionate intensity.

W. B. Yeats, 'The Second Coming'

The Pentecostal feeling – On enthusiasm – Quakers and Buddhists – A real live Charismatic – Liberation theology – Living in the 'time of change' – Sinners and converts – Opus Dei and the Neo-Catechumenates – 'Therapy for Normals' – Finding God in silence – The importance of offending people

Hoping John Wilkins might be of help, I told him about my visit to the Charismatic meeting in London. Some people, I said, had waved their arms around and swayed, and some had spoken in tongues – only nobody seemed to understand them, and one young man got up and said he had always wanted to be a terrorist until the Holy Spirit visited him, and now he had an impulse to embrace British soldiers. I could only wonder what would be the reaction of the rude and licentious soldiery. I find it annoying myself when people try to embrace me because they are overflowing with goodwill.

'I took away some literature,' I told John. 'It seemed to be very much concerned with me, me, me, me. Whereas once you tried to be, as it were, a receptacle for God, now you are trying to be a better receptacle for yourself.'

'I haven't found that at all in any of the Charismatics I have known,' said John. 'While it's not something that appeals to me very much personally, it is having a great effect. There have been

huge gatherings in Rome itself, and certainly it had the approval of
Paul VI – and of this Pope too, I would think.'

'You don't get the feeling that it somehow works against the
sacramental nature of the Church?' I asked, for, while the Church
was once centred round the Eucharist, I have the impression that
now the Pentecostalist feeling is stronger – people imagine God to
be present in themselves rather than in the Host.

'I can't see why it should,' said John, 'although I don't know a
great deal about it.'

'You think that they're not in opposition – that the reverence for
the Body of Christ hasn't been put aside in favour of the personal
sense of the presence of the Holy Spirit?' I asked.

'I wouldn't have thought so,' said John. 'But you do have to be
very careful with the Charismatics thing – any enthusiastic movement
raises questions.'

'When I was a wee girl in my convent,' I observed reminiscently,
'they were very, very suspicious of enthusiasm. Any postulant
found waving her arms about in the air was severely spoken to. We
were not encouraged to draw attention to ourselves.'

A Benedictine once told me that when one of their novices announced to the Abbot that he had had a vision he was told firmly,
'We don't have visions here.' This will seem repressive to those who
like the idea of visions, but true visions are few and far between,
Deo gratias, for too many would greatly impede the daily work of
a community. There is an idea that when someone claims to have
seen a lady in the wood the Church comes flying in to claim
her as the Virgin Mary. On the contrary: the Church is highly
sceptical of unexplained ladies.

'I dare say the Church has always been a little too doubtful
about enthusiasm,' said John.

'Quite rightly, in my opinion,' I said. 'Enthusiasts are exasperating
and exhausting. They cry, "You must get up at once and come and
see this wonderful view that I, in my unusually perceptive way,
have just noticed." You'd rather go back to sleep and look at the
view in your own good time. Besides, quite often the view that
they're urging you to gaze upon is an aspect of Disneyland. What
is speaking in tongues? Do you know?'

'In the Acts, if I remember correctly, what happened was that
people started talking in languages they didn't know, but others

who spoke that language could understand what they were saying. I'm told two things happen, although I've never seen them. One is that some people talk in a funny language – I don't know if you've heard that – and then others will talk and someone will interpret a language that they don't know. It would be worth going into that and finding out.'

'I must try and find a Charismatic to ask, because what we heard at the meeting sounded very strange.'

I have since asked Richard what transpired and he said that the people he had known claimed that the Holy Spirit had given them the gift of prophecy. One of them would babble, someone would ask 'What did he say?' and someone else would respond, 'He says God loves you' or 'Somebody here has just been healed of cataract' or some other remarkable piece of information. I said it sounded reminiscent of those spiritualist meetings where the deceased return to remind the living to feed the canary. He did not demur.

'I dare say it's a bit like a Quaker meeting,' suggested John, 'where you're meant to speak when the spirit moves you, but you always know that certain people are going to speak. Anyway, that's roughly how I see it.'

This did nothing to recommend the practice to me. In the few dealings I have had with Quakers I have found them to be lacking in charity and passionately respectful of money. Sydney Smith said his lifelong ambition was to roast a Quaker, while William Cobbett addressed them as follows: 'your whole sect live without labour, and by preying constantly, from the beginning of your lives to the end of them, upon the vitals of those who labour.' In one respect Quakerism is similar to Buddhism. People who are not religious but who do not wish to seem bigoted will say that, while they are themselves too rational and liberated to believe in God, they yet have quite a lot of time for whichever one of these disciplines they have chosen in order to demonstrate their broadmindedness.

*   *   *

I realised at this point that I was going to have to speak to a real live Charismatic. So I asked one to tea. She is called Kristina.

'You're a Charismatic,' I told her, having grown fond of this curious interview technique. The only proper answer is, 'Yes, I know.' But I went on, 'Can you tell me how that came about?'

'I was born into a Catholic family,' she said, 'and for most of my life had a Catholic education. My father was very devout and his faith meant a lot to him. I respected him a lot and used to copy him, hoping to become like him. Unlike most of my contemporaries I continued to go to Mass throughout my teenage years and at university I went to the Catholic Society. However, I felt almost ashamed of being a Catholic because of the current feeling at the time.'

'What was that?' I asked, intrigued.

'Mainly the sex thing,' she said. 'If you were a virgin it wasn't something to be proud of. Being a "good Catholic girl" did not fit in well with my social activities and I wanted to be viewed as an interesting individual.'

Oh dear, oh dear. The pressures of sexual liberation have stolen away one of the most basic freedoms. The freedom to be yourself *by* yourself. A priest upon whom I dote, since he is wise and funny and vital, was once asked when he was giving a talk, 'Are you . . . er? That is, have you ever . . . ? I mean to say . . . um?' 'I'm a virgin,' he responded cheerfully, which is far more courageous than announcing 'I'm a Stakhanovite fornicator.'

'I practised my faith,' she went on. 'I knew that was right but I didn't really know why apart from knowing that my parents felt it to be so. I had a lot of friends who did respect my views, but when you are the only one who thinks in a certain sort of way you do begin to doubt.'

'You were swimming against the stream,' I said sadly.

'I continued to go to Mass but saw religion as a bad thing and someone who was a Catholic as narrow-minded.'

I could not remember ever having been described, as a Catholic, as narrow-minded. Hypocritical, yes; narrow-minded, no. This, of course, reflects badly on my attitudes and behaviour and has led to people rebuking me with the old cry, 'Oh, you Catholics, you do and say such and such and then you go to confession and you think it's all right.' Unless you're a hopeless recidivist it is.

'When you say a "bad thing", do you mean from the point of view of the world?' I enquired.

'Yes, as something that was repressive, and that wasn't how I saw myself. My mother had a very strong social conscience and I knew that I'd had a lot of advantages so therefore I felt I had a debt to repay. From my schooling I got the feeling that you had to earn your way to Heaven – that when you died you'd be judged on what you'd done, and I lived in constant fear that I hadn't done enough.'

'You must have had a very odd schooling.' I was similarly taught, but was never left with the impression, evident here, that it was virtually impossible to 'do enough'. Indeed, trying too hard to appear virtuous was regarded as a sign of vanity.

'I remember when I was very young being taught the difference between venial and mortal sin – if you died in mortal sin you went straight to Hell,' she said.

'Did they never explain to you that even in mortal sin if you said at the very last second, "Oh God, I'm sorry", in a final act of contrition, then everything would be all right? I presume this teaching took place well after Vatican II?' I asked this question because I had assumed that after Vatican II few people any longer believed in Hell.

'Yes. I remember at the convent when I was about fifteen we did some work on the Sixth Commandment – and it had about ninety-five sub-sections, such as if you were at someone's house and a comedian told a dirty joke on the television you told them you were a Catholic and asked would they please turn off the television. If they didn't you were supposed to sit in the corner and say Hail Marys and hope that no impure thoughts would enter your head.'

I was puzzled by this, remembering Belloc: 'Wherever a Catholic sun does shine, There's good loud laughter and good red wine. At least I have always found it so, Benedicamus Domino.' The Liverpool Catholics I had been brought up amongst had a robust and earthy sense of humour. There was an innocence, arising from the absence of prurience, for no one brought up in a large family can long remain ignorant of the facts of life. I have found a similar realism amongst Jews and Muslims. The western fear and horror of sex and the concomitant attempt to redress the balance by paying it undue reverence are based in puritanism.

'The nuns at my convent', she continued, 'were very strict about petty things, but things such as compassion to people and equality went by the wayside. They seemed out of touch with the real world. At the state school there was a very weak RE teacher who had no class control. My mother was a convert and didn't really know a lot about the faith but went to Mass and did "good works" and my father didn't talk about his faith to us as children. All these different strands left me very confused. My father died when I was twenty-two and this gave me a great fear of death — had I done enough good to go to Heaven?'

My father died when I was twenty-six and took with him my fear of death. I watched him go. When my baby daughter died at two days I was stunned that someone so young could take this extraordinary step on her own. Then I realised that she wasn't on her own. When my son died at nineteen I wanted only to follow him and make sure that he was being looked after properly. This was due not so much to lack of faith as to purely human selfishness and misplaced motherly fussiness: I had grown accustomed to worrying about him. One's own death seems of very little consequence after one's children die. For the rest of your life you wait, rather as you waited through pregnancy, impatient for their presence. God in His goodness permits us all to die. An evil being might have condemned some of us to live for ever, eternally separated.

'I was working in London at the time on *The Universe*,' Kristina went on, 'and became interested in the Church in Latin America. I didn't have enough experience to be a foreign correspondent, so I decided to go and do volunteer work for the Church in Panama. I saw it as killing three birds with one stone: appeasing my guilty conscience – if I suffered for two years that should see me for the rest of my life; it would be a good, professional career move; and finally it was OK to be a Catholic there – liberation theology intrigued me because it seemed to lead to political action. But things were very different when I got there – no clear-cut situations, just life. There were nice people who were rich and some who were poor; and the same with horrible people, and I realised the poor could be as corrupt as the rich, they just didn't have the power.'

Liberation theology is a hybrid of Marxism and Catholicism and has had one unforeseen effect in some Latin American countries: if you were Catholic you were seen by the right-wing authorities as communist – and slaughtered. This drove many to fundamental Protestantism.

'So you had to look for the core of your faith elsewhere again?' I said.

'Yes. I realised that I had nothing to offer them and the kind of faith that I had was only valid in a pretty secure environment.'

'That it wouldn't take you through any real crises?'

'Yes. I couldn't really share my faith with them and from a practical point of view there wasn't much that I could do. I wanted to help people change their lives and be happy – and I realised I couldn't.'

'You must remember something I learnt a long time ago,' I said. 'You cannot suffer other people's pain. One of the worst frustrations in life is the impossibility of carrying the suffering of those you love more than yourself. As cruel as it sounds, they are entitled to their own sufferings because it is an element in growth. And everyone is given the opportunity to share in the sufferings of Christ.' How very unfashionable is this view when 'me' wants only to be more and happier 'me', and if we follow the tenets of the 'Prayer of Inner Healing' have even the trauma of birth retrospectively removed.

'I can accept that now I have faith,' she replied, 'but at the time I only saw things from a humanitarian, humanistic viewpoint. I was then invited to a Charismatic prayer meeting and I went out of politeness and curiosity. It wasn't weird, just a bit embarrassing, and I wondered why God, with all the terrible problems in the world, would be bothered with these people's little individual problems – such as finding a car-parking space. I felt that God made us and then left us to get on with our lives. However, these people felt that God was very close to them and therefore offered every situation and happening in their lives to Him and then prayed to Him to thank Him.'

'What if He let them down constantly? Could they handle it if their lives were a complete misery?' I asked. What I found odd about this was that Kristina thought it so novel. Nearly all Catholics I have ever known have constantly invoked God, the angels, the saints and Our Lady in every crisis in their lives, from a curdling sauce to a confrontation with a juggernaut.

'My first view was that they were mainly middle-class Americans with no problems. However, I found this not to be true. Many of them had lived bad lives but God had touched them through the Charismatic movement and they had become reformed. I was intrigued by the way they talked about God – I had never heard any other Catholic speak in the same way. Faith with my father was something private between him and God. They said a personal relationship with Christ was the most important thing and that faith saved you, not good works.'

I was unnerved by this Calvinistic remark. It is somewhat at variance with what I was taught. 'I always knew that if you had faith you would automatically do good works. The love of God comes into you and then you give it out – if you're not getting anything in, then there is nothing to give out. I think this is where the Church has fallen down very badly in our lifetime. You seemed to be so poorly taught that I'm not surprised that you needed an extra bit of encouragement.'

'I'm sure that it would be true for a lot of people of my generation,' she said. 'Because it was a time of change we didn't actually get taught the basic Gospel message. I didn't want to become a Charismatic – I had come to Latin America to find God amongst the poor people and in liberation theology, not with right-wing Americans.'

'You don't need to charge about looking for Him. He's everywhere,' I said. Kristina is perhaps a typical victim of the 'time of change'. She wasn't taught the basic Gospel message and nor was she taught sound Catholic doctrine. I begin to see how the Charismatic movement got its hold on people. There was a vacuum while the much-vaunted time of change wrought its havoc.

'I always had the problem of being worried about my "image",' continued Kristina, 'but God was deliberately giving me the truth in an unacceptable package and I had to ask which was the most important to me – image or truth. I said I was a Christian, but I wanted God to fit into a little compartment and not really to interfere with my life. Charismatics talk about "baptism in the spirit", basically a conversion experience, when the Holy Spirit begins to manifest itself in your life. It may not be a one-off experience but cannot be just an intellectual assent to facts. I knew that Jesus died for our sins but not what that *really* meant in practice. You need a sense of Christ's presence in your personal life.'

'This all depends on what you mean by a sense of Christ's presence,' I observed. 'A lot of perfectly good people who are in no danger of damnation just do not have that sort of experience. God comes in many guises and we must be wary of the "born again" who say that unless you have had it you can't be saved.' I once saw, on TV in Los Angeles, an American minister being interviewed by an Englishman. The minister said that unless you were born again, let the Lord Jesus into your heart, meeting Him face to face, then you would undoubtedly go to Hell. 'Do you mean', asked the interviewer, 'that if, say, Mother Teresa did not have this experience she would go to Hell?' 'That's right,' said the minister, contentedly.

'People are different, so it needn't be an emotional experience. With myself, I knew the facts, but had somehow missed the point,' said Kristina.

The insistence on 'religious experience', according to Don Cupitt, 'dates back at least to the seventeenth century . . . and the heyday of puritan scholasticism'. Calvin, dismissing the authority of the Pope, held that Scripture alone was to be our guide and anyone, with the help of the Holy Spirit, would be able to interpret it correctly. Here we see the start of the cult of the individual; and the individual, out on a limb, was scared witless that he would not be among the 'Elect' but would burn eternally in the flames of Hell. 'Thus', to quote Cupitt further, 'puritanism could lead people to attach great importance to sudden, charismatic, religious experiences, especially those which seem the most uninvited, unprepared-for and compulsive. Religious experience is like an orgasm from nowhere, warm and melting – and a very good thing to have because it is a pledge of final salvation.' People still mistake various sensations – from drug-induced hallucination to crowd-induced hysteria and indeed ordinary orgasm – for religious experience. A phenomenon known as the Stendhal syndrome can cause the susceptible to faint when they hear great music or see a great painting. Some claim that this is a religious experience – which it isn't.

'Yet when you meet somebody of faith,' continued Kristina, 'you *know* they have faith and it doesn't matter what their opinions are. After I had my conversion experience my faith suddenly became alive. Previously I went to Mass because it was a good thing to do rather than to get anything out of it. I also felt more able to read and understand spiritual literature – I could identify with the saints. The renewal is not just a modern thing happening for today, it makes you feel part of the Church as a whole, past and present.'

As it seems to me more like a piece from a different jigsaw, and I cannot relate it to the Church I knew, I had little to contribute here but remarked dubiously that it struck me as alien and unaesthetic.

'The Charismatic renewal', said Kristina, 'started from the Pentecostalists in America at the beginning of this century and has all the influences of sharing and therapy from the sixties. But God knew that was a way to reach people in today's society. The Church had become removed from people's everyday life and they needed to see how faith fitted in. The renewal does encourage you to talk about your faith, which is important if the Church is not to continue in its retreat.'

As it was during and after the 'time of change' that I stood open-mouthed watching the Church remove itself from me and my everyday life; as it had not previously shown any sign of being in 'retreat'; as this is the excuse put forward by the innovators for their antics, I was lost for words. The 'renewal' does not encourage me to talk about my faith. It causes me to wish that everyone would take a vow of silence, for I am not eager to hear about theirs any more than I am eager to watch their holiday videos. The faith of which they speak is not the faith I knew.

Kristina went on, 'I think there was confusion after Vatican II and religion wasn't culturally acceptable any more.'

'There was a strong streak of logical positivism in the sixties,' I observed, 'and still today a lot of clergymen don't like to say they believe in God because it makes them look credulous and idiotic.' Logical positivism, a discipline seriously stuck up its own cul-de-sac, is out of style but its influence lingers on, particularly among those clergy who wish it to be known that they have a grasp of philosophy.

'People do not like to live with the disapproval of those they see as their friends,' said Kristina. 'Faith was seen as old-fashioned, a crutch for those who were inadequate: for those simple souls who were uneducated and didn't know about sociology and psychology. Charismatics, particularly after their conversion experience, can be quite fervent and want to tell everyone about it and let them share in it.'

I have wasted an inordinate amount of time arguing with the invincibly ignorant. As somebody observed – if the Lord Almighty Himself came down and wrote *Mene mene tekel upharsin* in letters of fire twelve feet high on the floor in front of their eyes they still wouldn't believe. I still think that's taking scepticism too far but I must admit that if, say, Billy Graham came along and tried to convert me on the grounds that with a little effort I could be just like him my resistance would be implacable.

'This is the gift of faith,' said Kristina: 'when you have that everything somehow slots into place. You realise that it is not up to you to save the world, God will, but you have to be open to what He wants you to do.'

I agreed, but I had learned all that in the old Church. If I were now an unbeliever I should stay that way. So I asked about something

I had read in a Charismatic magazine. A woman had described how she and a number of people had sat on the floor under a blue net, thought about Our Lady and undergone a rebirthing experience.

'Because the Charismatic renewal is not a cohesive movement,' said Kristina, 'people can bring their own viewpoints. You can be very Marian in your outlook, or Jungian and concerned with in-depth analysis, or very psychological, or even fundamentalist with an almost Protestant theology.'

'This is what has happened in the Church at large,' I said. 'There are preoccupations with fads and fancies which people have tried to fit in.' Bit like trying to pack a suitcase when you're not sure where you're going. Would it be wise to pop in the ball-gown and possibly the kitchen sink?

'I see the Charismatic renewal', said Kristina, 'simply as grace from God in our century to bring people to conversion. Once this has happened you needn't really belong to it any more – you belong to the Church. The problem is the low level of faith in most parishes. If someone has just gone through the wonderful experience of conversion and is totally in love with Christ, then meets a lot of people who are not really interested in being Christians, he could be completely crushed.

I was not as moved by this sad image as perhaps I should have been. I was thinking of people living under alien tyrannies who had clung to their faith through thick and thin without the consolation of understanding from their peers.

'I think the prayer groups and suchlike exist to counter this low level of faith and give spiritual support,' said Kristina.

Nor was I much moved by this idea. Far be if from me to go along with Sartre's 'hell is other people', a most unchristian position (although I must admit I see what he means), but I am temperamentally averse to the display of emotion in public. I have seen in 'sharing and caring' groups evidence not of solidarity and strength but of individual weakness and inadequacy, seeking support and affirmation unavailable in society at large. These groups, despite their protestations, are necessarily exclusive. If they proselytise they seem to do so more in the search for recognition and acclaim than out of disinterested concern for humanity. They are unlike the religious Orders and Communities which exist both within and outside society, clearly defined in their disciplines, attitudes and aims and giving witness and succour from inside a recognisable and orthodox structure. It is unfortunate that the Church has been brought to a pitch where any activists can claim that they are needed to restore its inner life.

Without a shadow of doubt, Kristina means well and is sincere but her enthusiasm is, to me, irrelevant, not to say redundant. She went on. 'A lack of faith means you concentrate only on immediate problems because you don't think God is around to help, the priest becomes a sort of social worker and there is a loss of mystery. But God is powerful in every way. He chose to become a human being in Jesus Christ and be concerned about little everyday problems; and then to die on the Cross to allow us a relationship with God the Father through the Holy Spirit. This is the awesomeness of the Christian faith – that we can actually become brothers and sisters of Christ.'

'So what's new?' I asked. 'That was always the whole teaching of the Church. You were supposed to become Christ-like – "Not I but Christ lives in me". A person from Opus Dei announced the other night that they had made all work a prayer – the Benedictines did that centuries ago.' I suppose every generation has to learn the same old lessons but it's evidence of a lack of grasp of tradition when they seem to imagine they're starting from scratch.

'The Benedictines kept Christian learning safe during the time of the infidels but eventually became corrupt,' said Kristina. 'The Franciscans succeeded them but felt that the message had to be spread amongst the people. I see the fall in priestly vocations as part of God's plan to adapt the Church for our society. People aren't going to church as much and therefore the Gospel must be preached out in the workplaces.'

'Father de Foucault started that not all that long ago with the Little Brothers and Sisters of the Poor,' I said.

'Yes, but in a sense they were still "professionals". Perhaps the various movements – Charismatic renewal, Opus Dei, etc. – are what is needed today.'

I wondered why 'professionals' in the Church are in such disrepute. Does it spring merely from the notion of the 'priesthood of the people', or is it because, in Britain at least, the state is now meant to supply 'professionals' to cater for our every need from the cradle to the grave? The collapse of this worthy ideal leads me to yearn for the disinterested charities, including the teaching and nursing orders, which once proliferated.

'What do you think of Opus Dei?' I asked. 'The ones I've met seem to think they're on to something totally new. They think Monsignor Escriva has had a wonderful new idea.'

'The same could be said of St Francis. It is always the same Gospel but at certain points in history it begins to be forgotten. If you take things seriously and really live the Gospel you will be persecuted, but in our culture this won't be with violence. You will be called names and misrepresented – what I felt with simply being a Catholic and initially with the Charismatics. Neo-Catechumenates have had a bad press as well.'

'What do they do?' I asked.

'They started about twenty-five years ago. Someone who had had a conversion experience went to live among the poor in Madrid. He had no intention of evangelising or converting, he just brought his bible and a guitar. He began to explain to them, as a man of faith, about the Scriptures and their everyday lives. He noticed, as time went on, that their lives were changed through the power of the Scriptures and the word of God working through him. Then everything became more formalised and followers began to go into parishes. One of the liturgists of the Second Vatican Council was involved and so they have the most spectacular liturgies containing things which are missing from those of the general Church. Their font is in the floor and baptism is by full immersion. They have a huge table of the Eucharist in the middle of the church instead of an altar.'

That, I felt, was all and more than I wanted to know about the Neo-Catechumenates.

'It all relates back to the early Church,' explained Kristina.

'How I hate the "early Church",' I said, rashly. What I meant by this intemperate remark was that since we know very little of the early Church anyone can claim it was like almost anything – as indeed they do. Paul VI, in his statement as to why the changes in the Mass were made, gave five reasons. The first was to bring the Church's liturgy into line with the modern mentality, while the fourth was to return to primitive practice. The impartial observer might consider these aims to be mutually exclusive.

'You may have a preference for a certain form of liturgy,' said Kristina, 'but it is Christ to whom you are attached and whom your relationship is with. People may rebel against a lot of rules – just because something is accepted as the "norm" doesn't necessarily mean that it is OK. I went along with the rules of being a Catholic but did not have inner peace which they should have given me. *You* had faith and therefore you understood why things were as they were. This is the reason for many of the rules of religious life – to enable the person to die to self and then to grow in Christ. If you went into a convent and had no relationship with Christ the result would be screwed-up nuns ruled by tyranny.'

'If you didn't have faith you shouldn't have been there in the first place,' I said. Nor had I met any screwed-up nuns until after the 'time of change'. I recently read in a magazine an interview headed ' "We overcame their traditions, we overcame their faith": A contrite Catholic psychologist's disturbing testimony about his central role in the destruction of religious orders'. Dr William Coulson describes how he fell under the influence of one Carl Rogers, who was into something called 'non-directive psychotherapy with normal people'. During 1966–9 they introduced themselves to the Sisters of the Immaculate Heart of Mary in California. 'We inundated that system with humanistic psychology. We called it "Therapy for Normals", TFN. The IHMs had some 60 schools when we started; at the end they had one. There were some 615 nuns when we began. Within a year after our first interviews, 300 of them were petitioning Rome to get out of their vows. They did not want to be under anyone's authority, except the authority of their own imperial inner selves.' Dr Coulson goes on, 'There's a tragic book called *Lesbian Nuns: Breaking Silence* which documents part of our effect on the IHMs and other orders that engaged in similar experiments in what we called "sensitivity" or "encounter". . . . Sister Mary Benjamin got involved with us in the summer of '66 and became the victim of a lesbian seduction. An older nun in the group, "freeing herself to be more expressive of who she really was internally", decided she wanted to make love with Sister Mary Benjamin. Well Sister Mary Benjamin engaged in this; and then she was stricken with guilt, and wondered, to quote from her book, "Was I doing something wrong, was I doing something terrible? I talked to a priest—" Unfortunately we had talked to him first. "I talked to a priest," she says, "who refused to pass judgement on my actions. He said it was up to me to decide if they were right or wrong." ' Dr Coulson now devotes his life to 'lecturing to Catholic and Protestant groups on the dangers of psychotherapy'.

'The whole world and the Church are changing,' Kristina went on. 'Therefore they changed the rules – any sin would threaten your relationship with God and this is the only thing which really counts. They were trying to make the relationship more "adult". If, for instance, they were only attending Mass through fear of being in mortal sin rather than because of the love of God, then the teaching of the Church has gone wrong and something is missing. I think this is why God sent the present Pope – to pull it all in and try to control things. The Vatican Council wasn't a mistake – God is in control and sees the whole situation of the Church and what is necessary. Some of the movements are God's way of bringing alive the faith – the bishops were worried that the Church was full of baptised pagans who didn't go to church or had incorrect attitudes.'

'We've got a lot more pagans now,' I said. 'Goddess fanciers and earth worshippers, and far fewer people go to church at all.'

'There is the worry that these movements,' Kristina went on, 'the Charismatics and Opus Dei, may become more interesting for themselves rather than for the faith which they represent. The Charismatic renewal should enable you to be a full member of the Church, to want to read the Scriptures and give a desire to get closer to God – the "baptism in the spirit" – not just to attend a prayer meeting or sing "Praise the Lord". I was self-righteous and didn't see myself as a sinner – I experienced fear of the Lord. I didn't have Him as the centre of my life – I was like a Pharisee; it was all about image. I felt that perhaps a sinful life would have been more enjoyable and I needed God to help me realise that this was not so. But once the Church is renewed there will be no need for the Charismatic renewal. Initially after my conversion I had no interest in parish life, but I have since come to realise that the parish is the body of Christ and that I have a responsibility to participate in it.'

*   *   *

I asked my friend Alexander what he made of the Charismatic movement.

'The thing with the Charismatics is that you can attend one of the prayer meetings and feel great – but you can feel the same at any mass event. I was similarly worried about the Papal visit to Ninian Park nine or ten years ago – it was in a stadium and like a football match. You can get carried away by euphoria, which is the opposite of depression and usually its concomitant.'

'What is the mass hysteria that comes over people?' I asked, for there does seem to be little obvious difference in the manifest behaviour of people at an evangelical gathering and those at a pop concert. They all seem to go into ecstasies, weep, faint, moan and clutch each other.

'I don't know. Perhaps it is a misdirected search for the Divine. I want something for myself but am missing the mark, i.e. God.'

'I think you can only find God in solitude,' I said. 'You can worship in community but we're born alone and we die alone.'

'I would agree absolutely. One finds God in silence. You don't need to go anywhere. But then of course you have to come out, or at least carry your solitude inside you – that is prayer. The rule set down by St Ignatius Loyola was that each priest or nun or monk should pray silently for an hour each morning or whenever it is convenient. Lay brothers need only do half an hour. This meditation is very important, everybody should say silent prayer. If lay people don't have the time or technique, they can read the Scriptures quietly to themselves or say the Rosary. You have to start praying with the mind, but this should lead to prayer with both heart and mind, and then to pure contemplation, which is the highest form – purely the prayer of the heart without words at all.'

'For that you need silence,' I said, 'which is quite difficult to obtain in this world. People worry about you if you say you want to be alone.' They also usually refuse to believe you *want* to be alone. They think they must have offended you and you're sulking, or that you're going out of your mind and they'd better come and counsel you.

'Yes, both exterior and interior silence,' said Alexander. 'One wonders nowadays about people – do they ever shut up and just think? On a train I always have thousands of thoughts pouring through my head. If I'm doing something physical I'm still thinking – usually something totally unconnected: was St Thomas Aquinas the greatest philosopher; was Aristotle right? I remember once in Rome we had a morning meditation where you sat in church for forty-five minutes and all I thought about was the Kennedy rape case. One needs to slow one's mind down and think the thoughts of

God because the empty mind can then be filled with God. Yesterday's reading was from the prophet Jeremiah – you have gone after alien gods. 'Strange' was the word in the old translation. We have one true God, but other strange little gods crop up and distract us.'

He went on, 'The clergyman looking upon religion as purely sociological is making a terrible mistake; as is looking upon religion as purely philosophical, like Iris Murdoch – you pray but there is no God.'

'What a waste of time,' I said.

'Yes, who is she talking to? The idea of not talking about God too much because it puts people off is the greatest mistake of all. The Church does not talk about God enough. For example, everyone knows that Catholics are against abortion, this has been publicised well enough, but not by the clergy. All the leading lights in the anti-abortion campaign are lay people. The same with contraception. If you stop talking about God, what do you say? A lot of hot air. In every one of these debates you should ask "Do you believe in God?" and start from there. The real argument is with the reputation of atheism and agnosticism, and this is where the Church is not doing enough. It's hedging its bets.'

'No one wants to offend anyone by saying "There *is* a God",' I said. 'It sounds argumentative. Except for the "born again", who think they've discovered Him.'

'When Durham said there was no physical Resurrection I think the Catholics made no comment whatsoever because they didn't want to upset the Anglicans because of the ecumenical thing – a very bad move. They should have gone in with all guns blazing, saying it was an article of faith that there was a Resurrection; it was not impossible even from a philosophical point of view, and on this Resurrection all our faith depends. Durham says they have experienced hope: Jesus is alive – really He is dead, but ... This is what he thinks the disciples said to each other on Easter Sunday morning: the fish are gone but their stench lives on. Jesus is dead in His tomb but He is alive really. *Rubbish!* You cannot take away the miraculous element in Christianity. If you do you are left with nothing but a group of well-meaning people who have got absolutely no one.'

I brooded for a moment about ecumenism, for I fear I do not see its appeal. Mindless ecumenism is another manifestation of the human inability to accept or tolerate the 'other'. Genocide, the murder

of heretics or believers in different faiths, commination are out of
style in some quarters, although by no means all. Now, confronted
with difference, we try to minimise it, a move which has led to
the incorporation and wider dissemination of error rather than the
hoped-for 'better understanding'. Among Catholics it has been a
fawning, one-way process; for few other denominations have made
much effort to concur in Catholic belief. It has been a waste of
time; for the Church of England, to which it was hoped we would
grow closer, is disintegrating before our eyes, while many of its
disaffected adherents are turning to Rome for security: an irony
in view of the fevered attempts of much of the Roman Catholic
clergy to protestantise and mutilate the Faith. I have never been
in favour of ecumenism, either wide or narrow, for it reminds
me of those promiscuous bouquets concocted by florists wherein
bullied blossoms, chronologically and geographically incompatible,
wilt miserably. Daffodils, chrysanthemums, lilies, carnations lose all
particularity and appeal when lumped together. Ecumenism, like
tourism, ultimately destroys what it seeks to make more available. It can lead to syncretism and when the boundaries become
totally blurred nobody knows where he is. It may seem like a
sweet idea – but it doesn't work.

Alexander continued, 'They are frightened of offending people
– but we have got to offend people. If I say to you, "There is a
God," and you dispute this, and I reply, "Well, there is, and there
are seven arguments to prove it," and you still doubt it, I think
I have a right to offend you.

'If we look at fundamentalist Protestantism we have to say – and
this is harder – they are on very shaky ground and are causing untold
misery to thousands of people. Catholics are very frightened of being
drawn into an argument in which they say our fundamentals are right
but yours are wrong. Then we get to the real fundamentalist who had
Divine Revelation. We have to find real revelation even if we don't
understand it completely; that is how Catholic doctrine develops –
"Thou art Peter and upon this rock I will build My Church." This
is important, there are certain things which are essential.'

'Everyone has lost his nerve,' I said.

'If you keep quiet you can be all things to all men. But there are
certain truths that are eternal and cannot change. People do but
truths do not. There is absolute truth despite what Lady Warnock

says. There is the law of gravity and there are religious truths, and they are not going to go away, even if they are deeply unpleasant to us, another frightening thing.'

These views seemed about right to me.

I could see very little point in the Charismatic movement and my search was leading to the impression that there was nothing to be found – only that something had been lost: that something had been put aside and a changeling put in its place.

So I went back to church.

9

Priests and the People of God

> *Once the layman was anxious to hide the fact that he believed so much less than the Vicar: now he tends to hide the fact that he believes so much more. Missionary to the priests of one's own church is an embarrassing role; though I have the horrid feeling that if such mission work is not soon undertaken the future history of the Church of England is likely to be short.*
>
> C. S. Lewis

Pastor Ignotus and the parishioner – What is a priest? – Dog collars and tie-dyed frocks – Evolution and entropy – Is there a devil? – Babel – Empowerment – On sharing the sandwiches – Ministers of the Eucharist – 'Weaving the Web'

The Tablet of 28 November 1992 contains a piece by someone calling himself Pastor Ignotus. Pastor Ignotus writes in very short sentences. Like this. He begins, 'Paul Hardwick is not pleased with me. He is a good man. I like him. Perhaps he likes me. But he is not pleased. It became obvious at a recent parish meeting.'

Pastor Ignotus, according to his article, had called a meeting to help him 'get to know people more quickly and float a few ideas for the future'. One wonders what he had in mind. I have visited churches where the priest has been inspired by Good Ideas and the result has always been regrettable, to say the least. 'I have no plans for sweeping change,' he says. 'Changes there must be, but I believe they must happen gradually, born of the trust between people and their priest.' (Already I suspect that I would not buy a used car from Pastor Ignotus.) 'We met in our school hall. There were almost eighty of us, which was encouraging. A drink and a bite to eat had been laid on as well. All seemed set fair.'

He continues, 'We talked about various aspects of parish life, but came unstuck when discussion turned on our need for eucharistic ministers. We have none. Views were exchanged. Some people had doubts, but most approved: after all they had been to other parishes and seen lay ministers assisting there. So far so unsurprising. Then Paul climbed slowly to his feet.'

Good for you, Paul, you think as you read. Get right in there, swinging.

'He is a tall man,' observes Pastor Ignotus patronisingly. 'I met him after Mass the first Sunday I was here. He told me he had become a Catholic forty years ago and joked about having cast off the limp Anglicanism of his youth. He recalled with a twinkle in his eye the Latin liturgy, doctrinal clarity, and the moral confidence of those days. I suppose these were signals, but I was not prepared for what was to come.'

Pastor Ignotus is a touch slow on the uptake. He may not have noticed, but there are many of us who, like Paul, regret the subjugation of common sense and certainty to the sentimentality and lack of realism now so prevalent among the *bien-pensant*.

'"Forgive me Father," Paul began calmly, "I don't mean to be rude, but really I cannot stand this nonsense any longer." Everyone could hear the emotion thickening in his voice.'

The word 'everyone' is meant to indicate that Pastor Ignotus was not alone in his perception and must not be held solely responsible for his reaction.

Paul continues, '"I am sure you mean well, but these ideas of yours, what do they amount to? Either they're happening already or they're a waste of time, superfluous extras dreamt up by bureaucrats who haven't a clue about what the Church is really like in the real world." He warmed to his theme: "You're a priest. You give out Holy Communion. That's your job. We'll help in any way we can. Just tell us what you want. But don't try to hand over to us the work that you should be doing."'

Pastor Ignotus adds: 'There was more, but I think I have caught the spirit of the onslaught. As he spoke, it was obvious that he was not really concerned with whether there might be lay ministers of the Eucharist; the target of his attack was more fundamental; the trigger had been my remark, as I introduced the topic of eucharistic ministry, that it was not a device designed to cope with the shortage of priests, but flowed from the very nature of the Church as a life in which we all share through our baptism. He was reacting to that vision of the Church. I tried to reassure him.'

After a while Pastor Ignotus goes on trying, this time to 'explain as well that there is more to our Christian life than what is done – there is the reason for doing it; and there is more than the reason – there is the living reality which gives rise to the reason. I offered an example: when we feed the hungry, we act for a reason, our obedience to the Gospel; and the Gospel does not issue arbitrary commands, but flows from life – we act because we recognise the starving as our brothers and sisters. In other words, our lives as Christian men and women supply the causes which prompt us to act. Life, cause and action form a seamless robe.'

Paul, writes Pastor Ignotus, 'was having none of it', and who can blame him? Had I been the recipient of that speech I'd have been going 'Eh? Pardon? What?' Does Pastor Ignotus think we have to recognise the starving as our brethren before we realise they need to eat? And if he meant that we must feed the hungry because God bade us to, why couldn't he just say so? Paul, obviously a man of sound sense, would be well aware of it already, 'and when someone else, in an attempt to help, referred aptly to collaborative ministry, he exploded with disgust: "All that means is a secularised clergy and clericalised laity." And in the anger I saw the fear!'

I don't see any fear. I see a perfectly proper exasperation with ill-explained and superfluous innovation. Pastor Ignotus proceeds to get more infuriating by the minute.

'The small party afterwards was enjoyable, but more subdued than I had hoped. Paul is plainly the exception rather than the rule. The others know him better than I do. Some of them made a point of having a quiet word with me. "Don't worry about him. He gets like that sometimes," they said. But I do worry. And I went home to the presbytery that evening feeling a bit bruised and saddened. Here is a servant of the Church, who is both faithful and frightened. That should be a contradiction in terms. How can I help him overcome his fear? I saw Paul at Mass the next day. He is there most days. He will stop and chat cheerily enough. He is a good man. But, for the time being, the barricade is in place and secure around him.'

I suppose I should feel grateful to Pastor Ignotus. If I had tried for months to encapsulate all that is most exasperating in the attitudes of the innovators I could not have improved on the above. In another edition of *The Tablet* (which I have come to think of as saponaceous), Pastor Ignotus writes of 'little Heather' who comes scampering up to him, her little eyes sparkling, crying 'You come to *my* church, don't you?' 'Yes, Heather, I do,' replies Pastor Ignotus, heavily. This touching scene inspires in the unregenerate only an overwhelming urge to smack little Heather and throw cold water over Pastor Ignotus.

I went round to our local church and seized upon my friend.

'Why is there now a carpet in the church?' I demanded. 'It has long puzzled me.'

'A carpet?' he responded. 'To keep people's feet warm and to contain the sound, I suppose. It has something to do with acoustics. I much prefer it; it has a kind of softer and warmer feel to it; we are the ideal church for where the liturgy is at the moment. I think the primary concern should be that people are as comfortable as possible. You should feel at home in the church.'

'I don't feel at home,' I said with heartfelt conviction. 'Nor do I get any feeling that I'm in church. It doesn't feel too different from McDonald's or the bank, and the local post office has got a new carpet too. If I merely want to feel comfortable I go to the pub. And it seems strange to have the priest facing the people. I used to have the feeling he was addressing God, but now it's more like some social event – "Hi, guys, how're ya doin'?"'

'But what *is* a priest?' asked the priest, not, I think, rhetorically. 'You can either say that he is someone zapped from on high to do a given function; the bishop laid hands on him and he was someone very special because he had been called from outside. But if you look at the history of ordination, at the tradition the Elders passed on in Hebrew times, the laying on of hands is passing something on from the community. That element was lost and is now recovered. If you take the idea that the priest in some sense embodies Christ to the people, there is no problem with that.'

Is this the message of Vatican II, I wondered.

'Where is Christ to be located?' he went on. 'If you locate Him beyond the rainbow in a kind of theology coming from on high it makes perfect sense to face away from the people. If, on the other hand, you see Jesus as present within the community, then that is what should be made present in the priest – the embodiment of Christ in the community. That is what a priest is all about. So when the priest faces the people what you have is precisely that – the one person who is given the power to embody the people *and* Christ in his people.'

'I always thought the priesthood derived from Christ through the Apostles,' said I. 'And I thought the priest *was* called. It used to be known as a vocation. But, while we're on the subject, can you tell me why you don't look like one?'

'What does a priest look like?' asked the priest.

'A priest looks like a person in a dog collar and a black suit. You can tell him at a glance,' said I. One of my friends, a priest clad in dog collar etc., was once leaving a prison where he had been visiting one of his flock when he was accosted by a person in a vast black limo. 'You a Catholic priest?' enquired the gangster (for such he was), and on learning that his supposition was correct he requested my friend to get into the car. They drove around while the gangster made his confession. This gangster might have died unshriven if the good Father had been wearing jeans.

'Well,' said my young friend, 'there are certain occasions on which I do wear priestly garb – when I'm going to hospitals, for example – but simply because it's easier to get in and you're not asked too many questions, particularly if you are in a hurry. I don't think it's important, priestly garb. Vestments are another thing altogether. But the wearing of the black and a little bit of plastic round the neck – people said in the past that it made a barrier. I've always felt uncomfortable in it, though I'll wear it at home when I'm forced to. I think it acted as a shield, an emotional shield that people could retreat behind, and that I wouldn't want to do. This isn't to decry priesthood: I must make that clear. I do think the priesthood is very special, but as a priest I don't perceive myself as any more special than anyone in my congregation or indeed anyone, period. I believe I have a special function as a priest, but I think that somehow the priesthood is inside, it's not outside. I also think that everybody is called to be part of the royal priesthood – that's what the baptism promises are all about – and so in that respect the day-to-day being a priest to other people is the job of everybody.'

'You're taking a sort of rabbinical view?' I asked, somewhat at sea, for I find myself unable quite to grasp the concept of the priesthood of the People of God.

'Not exactly. I would still say that a priest is ordained – there is that about a priest which is different from others; but I wouldn't place that on a pedestal and say it's above others – it's a functional difference.'

I tried to gather my wits. 'I think here you are failing to take into account people's need to revere and admire: and if the priesthood – and indeed nuns – aren't apparent, then they choose other icons like Madonna and Michael Jackson. There is in human nature a need to revere. If they don't find Christianity sufficiently interesting they start saying their prayers to Elvis Presley. Or they go around looking for something else and end up in orange robes, painting their noses gold. At the worst they give all their money to some madman and end up committing mass suicide.'

'It's a very good point,' said the priest, 'but there's also a sense in which it is escapism. Also I would ask what they are revering. Is it the clothes or the function of the person?'

'Well, I think a uniform does define your function,' I said. 'It makes it clear. That's why they were invented. It's quite useful in warfare too. Saves you from shooting your own side.'

'I'll agree with that. Sacramentally it does define your function and, in particular, with the Eucharist. But other than that I would say no. People should be encouraged to say, "Well, look, you were baptised, you're part of the Church: come to us – it's your responsibility to be Ministers of the Word, Ministers of the Eucharist. That's your job, that's what it means to be baptised; go ahead and do it. Don't believe any more that it's this little caste of priests that is supposed to do it." Otherwise not only is it bad theology, it can't be fair to the only Church. But the way the Church is now moving, the Spirit is guiding and it's back to *you*; it's *your* job. Once you could say there's somebody up there, this wonderful person, it's his job, he is the professional Christian, not us. I say "No, *you* are."'

I remembered here the time my daughter received her first Communion: the priest, wearing a tie-dyed frock, suggested with the statutory friendly smile that, since we had borne and reared our children and loved them dearly, we would ourselves like to administer the Sacrament. I suggested, in my turn, that he should do it himself in the proper, time-honoured fashion. His smile faded. I feared my daughter would be angry with me for showing her up but the child, for once, was quite proud of me.

I returned to our conversation. 'Well, it may be good theology, though I doubt it – it seems foolish, not to say perverse, to centre God in mankind, and anyway it's poor psychology,' said I.

'Is it poor psychology to encourage people to undergo a process of grace, to become themselves, to experience the full freedom they have under God in the world? I think not.'

I should have pressed him to explain what he thought he meant by this, but I said, 'I think you are being a bit hard on the old-style sinners – the ones who rolled out of Mass into the pub. It may have been reprehensible, but they knew why they were there. You'd have terrible trouble persuading one of them he could be a Minister of the Eucharist. Seems to me you're demanding too much of many people and making them feel more excluded and unworthy than they ever did before. I, for one, knowing what I do of myself, would not feel competent to administer Holy Communion.'

'Jock Dalrymple', said the priest, rather puzzlingly, for I am not familiar with this name, 'once said, "Christ came to disturb the comfortable as well as comfort the disturbed", and that's fair enough. The trouble I have with this image of the old Church – that supine mass of people who came to worship; great, marvellous – but it was all up there, and in places where they had paid choirs somebody else was paid to do their singing for them; the priest was paid (though not much) to do the praying, and that sort of thing. Yet the whole basis of the Christian faith is that the spirit is alive in every single person – which is what baptism is all about.'

'Do you think that within this feeling there is a fear and dislike of authority, hierarchy, patriarchy?' I enquired, failing to protest that I had never in the past understood my role in church as comprising one of the 'supine mass of people'.

'It's a necessary entailment, I think. I have nothing against legitimate authority – I don't think that anybody, no matter what their position in the Church, would say that the Pope wasn't the Vicar of Christ, didn't hold that particular Petrine function in the Church. On the other hand, people say that the time has gone in human history when a single group of people can say, "This is true and your function is to obey." Now people are asking *why* – they want to know *why* to believe it. That seems to me to be an evolutionary advance.'

'Then it's a pity evolution hasn't provided the answers,' I said. 'People have *always* asked *why*, and, on the whole, answer came there none. I was taught that you had to have faith. You could ask as many silly questions as you liked but they'd all been asked and answered to the limits of our understanding over the course of centuries. I can't think of any valid new questions. You too seem to be saying *vox populi, vox Dei*, invoking the idiot beast, democracy.'

'I wouldn't actually say it's democracy. In fact, if there was ever a referendum to have decisions in the Church made democratic I think the vast majority of people, myself included, would say no. But on the other hand I want people to be treated as adults, and for people to take their baptisms very seriously. That implies people growing and having their own informed decisions. The Church has always taught that conscience reigns supreme and that people have to exercise it. Many's the time I sit in confession and hear the same old stuff time and time again. Every now and then I say, "But do you think it's a sin?", and there is absolute silence on the other side as the person tries to assimilate the question; then they'll say, "No, but the Church does." What's happening now to the old way of approaching Church organisation and ethics is that people are questioning things. That's not democracy: that's maturity.'

I found this ironic, bearing in mind the infantile ambience of many of the new proceedings. Beryl Bainbridge quite often drops into this church out of curiosity to see what they're doing, then comes flying round to tell me. One Sunday she caught a priest in mid-sermon. He was holding his index fingers a handbreadth apart and telling the congregation, 'God doesn't love you this much.' He widened the gap between his fingers to two handbreadths and said, 'And God doesn't love you *this* much.' He flung his arms wide and declared, 'He loves you *this much*.' 'Do they think we're mentally defective?' wondered Beryl, sitting down and looking round for the Scotch. I am increasingly convinced that by 'love' God means something quite different from our understanding of the word.

The church noticeboard advertises a 'Ceremony of Reconciliation' with the word 'Confession' in brackets. One day, bowed down under an awareness of my failings, I went to unburden my soul. Having conducted an examination of conscience I announced *sub rosa* that, on reflection, I had to accuse myself of having fallen short in virtually every aspect of what was required of me: I was, to say the least, inadequate as daughter, wife, mother and Catholic. Picture my astonishment on hearing my confessor suggest soothingly that he feared I was suffering from 'low self-esteem'. He advised me to go away and talk to God in my own words. I said I'd been doing that and didn't need him to tell me. What I wanted from him was absolution and a penance. He grudgingly gave me one 'Our Father', but guilt can only be relieved by painful penance. An atmosphere of humid cosiness merely aggravates the condition. Over-indulgent confessors, like over-indulgent parents, do their charges no favours, and I had no one to blame for my failings but myself.

It was interesting to be told by the priest that many parishioners confess to things that 'the Church considers sinful' whereupon he asks them what *they* think. One might almost get the impression, in this parish, that the Church no longer considered *anything* sinful. However, the priests do not, so far, follow the practice of another priest, further north: he invites his flock to pick up a pebble at the church door, squeeze it and drop it in a bucket. These pebbles, he says represent their sins and he absolves the bucketful.

I continued, 'Do you see very much evidence of maturity in the population at large?'

'I would say yes, on the whole. More so than in the past. One of my favourite images of western society is that it's going through adolescence. In the past both adults and children did as they were told. There was authority and they obeyed it.'

'Do you think people are evolving?' I asked.

'Yes, very much so.'

'Do you have any evidence for this?'

'Oh yes, of course – where would you want one to start?'

'Well, how about starting with what's going on in the Balkans? And, now I come to think about it, almost everywhere else as well.' I had been watching the television news again.

'Yes, that's absolutely dreadful. There'll always be exceptions to any kind of rule. I would never say that the stage of evolution we've reached has been perfected.'

'I think I go much more for the second law of thermo-dynamics,' I said combatively: 'that everything is conspiring to turn us all back into dust. "Dust thou art and unto dust thou shalt return." God assuredly made up entropy when he made up everything else.' I take this law to be illustrated in the fact that none of us is getting any younger and you can't unscramble eggs, and sum it up in the simple observation 'Things get worse'. Think of the NHS, of British Rail and the general state of Britain as a further example. There is a passage in my favourite reading, the Book of Job, 'Now I shall lay me down in the dust and if you seek me in the morning I shall not be.' This is why the Resurrection is so magnificently startling.

'The trouble with that', said the priest, 'is that nowhere in the equation is life put in, conscious life.' ('What?') 'It's always assumed that the universe will plod along as though life never happened. But it seems self-evident that life *has* occurred; and life gets higher and higher and bits of matter get more complex and more conscious.'

'I know life has occurred,' I said, 'or we wouldn't be sitting here arguing about it, but which bits of matter get more conscious?'

'Well, that's what evolution is – a movement to consciousness. Very little, then gases, earth, plants, moving animals, human beings – the history of evolution.'

'I'm not unequivocally convinced by evolutionary theory,' I said moderately, for the way I was hearing it propounded made it sound like unmitigated tosh. 'Do you believe in life after death? Do you believe in the Resurrection?' I went on.

He did not pause to ponder. 'I don't believe in souls transmigrating anywhere. I don't think there is an ethereal part of a person that wafts off at the point of death into the hereafter. I don't believe that for two reasons: firstly there isn't one shred of evidence to suggest it; and secondly, if that was the case and you never died, then you could never rise again. I do believe in the Resurrection. I'm not really sure what happens when you die. I prefer the language of sleeping and resting, which has always been the Christian tradition: rest in Christ, sleep in peace. I also believe in something to do with going back into the process, and evolution achieves this – that is our resurrection.'

'Personal, physical resurrection?' I asked, not hopefully, for he appeared to subscribe to some totally different faith from my own. Also I was getting a little confused as to which of us was keener on dust and chaos, while the word 'process' had alerted me to the probable roots of his 'theology'. I'll explain why in the next chapter.

'Personal and physical resurrection, but not as separate from anything else. The Hindu understanding of sin means "separation from". The English word "sin" means to do without, and I think basically that is what our big illusion is: that somehow we are separate from everything else. When people get to talk about life after death, they assume that life-after-death/resurrection produces a kind of discrete personality. It seems to me that what we are heading towards is a greater unity. The New Testament references to risen life are not about individuals but for the Church as a whole, the whole community. This is a very broad definition of what I mean by "Church" – far more of a unity thing. That separation which exists between ourselves and everything around us, that's what disappears.'

Since my knowledge of Hell lies in my memory of what it felt like to be a vessel of evil afloat in a sea of evil, aware that if through my own will I should destroy my individuality I would be subsumed and lost eternally, I did not find this reassuring.

'Do you believe in the devil and in Hell?' I demanded.

'If the question is do I believe there is an objective person outside the human way of thinking, outside of this world – the devil – then I would have to cross my fingers and say I doubt it. The question in fact would be irrelevant, because it's whether or not the word has meaning. I think the word "evil" has enormous meaning: we find within ourselves a depth which we simply don't like and call it "evil" and we personify it as the "devil". But that doesn't mean it doesn't enjoy a real existence.'

'Would you take that further to say that the goodness we find in ourselves we call God?' I asked.

'We don't require a devil to explain existence at all, and existence does imply somebody outside the system. If anything is evil, it is in the classic Thomist view – the absence of full grace.'

'I think of it as the absence of God,' I said, with memories of Hell.

'Absolutely – if you go to absolute zero what you are left with is nothing. A great analogy is hot and cold: cold simply doesn't exist in its own right, and absolute zero is a total absence of heat. I think it's very similar to evil and the devil – evil is the absolute absence of being; and if you want to say the devil is absolutely evil then you are literally talking about nothing at all – the absence of everything that is good.'

And here, for a moment, we were not so far apart in our views, although I am inclined to believe that Satan still goes 'to and fro about the world, walking up and down in it'.

'Where do you think the Church is going?' I went on.

'I think the Church is moving from a kind of entrenched fortress to what it should be, a servant of the world. In the past, people tended to view the Church as a number of images – the rock, the veritable fortress, the drawbridge of which could be drawn up against the world. Malcolm Muggeridge once said that the reason he became a Catholic eventually was because of the moral certainty the Church seemed to embody. I think that is beginning to crumble.'

'How profoundly unfortunate,' I said, never having thought of the Church as merely the 'servant of the world' but more as a machine for the worship of God. And all my life – and I do not think I am unusual – I have had a desire for moral certainty. Nothing that I would impose on others, but somewhere that I could stand, and from where I would be able to love without doubt and without unreal expectation; untroubled by the hope of reciprocity or the fear of rejection. Also, to my mind, the world, the flesh and the devil go together as neatly as bacon, egg and tomato.

Charles Glass wrote in *The Spectator* of 12 February 1994: 'Pressures on the priest are many: he hears our sins; he responds to our spiritual needs in an age when families and communities offer us less; he is the barrier between faith and despair; and he serves, in Oswald Spengler's words, as a "hand with which even the poorest wretch could grasp God's . . . this visible link with the Infinite." The Catholic faithful are losing that visible link, and they demand to know what will become of the Catholic Church. It is meant to be the "one, holy, Catholic and apostolic church", a changeless rock in a turbulent sea. The post-Vatican II Church seems more a ship shifting in the waves, while its helmsman fights the wind, the crew deserts and the passengers fear for their lives.'

'I'm not averse to the crumbling,' said the priest, unaware of the darkness of my reflections. 'It's that siege mentality that it had in many ways – that it was absolutely right on all possible subjects – that is now going. Now it is entering into dialogue with other faiths and spiritual traditions, which I think is the beginning of a proper dialogue with the world.'

I smothered a scream. 'I don't believe in dialogue,' I said. 'All my married friends, when things go wrong, say, "Oh, we'd better talk." I say don't talk – if you talk, you'll tell each other what you really think about each other and end up with no marriage at all. Keep your mouths shut. Look at businesses – they're always "in meetings". There is wild inefficiency and nothing ever gets done.' Talk, chatter, babble are the curse of the western world. Bureaucracy, the endless forms we have to fill in, are all one aspect of this meaningless *talk*: intrusive, profitless, legalistic and barren. No one ever really listens to anyone else *talking*. The only real, true, human response to anything that another human being says or does is wordless, or at best: Oh, I know what you mean. No one ever listens to anyone else talking: they wait for the opportunity to talk themselves, rehearsing their next utterance. Look at the Houses of Parliament. They don't *parler*. They just tell lies and no one listens to them. I didn't say this.

The priest went on, 'The Church is a bit like that. I spend my entire life at meetings at which nothing ever gets done. Talking of the future of the Church, I would say that some of the young minds that are coming out are very good. In many schools we have simply lost the battle – people haven't the foggiest about religion and simply aren't interested. But in other areas and other people you see a kind of flowering of both intellectual and spiritual energy that you wouldn't have seen in the past – empowerment.'

'I hate that word,' I said, simultaneously marvelling yet *again* at the young who imagine intellectual and spiritual energy to be an innovation peculiar to their generation (like sex, intelligence and a sense of humour).

'I guessed you might,' said he percipiently; 'but people feel more power is with them in many ways.'

'But some say power corrupts,' I said, wondering why those who claim to mistrust it are so eager to bestow it elsewhere: why, if they think it corrupts our leaders, they imagine the previously led will handle it differently. The evidence is all against this hopeful proposition.

'It depends what it is for,' said the priest. 'People feel it's their Church and their responsibility – that is a kind of empowering. Those who go on about how bad religious education has become say that people aren't taught the catechism and what they call the fundamental truths of the faith. Then, when you ask them to list the fundamental truths, they come out with things like the immortal soul and transubstantiation. Those aren't the fundamental truths of the faith; they have always been open to interpretation.'

'Yes they are and no they haven't,' I said, putting my foot down. There are times when one has to state one's beliefs clearly.

'People are thinking for themselves,' he went on, ' "Yes, I want to remain Catholic, I want to be active within the Church, to have a spiritual life, to think things through." I think this is marvellous, this is something that is new. I see a lot of those kind of spring shoots coming through an otherwise rather barren field. There are tremendous grounds for hope. The Church may become a community of mature people, brought together by their baptism and active in the service of the world and their love of Jesus.'

As I have seen no evidence of this, but rather many disparate factions splintering away and inventing new – and, by virtue of their frequently risible rituals, necessarily exclusive – groups, I demurred. 'I can't see it myself. I prefer to have some certainties, rather as when I'm walking somewhere confusing I'd like to have a line of breadcrumbs to follow. I don't want to have to keep stopping and thinking for myself: I want a structure. I've got other trivial things to think about – I've got to think about and cope with the complexities of the world and bureaucracy and trying to stagger on and make money. I don't want to have to sit down and think out a new theology for myself. I was perfectly content with the Church I knew and am deeply fed up with the twaddle we're so often subjected to now.'

'Yes, as I said,' continued to priest, 'it's adolescence – the crisis of adolescence.' And it was admirable of me not to clout him with the bottle.

I said, 'No, it isn't. Christ said we must be as little children and I'd rather be like a little child. I'd rather live by the faith than by reason. Adolescents are rebellious and deeply tiresome. He never said we should be like adolescents.'

'He said the best approach to faith was simply to trust; that's what the word "faith" means in Greek.' (Here we were in accord, for 'trust' has connotations of endurance, whereas 'faith' can be corrupted to fanaticism and the throwing of weight about.) 'I am very keen that people don't feel alienated by what is happening in the Church or what will happen in the future. Without stepping on anyone's toes, I'm all in favour of a couple of disturbances; but, as I said, people must begin to take their baptism seriously. It's the same Church. It saddens me that people will come to Mass late and stand at the back and go after Communion because they have done their duty. They've obeyed the Church, but where has been the personal engagement in what has gone on?'

I took a deep breath and tried to explain my reservations about the innovations. 'I always took my baptism seriously,' I said, 'and

I used to feel much more personally engaged when the Latin Mass was universal. I don't feel involved at all when the priest seems to have elected to follow Mickey Mouse and there are people playing guitars and prancing in the aisle and everyone is doing his own thing – or whatever they call it now. There's a lack of awe, a lack of silence, and sometimes you feel you might just as well be at a chimpanzee's tea party.'

'But the problem with the "I must be told what to do" approach is that it abdicates personal responsibility: for existence, for the world, for our faith in God and in other people,' said the priest.

'No, it doesn't,' I said, 'and anyway I like heroes, people I can look up to and follow. This may seem childish, and no adolescent would admit to it, but I think it is a basic human need. I don't want to think of myself as being as good as anybody else or as competent; I want to know that we have teachers and mentors who live up to an ideal and who make it seem to me possible to do.' Saints are out of fashion in many circles at present: perhaps because they are seen as élitist.

'I think that is very true,' said the priest, 'and I thoroughly agree with you – and of course the greatest mentor is Christ. Paul VI once said that no man/person any longer listens to teachers, they listen to witnesses; and if they do listen to teachers it's because they are witnesses as well. I think that's absolutely right.'

It seemed to me only to be a denial of the realistic and sensible old instruction 'Don't do as I do, do as I say'.

'Are you saying', I asked, 'that the only thing we can do, the missionary thing, is to be as good as we possibly can? Set an example, and if other people think it's a good idea then fine?' I have always fled like a hare from evangelisers. And I have always been attracted to people who evince holiness and quiet certainty. These are now in short supply, having been replaced by the *unco guid* who smirk and nag at you. These usually call themselves Christians, although there are also atheists and New-Ageists who go to some lengths to convince you of the rightness of their cause. I am ambivalent about missionaries, for often they seem less concerned with the salvation of souls or the material well-being of those they seek to convert than with imposing their own ideas of propriety and value on the benighted heathen (although there are undoubtedly many who would benefit by being released from the fear of certain unpleasant elementals and demons.) Nevertheless, if I were visited by a total stranger who insisted on driving an airstrip through my ancestral burial grounds without explanation or apology, I should feel entirely justified in eating him. Common sense and courtesy are sadly wanting in many enthusiasts, as are ordinary intelligence and any genuine awareness of the numinous.

'Brilliant. Couldn't agree more,' said the priest. 'One of the things that always depressed me – though I must give ourselves credit, it's much more a Protestant thing – was the soup kitchens, particularly in North America, where you could only get anything if you sat through a service first. That seems so wrong to me. If we believe that Jesus is present in people and that it is important to save people, it makes no difference what they think. The fact is they are in need.'

I was surprised to hear him speak so dismissively of Protestantism. I have never been troubled by the remotest desire to placate a Protestant but I would have thought, bearing in mind the nature of his taste in liturgy, that he would be in more sympathy with them. I said, 'If people are hungry you feed them. I can't imagine why there should be any further debate about it. I know people who worry about their own motives in giving to beggars, but if you're hungry a loaf of bread is a loaf of bread whether it's donated by Lady Bountiful Muck or the Angel Gabriel. What about the poor in your own parish? How do you cope with them?'

'With great difficulty. The need is too great and the resources are too few. One thing we have done is to develop a deal with the drop-in centre. So we have volunteers who help share out sandwiches at the parish centre offices. Sometimes, but very rarely, we give money to help people, particularly around Christmas time. The twin danger is drugs and alcohol. To give out money is sometimes a very bad thing to do, because you might be assisting people to kill themselves. And it actually follows sometimes that to give out food is the same, because you are freeing the money they have got to be spent on things which are suicidal. I know it is making a judgement on people, but I think you have to after a while.'

I'm not sure about this. It seems to me natural to feed people who say they are hungry and even to give a quid to anyone who holds his hand out. A group of Hare Krishna followers are, even as I write, doling out rice and lentils just round the corner, to anyone who asks. Janet says she's seen pigeons turning up their beaks at it, but she is biased, as they must be, by an aversion to curry.

'Would you say that the laity is now taking a much greater part in parish life than it did previously?' I asked.

'Very much so, and increasing. The way you actually have parish renewal is to engender as many groups as possible, which are incorporated into the whole parish group. This allows people to feel more a part of it all. In addition to the ministries (readers, Eucharistic Ministers, etc.) you would have people making banners, the Legion of Mary, and Mothers and Toddlers. The parish centre is used for all sorts of groups, some of which are loosely attached to the parish, others of which are not, such as AA. We also have Scripture courses during term time, low-key theology courses. For the ministers we have Days of Recollection and that sort of thing.'

'I thought there were always these groups,' I said, thinking that the hounds of Hell would not have persuaded me to join any one of them any more than I'd have joined the Girl Guides or the Hitler Youth, for I am not by nature a joiner. 'Tell me about the Ministers of the Eucharist?'

'We have thirteen of them, I think. One of the greater reforms of the Council was to hand the Sacraments to the people. In the past, people used to consider that only the anointed hands of the priest could touch the Host, which really has no historical precedent. In the early Church people would bring their own bread and wine to the altar – the origin of the offertory procession. The only reason for a tabernacle was so that the Sacred Host could be preserved for those who could not arrive in time for the Eucharistic celebration – they could have it sometime during the week. The idea that the Eucharist belongs to everybody has been restored: that everybody is the Body of Christ. What happens at the altar in the act of worship which is the Mass is that the presence of Christ, which is within people, is placed on the altar in gifts made holy and blessed and then given back to the people.'

This did not sound to me remotely like any Catholic doctrine with which I was familiar. The Real Presence? The Sacrificial Victim? Where had they gone? I said restrainedly, 'Many older Catholics are shocked by what appears to be a lack of reverence. They feel that the Eucharist has now lost a lot of its meaning.'

'Some do, but others have been quite liberated by the changes. In the past, particularly with the Tridentine Mass, there was a great deal of mystery and mystique attached to the celebration of the

Sacraments. A lot of people liked that and there was obviously a place for it, but it would not be good theology if that was the case all the time because the reality of God is not something out there, shrouded in incense and mystery. The reality of God is that which is present in the ordinary and everyday situations of people's lives.'

'I always thought it was both,' I said.

'I would not say that people are becoming less reverent to the Eucharist: I would say that there is an evolution in the understanding of what the Eucharist means and in what the Church means by it. Remember that the people in many ways are separated from Church life and participation, and what has happened is that people have been drawn far more into the mystery.'

'Sadly, many thousands fewer people,' I pointed out, 'and the mystery is disappearing or, rather, is ceasing to be recognised.'

'I do not see a massive decline in Catholicism. There is in other denominations and there may be other reasons for that, but there is only a small decline in Church attendance. I am sure we can find historical precedents: affluent and materialistic societies tend to lose a sense of religiosity and spirituality. I do not necessarily think it is because of the changes that have occurred in the Church. On the contrary, if the Church had carried on as it was, it would now be facing a far greater crisis.'

'No, it wouldn't,' I said with absolute conviction. 'There were more priests, more Masses and much larger congregations thirty years ago, and people would go to church on their own just to be in the presence of the Blessed Sacrament. There was a sense of holiness, of the sacred. With the re-ordering of church interiors you often don't know where the Blessed Sacrament is. You think to yourself: Where have they laid Him?'

'In those days, one's life was very carefully organised,' said he. 'Today it is far more a question of a person finding his own growth, a community's own growth and a person discovering his own identity within the Church. Things aren't so fixed any more.'

'Sounds like psychobabble to me,' I said, wondering why he supposed one's life had been so 'carefully organised'. Mine never was. 'But to get back to the liturgy – I think people lost, in a way, not only the sense of reverence, but also the sense of excitement. The form of words is banal, if understandable, and paradoxically meaningless. And not nearly as compelling.'

'The implication is that that which you do not understand is more compelling?'

'No,' I said. 'I just don't want it spelled out to me as though I were a not very bright two-year-old, and besides people like a bit of theatre.' I thought of something Alexander had said of the mistaken notion which seemed to be prevalent at Vatican II that, if there is less to believe, more people will believe it. I also thought that the greater the insistence on 'ordinary language' the further you get from the truth and the deeper into human error.

'They do, but there are still quite a lot of places where there is theatre, if that is what people really want. There is the Cathedral High Mass; Brompton Oratory and other places have sung High Masses and all the works. I am not opposed to people doing their own thing. In that respect I think the Church is wide enough to encompass every person's spiritual needs.'

'Archbishop Carey just said that about the C of E, and look where it got him. What do you think people get out of this new Mass? Cardinal Ratzinger has said that it's the new Mass which has been "reduced to a show".'

'It should be the summary and source of their lives. I think they get more out of it really than people did in the past, because, without wishing to be cynical or whatever, it was a bit of a spectator sport. One went in and it was all done for you, even to the point of not being able to hear the words. People who had their rosaries and prayerbooks tended not to bear much relation to what was going on at the altar or in the sanctuary. Now people get out of it a sense that it *is* them, that it is Jesus who is present in their lives.'

'Nuts,' I said gracefully. 'And why is it, then, that I can stand about two minutes of the way some priests now say Mass and then I get in such a rage that I have to leave before I disgrace myself?' I feel like Jenny Geddes, although doctrinally her polar opposite, who slung a stool at the preacher because she considered him too 'high'.

'Depends what makes you angry.'

'I think it begins when the priest says, "Good morning, every-body", and the congregation immediately responds, "Good morning, Father." That is the first moment. It makes me feel as though I'm back at primary school, not like an innocent child – just retarded and pityingly patronised. Then I do not like those ladies who remind me of head prefects doing the readings. In fact, I don't like any of it. I try to go to the local church and then I get into a temper because I have to plod all the way up to the Priory. It doesn't make for a prayerful state of mind. I used to concentrate much more on what was happening on the altar in the old Mass.'

'Well, one would have to say, "Let's whizz back to the early Church."'

'That's what they always say. I can't quite see the point myself. What about the accretion of wisdom, of spiritual growth, over the centuries? Is that to be discarded? Are we to assume that the Holy Spirit has been absent until now? You get the feeling, paddling round in the bathwater, that it's pretty hard to discern the baby. How about *Weaving the Web*?'

The authors of *Weaving the Web*, which is designed for use in Catholic schools, write: 'Religious education is not *primarily* concerned with maturing and developing Christian faith. Its aim is to help people to be aware of and appreciate the religious dimension of life and the way this has been expressed in religious tradition.' They explain that pupils are being gradually introduced, by a 'drip-feed process, to the principal beliefs and practices of the major religious traditions'. I don't know what it does for the other religious traditions but it presents a bizarrely distorted view of Catholicism. As Piers Paul Read has observed, 'No one, after studying *Weaving the Web*, could recognise the Catholic Church as it is described in Vatican II. And it is difficult to see how any Catholic child, after three years of its "drip-feed process", could see any reason to be a Catholic rather than a Mormon, a Muslim or a Boy Scout.'

It was the religious educators and the bishops of Liverpool, my poor, beloved, benighted Liverpool, who produced *Weaving the Web* and another publication called *Here I Am*. Its stated aims and intentions are apparently worthy but the authors are clearly concerned with 'demythologising' the faith, as Michael O'Brien, the editor of *Nazareth*, a Catholic family magazine, points out. 'The child is informed that baptism is primarily an "invitation" to enter the community of faith. No mention here of liberation from sin and death. But strong links are made to Islam and Hinduism. A story about a salt doll who plunges into the sea, and who exclaims in wonder, "Now I know who I am!" just as he dissolves, is intended to symbolise the immersion of the human person in the community. It is actually more expressive of the dissolution of the self, and as such it is an effective agent of monism, the pagan view of existence as a vast organic being in which all divisions and distinctions are ultimately illusions.'

I was very much astonished when I read about the salt doll, and had to sit down for a while, for the story perfectly describes my experience of Hell.

The priest told me, '*Weaving the Web* is supposed to be the basis of a religious course. It is presumed that the teaching is in a Catholic school by a practising Catholic and it is used as a basis upon which to draw, and that is it. It is not supposed to be the sum total of the territory of the course. If it is seen as I have outlined, then all the objections to it tend to fall flat. In its favour, as it stands, I think we should be teaching our people about other faiths and showing what is common; and also that we should be teaching the truths about the Catholic faith. I feel there is a sense in which people's spirituality has been undernourished, certainly by us, and in particular by what Jesus called the World; and that is very bad. There are a number of factors. It is not just materialism or changes that have occurred within the Church, it is far more of an emphasis on the day-to-day. The only time people ask themselves "Why am I here?" type questions is when a bus is bearing down on them. People say we should have more religious teaching in schools but that is not necessarily the solution. Perhaps we should teach philosophy and how to think properly. That would have a far greater effect than forever jiggling around with the religious curriculum which you will never get right anyway. People are not trained to do anything other than find themselves a career and survive. They are never taught to ask themselves the eternal question and that, more than anything, is the real problem.'

'I don't think the tinkers or the chronic alcoholics who abound round here would be all that grateful if you tried to teach them philosophy. And we were always taught to address ourselves to the eternal question anyway. Nothing new there. When I was a postulant we were encouraged to sit down and think about our death, but you don't get many people – religious or not – recommending that now. Death is now regarded as a most indelicate topic. Mind you, I still don't think about much else.'

'That's a good thing to do. Without being morbid, there's that old adage: "Live each day as though it were your last and one day you will be right." It's a sound thing. It's not a question of Hell or

Purgatory that's important, but what gives my life meaning.'

According to Father Robert Burns, CSP, 'Many newly ordained priests are either formal or material heretics on the day of their ordination. This is so, because their teachers embraced modernist errors and passed them on to their students. Their students, after ordination, in turn, propagated these errors, either in catechetical teaching or in pulpit preaching.'

I could not find words to tell this young person how profoundly I disagreed with him: how mistaken was his impression that Catholics previously had felt their spirituality to be 'undernourished', how many had gained succour from the practice of their faith; how, where there had been gold, there was now dross. And he had, I surmised, been reading Teilhard de Chardin and quite possibly Matthew Fox . . .

Getting to Heaven

You can't get to Heaven in an old Ford car,
'Cos an old Ford car don't go that far.

Popular Song

Teilhard de Chardin and Matthew Fox – The New Age
– Don Cupitt's doughnut – Process theology – Salvation
through prayer – Loving your neighbour – Salvation
through holiness – The community myth – Nuns and their
habits – The Church past and present – The destruction
of the monasteries

The Jesuit, Teilhard de Chardin, wrote: 'If by consequence of some
internal upheaval, I come to lose successively my faith in Christ, my
faith in a personal God, my faith in the Spirit; it seems to me that
I should continue to believe in the world. The World (the Value,
the Infallibility, and the Goodness of the World); such, in the final
analysis, is the first and only thing in which I believe. It is by this
faith that I live, and it is to this faith, I feel, that at the moment
of dying, I shall above all doubt abandon myself! To this confused
faith in the world, one and infallible, I abandon myself, wherever it
may lead me . . .' Nowhere, I should think.

Teilhard de Chardin's vision of what is desirable also sounds to
me very like my own vision of Hell. If I didn't believe in God I
should find the world insupportable and see no reason not to hang
myself. Optimism based on fantasy is a palimpsest of despair. The
books of de Chardin are similar to Stephen Hawking's: many people
buy them, few read them, and fewer understand them. Hawking also
appears to believe that once we figure out how the world works we'll
know the mind of God. It seems nobody was listening when God
remarked that His ways were not our ways, nor His thoughts our

thoughts. Nevertheless the views of de Chardin have, in one form or another, filtered through to the masses and lent themselves to the neo-paganism which some regard as what he called 'better Christianity'. He is very much part of New Age thinking, not a million miles from those who see God in the tree or the rock or the river, as though He were a dryad or a naiad or a garden gnome. This is not optimism but a sentimental illusion, a retreat into fairyland and the confusion of New Age, science fiction and pagan mythology aggravated by a tendency to religious syncretism: unwholesome and lacking in nourishment for mind or spirit.

Matthew Fox, an ex-Dominican, runs something he calls an Institute for Culture and Creation Spirituality in California, where he employs a witch who calls herself Starhawk and says things like 'At this moment in history, the mythology and imagery of the Goddess carry special liberating power. They free us from the domination of the all-male God who has so strongly legitimised male rule and, by extension, all systems of domination.' She would undoubtedly go down a treat with some members of the CWN.

Matthew Fox says, 'The idea of private salvation is utterly obsolete . . . the cosmic Christ can be both female and male, heterosexual and homosexual . . . I believe there is a need to recover the sense of both lust and chastity as powers and therefore virtues within all people.'

'This is the dawning of the Age of Aquarius' went the 1960s song. The idea being, I gather, that we are moving from the Piscean into the long-awaited 'New Age'. This might make more sense – although 'sense' is not precisely the word in this context – if the astrologers were in agreement as to the dates involved: some hold that it all began in the eighteenth century, while others maintain it won't begin until the year 3550. In the meantime it seems that millions are of the opinion that it's all happening now, having inaugurated itself in the 1960s (round about the time of Vatican II), the Haight–Ashbury district of San Francisco being the epicentre. It is possible that I've got all that wrong since the whole subject is implicit with doubt and madness. It embraces earth worship, the Goddess (whoever she may be), sex-magic, witches, pyramids, fairies, crystals, dolphins, tarot, channelling (what used to be called mediumship), flotation tanks, transcendental meditation, eastern religions with gurus, 'new energies percolating the dense atmosphere of the earth', ecology, aliens, corn circles, circle dancing, deep breathing, rebirthing, Red Indian (now Native American) lore, cairn building, numberless esoteric therapies and God alone knows what else. Oh, and healing, hands on or at a distance.

It has infiltrated most areas of everyday life, but its most damaging effect is perhaps its insistence, derived in part from psychoanalysis, on the precious quality of *Me*. You must love and trust yourself, prescribe the practitioners, and then everyone else will proceed to love and trust you. This is demonstrably untrue and a cruel distortion and simplification of the case. The advice is not that you should strive to be a better person but that you are already implicitly godlike. The Christian position is that we are made in His image and are members of the Body of Christ. New Agers are in favour of Eastern religions rather than Christianity, define deity as the universal spirit within humanity, look for guidance from within and believe each individual creates his or her own reality – but that isn't what they really mean. I'm not at all sure what they do mean. They talk a good deal about the necessity of nurturing the 'inner child', which I suppose also arises from the dubious theories of psychoanalysis, and are very much given to wish-fulfilment.

Those who believe that the Age of Aquarius, which will bring about 2,000 years of universal peace, is already with us cannot, one feels, go out much. Mindless optimism, a refusal to face facts, is distinct from Christian hope. 'Things get better' is the message of the advertising agency selling anything from detergent to life insurance and is patently untrue.

Thinking that I should familiarise myself to some extent with more of the tenets of New Age, I went out and spent good money on a few books dealing with these matters. I wished I hadn't. Reading them, incredulity gave way to mirth, and mirth to depression. In their blind subjectivity they are like a sort of pornography of the mind: exaggerated, bizarre and ultimately inhuman, dealing as they do with unreal and unanswerable desires – horrid fantasies of darkness represented as the path to fullness and enlightenment. Even the lines 'I ask a fairy from the wild, Come and tend this wee rose child', which the modern witch is advised to recite as she goes about her gardening, strike me as resembling pornography in being truthless and perverse, and making you sick.

There were New Agers around in my childhood but they were then mostly referred to as the 'amber beads brigade'. They were typified by sandals, beards, homespun, nutcutlets, elder-flower cordial, ecto-plasm and free love. They believed in fairies and held seances and were considered a harmless source of amusement. Rosicrucians, The Golden Dawn, Madam Blavatsky were all mixed up in their beliefs and many of them claimed to have Red Indian spirit guides. Now some of these much-wronged native Americans are growing restive. Reuben Snake, Director of The Native American Religious Freedom Project, calls the New Agers 'pseudo-Indians exploiting our culture' and trying to imitate Indian religion.

While some theologians dance with paganism others aspire to a godless religion. Theologians can do more to destroy faith than the devil himself, for the people tend to imagine that they speak with authority and can be trusted. They are more dangerous than the rationalist who denies with commendable simplicity that God exists at all. You know where you are with a rationalist. Theologians can be confusing.

On the one hand we have clerics begging for inclusive language on the grounds that the person in the pew is too dumb to under-stand that the word 'man' embraces all mankind. On the other we have theologians expecting us to follow their impenetrable thought processes. They usually admit that God is unknowable to our limited faculties but proceed to speculate, painstakingly stripping off onion skins of possibility until even the smell is dissipated.

'Yah, and I think what would interest me is if we could probe a bit further into this business of "I can't believe" which is in a way also "I won't believe" and is related to this business of undervaluing and that one of the great issues it seems to me is how without a clearly defined faith in shall we say a "religious" sense or in a cultural sense to restore this issue, no, not this issue, this vision, this commitment, this faith that, look here, people matter more than the way they're being taken at the moment, do you see?' As the previous Bishop of Durham so memorably put it in a television programme.

I have some sympathy for the bishop but I cannot see what he was getting at here. I have been told that all sensible Christians now share the views of David Jenkins but, since it is hard to know precisely what his views are, I don't see how they can. The popular impression is that he doesn't believe in the Virgin Birth or the Resurrection, but sometimes he seems to indicate that he does – in some sense. I would have thought that either you do or you don't and the more you tiptoe around the issue the greater the confusion. However, I do not believe that it was the wrath of God which demolished part of York Minster shortly after the bishop was consecrated.

Don Cupitt lectures in theology at Cambridge. He once took part in a television debate about truth and dogma which included A. J. Ayer. Somebody said that Cupitt didn't care much about dogma, and just before the fade-out Freddie was heard to mutter that he didn't seem to care much about truth either. He is described as a nihilist or a textualist theologian and suggests that the universe resembles a 'torus' or a doughnut with a hole in the middle. 'Sliced horizontally along its circumference, it is one circle; sliced vertically along one of its diameters, it is two just touching circles.'

I meant to go and buy a doughnut and do a practical experiment but only American doughnuts have holes in the middle. Where I live you can only get English doughnuts, which are uninterrupted except for a dollop of jam hidden away inside. I got in the most unspeakable muddle contemplating this doughnut, for while I am interested in confectionery my grasp of geometry is tenuous. We drew diagrams, bearing in mind the flattened nature of the American doughnut, and found the result of slicing it more elliptical than circular: I wondered, supposing the thing to be spherical in the English style, how many diameters it would have, and found myself with a vision not of bliss but of a bathbrush bristling with diameters in all directions. I could not see that this doughnut held out much consolation for suffering humanity. Cupitt tells us that 'the torus image will be the new religious object. Contemplating it, and our own immanence within it, will give us the same feeling of drowning in bliss that we get from Claude Monet's last paintings. Here Buddhist thought, process theology and mysticism converge. A new synthesis can be reached.'

Apart from the fact that I am not affected in this way by the work of Claude Monet, I am not encouraged by talk of the 'initial singularity of physics' and 'streams of energies'. It has little relevance to my day-to-day problems. I think, on the whole, I'd rather stay with God the Father, God the Son and God the Holy Ghost. As for process theology, which began with A. N. Whitehead and was taken up by Teilhard de Chardin, I am told that since its smartest exponent, one Schubert Ogden, retired it has gone the way of the flared trouser and is no longer fashionable.

In *Christian Reflections* C. S. Lewis wrote:

> As J. B. S. Haldane says, in evolution progress is the exception and
> degeneration is the rule. Popular Evolutionism ignores this. For it,
> 'Evolution' simply means 'improvement'. And it is not confined to
> organisms, but applied also to moral qualities, institutions, arts,
> intelligence and the like. There is thus lodged in popular thought
> the conception that improvement is, somehow, a cosmic law: a
> conception to which the sciences give no support at all. There is
> no general tendency even for organisms to improve. There is no
> evidence that the mental and moral capacities of the human race
> have been increased since man became man. And there is certainly
> no tendency for the universe as a whole to move in any direction
> which we should call 'good'. On the contrary, Evolution – even if
> it were what the mass of the people suppose it to be – is only (by
> astronomical and physical standards) an inconspicuous foreground
> detail in the picture. The huge background is filled by quite different
> principles: entropy, degradation, disorganization. Everything suggests
> that organic life is going to be a very short and unimportant episode
> in the history of the universe. We have often heard individuals console
> themselves for their individual troubles by saying: 'It will be all the
> same 100 years hence.' But you can do the like about our trouble
> as a species. Whatever we do it is all going to be the same in a few
> hundred million years hence. Organic life is only a lightning flash in
> cosmic history. In the long run, nothing will come of it.

Shortly after I had spoken to the young priest, I received a letter
from someone who had heard that I thought of life as 'doing time', as
something to be endured before the release to Heaven. It was a well-
meaning letter, assuring me that death was not the gateway to another
kind of life, that the Bible tells us the dead have no more thoughts and
no more feelings, but also promises that we can be re-created from
the dust, restored to human perfection and will all live on earth as it
was before things went wrong in Eden. This sounds similar in some
respects to the opinions of the priest. The odd thing was that my
correspondent is a Jehovah's Witness. On a purely practical level it
is difficult to see how the earth, which we are told is already over-
crowded, could accommodate everyone who ever lived, but perhaps
we are meant to believe that only the chosen few will be restored to
their smallholdings while the rest of us continue to contribute to the
nitrogen cycle as fertiliser. The Jehovah's Witnesses were founded in
1872 by Charles Taze Russell, a Pittsburgh draper. He held that the

man Christ is dead for ever and that His body might have been dis-
solved into gases. I don't know how this enthusiasm for gases, shared
by the priest, arose. The word 'gas' comes from the Greek *chaos*.

I am also informed that the priest reveals a mythical understanding
of Church history and that the earliest Patristic writings – the
Epistle of St Ignatius of Antioch and the Letter of St Clement
to the Corinthians (both written around AD 100) – stress the
authority of the bishop over self-appointed demagogues. The latter
also shows the third Bishop of Rome cheerfully intervening in the
affairs of a local church in Greece.

*   *   *

Having now got the impression that there was very little point in it,
I asked Alexander why he was studying for the priesthood.

'I was incredibly young,' he said, 'probably about fourteen, when
I knew I had to become a religious – not a priest, a religious. I
kept it a secret for a couple of years and then finally, when I was
going to leave school, I told my parents that I didn't want to go
to university because I wanted to join the Order that was running
my school. My mother said I was far too young and wheeled out
a number of priests who said the same thing. But to me it was so
blindingly apparent that the idea of waiting just didn't make sense.
She begged me to become an accountant like my three brothers – a
sign of the bizarreness of the whole thing.'

I said we already had far too many accountants and wondered
why anyone should want to add to their numbers.

'It also seems bizarre to want to become a religious,' said Alexander.
'Because it means denying yourself some of the ordinary things that
are quite pleasurable – when to get up in the morning or whether to
lie in for another half an hour – you are negating a basic freedom.
You are trying to do without egoism and generally if you look
at priests and nuns who are unhappy it's because they find it
impossible to do without their own way in the tiniest things. The
greatest quarrels in monasteries and convents are on these grounds:
"I want the car", "Oh, but so-and-so's got it", "But I must have
the car". Tiny battles of will.'

'So why did I want to do this which seems so unnatural? I
think because this life that one leads on earth is not particularly

important,' said Alexander. 'I remember seeing a TV programme about a wonderful priest called Father Benedict Glyn, who was about ninety-four and a monk of Mount St Bernard's. He told a story of a priest in a railway carriage with several other headmasters and they were discussing what their schools prepared the boys for. The monk said his prepared the boys for death, which sounds rather macabre and old-fashioned, but that basically is it. This life here, which seems so real to many people, is not so important. The reality is somewhere beyond, and what really matters is saving one's soul.'

It was interesting to compare this with the convictions of my previous interlocutor.

'I'm not saying that people who don't become clergy or religious are not concerned with this. Some can do it in marriage; however, I could not turn away from this call. "Call" sounds like a very odd word and you can imagine a Cecil B. de Mille-style voice booming through the clouds and old men with white beards and so on. But it comes from introspection and reflection and the realisation that what is important is not the here and now, but what is to come in the next life. It's only when you have worked out that what is important is *God* that the here and now becomes important because it is created by Him. The starting point is God; I must do everything in my power to find Him, and the continuation of this is a religious life. Nowadays people think that is rather a bad way to find God and that you're better off living on your own or like a hermit or having your own freedom to find Him. For me, the religious life is purity, the best way, and why I became a Rosminian. It's rather an odd Order because it has no earthly purpose in that it has no fixed work. Its purpose is purely the salvation of the souls of its members through whatever Divine Providence sends us.'

Alexander continued, 'I taught for five years and did my very best, but the actual work, marking exercise books etc., was not an end in itself. Nothing here is. It is the means to an end, and that end is the glorification of God. A lot of people find it absolutely nuts, especially nowadays. They say that you should be more concerned with your neighbour.'

'Presumably you pray for the souls of other people?' I asked. 'Is that part of your ministry?'

'No,' he said, 'I don't very often, I'm afraid. I used to pray through long lists of worthy and unworthy people but I think one doesn't

actually need to target it in that way. One just needs to do the will
of God and all other things will fall into place.'

*   *   *

Stunned afresh at the disparity of view now rampant in Catholic
circles, I went back to Stuart and asked, 'Do you think that some
priests are especially gifted with, as it were, a special relationship
with God? I don't suppose that all priests have a constant sense of
that relationship.'

'Some people, lay as well as priests and religious, seem to find
prayer and a continual sense of the presence of God easier than
others. Even the most renowned mystics don't have a constant sense
of that relationship. It was St John of the Cross who coined the
phrase "Dark Night of the Soul". Having said that, the Catholic
Church has always had rather strong expectations of a spiritual
life in its priests. It has always, I think, certainly today, expected,
propounded and assumed that priests will say Mass, the whole of
the Divine Office and have a substantial period in private prayer
daily. We are clearly taught in the seminary that without a full
spiritual life our priesthood will end in disaster. For the active
as opposed to the contemplative priest there is a complementary
expectation. That is that you will be actively and usefully involved
with the people entrusted to you. So there is a balance. You will
have direct contact with God in prayer, and you will have direct
contact with God in people, important encounters with people who
need you and make demands of you.'

'But it must, in a way, be a distraction living in the world trying
to combine a practical with a prayerful existence. Is it very hard?'

'No, in the secular priesthood both are vital. "Love God and love
your neighbour" is the absolute command. It is one complete whole.
Prayer which doesn't lead to and from encounter with people would
make no sense if you want to be a parish priest. A monk lives a full life
through prayer, doing his work and living closely and permanently
in community with his brothers. An active priest, which is what I
want to be, lives a full life through prayer, appropriate involvement
with his people and good and close friendships. If these things are
all there then it seems to me that a major part of what people seek
and sometimes find in sexual intimacy is provided. "Seek ye first

the kingdom of God and all these things will be given to you." No priest ceases to be sexual, but when the deeply important human needs are met, then celibacy, if it works, is *the* most powerful sign of the authenticity of Christianity. If it constantly failed to work there would be something seriously wrong with Christianity.'

*   *   *

Having by now been confirmed in my impression that there *was* something seriously wrong, if not with Christianity, then certainly with the Church, I asked Peter Hebblethwaite if he was still a Catholic.

'Yes,' he replied, 'although I have never been described as devout.'

'Has your faith been changed or shaken? How do you feel about once a priest always a priest?'

'I agree with it,' he said.

'Could you still give someone the Last Rites – if I dropped dead now . . . ?' I asked him.

'Yes, in an emergency.'

'That is rather consoling,' I observed.

'The powers, to use that word, are in here, but they are, as it were, in the deep freeze. I am a good instance of this. I have received all seven Sacraments. I had received five up to and including my priestly ordination. In the time of Paul XI you could be legitimately dispensed from priestly celibacy, which I was; and therefore could be married in a church with a Nuptial Mass. The priest who presided at our wedding said during the course of his sermon that the Society of Jesus had not lost a son, it had gained a daughter. So that was my sixth Sacrament. Then I collapsed with a ruptured blood vessel in a television studio in Norwich – it was rather nasty so I received my seventh Sacrament. Therefore I am in good standing. If I go to Rome, I can have lunch with the General of Jesuits; he invites me. In some ways I am in a better position.'

'So you have kept your old friendships?' I enquired. 'You've lost very little?'

'What I've lost probably wasn't worth having,' said Peter. 'There are curmudgeonly priests here and there.'

'Do you think it's possible to be a saint if married? On the other hand maybe you have to be,' I said, seeming unable to shake off my opinion in regard to this state.

'There is a famous old saying,' said Peter rather enigmatically: '"We bishops will be astonished when we get to Heaven to see who is there before us. Our mitres will fly off our heads in astonishment when we see the riff-raff." But being a saint is only another way of being saved. You can't be saved unless you are holy. I believe in the Communion of Saints. The most simple definition of the Church is in Acts 2:22. It speaks of what the early Christians did. They studied the doctrine of the Apostles, shared prayer and communion in the breaking of bread. Communion means fellowship. Those three things are in the liturgy.'

'I have problems with the idea of "community",' I said. 'I live in a place where there are quite a few Catholics – yet I never meet them. I go to church and there I see people I never meet in the ordinary way. I have to shake their hands: I have nothing against them, I wish them well, but I have no sense of community at all. The word itself has lost meaning. There are few real communities left in this country. In the cities the little houses were cleared to make way for high-rise blocks and in the countryside whole villages have been depopulated. There is still much talk of community – we have ethnic communities, the gay community, even the international community, and that mythical community into which the mentally ill are released to fend for themselves, but it's only a nostalgic word.' (My favourite is 'the homosexual, sado-masochistic community'.)

'Suppose you lived in Kensington?' suggested Peter. I think I must have given the impression that I suffered from an arcane form of snobbery. Come to think of it, I do. I won't go to Country and Western Masses. The problem never arose when the Tridentine Mass was universal, identical in the loftiest cathedral or the humblest convent chapel. The levellers have brought a new element of class-consciousness into the Faith. They detest beauty and grandeur and prefer to see us making fools of ourselves.

'I don't think it would make any difference. If I don't know them personally, I don't see the congregation as any different from – say – the people I'm with in the supermarket. I'm benevolently inclined towards them unless they start mugging me or something, but I don't feel close to them as I do with people I know. I suppose it was different in small country parishes where people relied on one another, and if two parishioners fell out it would be a scandal so they'd have to be reconciled. But the size of this parish means that our paths never cross. There'd be no particular point in me going to church to look for support from other people. If I was needed to help in some way, I hope I would, but nobody's ever asked me. I only go because of God, not the other people.'

Once as I was leaving the Little Oratory I wondered why I had such a sense of peace, of completion and satisfaction. One of the reasons, I realised, was that no one had smirked at me or attempted to wring my hand. I had been spared the all too prevalent spurious *bonhomie*, the sentimentality. The atmosphere of awe, reverence and holiness had been unimpaired by the imposition of assumed chumminess. We left singly or in small groups but we all knew where we had been, why and what for. I seem to find it impossible to visualise myself as a parishioner – it's too parochial. I prefer the sense of space and air and light that comes from belonging to the whole Church, not just to some club.

One day I went to a parish party taking a friend, I expected that the poor of the parish would be there; the homeless, the mad, the alcoholic – but they were not. The other guests were respectable young persons; nurses, social workers (as unmistakable in their sphere as PR girls are in theirs), a sprinkling of couples with babies in haversacks, some of the trendier type of priest – the non-authoritarian type whom you can't recognise from their garb – and at least one aspiring Buddhist. I was disillusioned, for while I have no time for the progressives I did expect them to put their money where their mouths are and ask in the people from the streets.

My friend said we were witnessing a common phenomenon: when a leader, be he priest, rabbi or swami, determines to make himself more accessible, more 'human', he gathers followers around himself and immediately an air of exclusivity materialises. His wider purpose is diminished in proportion to his particular friendships. He and the groupies become part of each other and the rest of us are left out. Not that we mind, for the atmosphere of self-righteous mutual congratulation is not appealing. The human being is capable of maintaining only a few particular friendships; if he wishes to be available to all, they must be eschewed.

'I would take it from the other position and say that everybody has a potential ministry in the Church,' said Peter. 'You will be ministering without knowing it or calling it that. What does ministering mean? Helping people somehow to God. Making your faith, hope and charity more credible.'

I don't have an evangelising bone in my body but I said that on the whole I did try to be kind.

'Then, even if you don't call it that, you have been exercising a ministry,' said Peter. 'Jesus said, "I came not to be ministered to but to minister", and that is true of not just priests but everybody. The priestly ministry should be vividly encapsulated as an expression of that which we all have.'

'There's a lot to be said for unmarried priests,' said I, now seeming incapable of descending from this hobby-horse, 'for all single people, because there's always a problem with couples – you tend to prefer one to the other and a couple can seem far more exclusive even than a remote solitary.'

'That doesn't really alter the point I'm making,' said Peter. 'I'm trying to relate this general ministry to the priestly one. The priest is separated by his celibacy. The accidents of his dress and dog collar were only introduced in 1850. In 1849 the General of the Jesuits, a fierce old Dutchman, visited London to plant a few trees after fleeing revolution in Rome. He was shocked to find the clergy weren't wearing Roman collars but the traditional chokers. He imposed the Roman collar, but some refused to wear it on the grounds that it wasn't traditional but a new-fangled innovation. It is very strange that it has now been taken up by others, even rabbis in some cases.'

'What do you think about this idea that by your uniform you are recognised?' I asked. 'I find it very useful. As a child I was told that if you were lost you should go to a policeman, a priest or a nun, nobody else.'

'You should meet Sister Beatrice,' said Peter. 'She's about eighty and she said the happiest day of her life was when she was able to cast off her habit.'

'I've known other nuns who found it very disruptive, so tell me more about it.'

'I suppose it would be in the sixties and she had been doing the soup run down near Waterloo Station. For the first four or five years she went in her habit and she received the most enormous respect: everyone moderated their language, and so on. Then, when she started going dressed like everyone else, things changed and she was able to talk to them and learn what their problems were and how to help them, even though their language was now unmoderated and truthful. I think that is the problem about the religious habit: it cuts you off and excludes you from the reality of people's lives.'

'It is probably very salutary, making people mind their manners,' I observed, and I thought of my Liverpool relations who had never shown signs of being intimidated by the habit but would not have sworn in the presence of a nun.

'No, not if you are only going to be taken for the uniform, not the person,' said Peter. 'I don't think many nuns were forced to divest themselves from their habits.'

'Well, some of them were,' I said. 'Mostly, now, when I see a sister in a habit I assume she's an Anglican or maybe a transvestite on its way to do a kiss-o-gram.'

*   *   *

Thinking of nuns I turned back to Sister Anne, who had told me that her community had had trouble trying to decide how to modify their dress – chopping off bits here and there – until they opted for the skirt, shirt, etc. Janet, who amongst her other capabilities is also clever with her needle, says she could have run them up a nice little habit in which they would still have looked like nuns without tripping over hem or scapular or getting their bonnets stuck in lift doorways. (One French sisterhood had its apparel designed by Schiaparelli or someone, but perhaps that's going too far.) I asked if there were many postulants offering themselves.

'An increasing number of women are interested in devoting themselves to religion, but at eighteen are not sure if and when they want to join a religious Order. My students can only teach when they leave, and, whilst they are very good, not everyone who studies theology wants to teach it. I'm making a statement here, not judging. The sort of woman who would traditionally have joined a religious Order is there, but she is not attracted to committing herself to us. She's attracted to commitment, but isn't finding any role or answer because the Church cannot afford to pay her. My views', she continued, 'have grown from talks with students who have done the same theology course but have seen that only the men are elevated to the priesthood. There are an immense number of reasons why, but they don't make any sense to young women who have offered themselves to God.

'I see an increase in the number of dedicated lay men and women who are prepared to learn their theology and go and teach and want to do something for the parish – to cast their nets upon the water. But the Church doesn't seem able to use them and still talks about the lack of vocations. Is this a defect, or a sign that the Spirit is telling us something else? Celibacy is certainly tied up in this, but that for the moment is a separate issue.

'It was Thomas More who said that we have to serve God from the tangles of our minds and I think that is true. The Church is tangled.'

'You never said a truer word,' I agreed.

'But there are so many good things going on and they are meshed up with so many others. The greatest sin is that against hope, against the Holy Spirit – pessimism. I think the signs of the times are fairly pessimistic but you do meet great things going on quietly.'

I wondered where but was loath to reveal the depths of my own pessimism. 'The fall in congregations is alarming,' I said.

'Research into nineteenth-century Catholicism', said Sister Anne, 'has looked at the so-called myth of the swelling of the ranks of Catholics in England by the Irish immigrants. What it covers up, however, is that when the Irish came over before and during the famines they were not practising Catholics in the sense of church attendance on Sundays. They were deeply Christian and deeply Catholic but hadn't acquired, through penal times, the habit of regular church-going. The whole parish structure had to be set up in Ireland as well as in England. So, very slowly, after the restoration of the hierarchy in 1850 as the English built schools and churches in parishes, the Irish came back to the formal practice of their faith.

'The Church as we now know it – the structures, the pattern of devotion and Catholic practice – was actually set up in about 1885 and lasted until Vatican II. But, previous to that, the Catholic communities in England were actually living on quite good terms with their neighbours; the age of persecution had died down, they were beginning to get their rights back, and there's evidence, for example, of Catholics contributing to ecumenical schools for the poor of all denominations. Then you get locked into the restoration of the hierarchy, with the Catholic school and church systems, plus the Methodist evangelical thrust and its subsequent problems; which results in a separatism that wasn't known in the previous century.

From about 1770 you had control of the Church, the gentry often treating their bishops and priests as servants, with a rural Catholicism surviving throughout the penal times in the great houses. With industrialisation, many Catholics went to the towns and gradually the shift was towards clerical control of the laity.

'Until Catholic emancipation, which didn't come formally until 1829, the lay Catholic noblemen didn't see any reason to consult the bishops; but nor did they ask the laity about setting up the hierarchy. This is interesting because one imagines that the patterns for Catholic devotion, to St Jude and St Thérèse for example, and convent schools are long established, but this is not so.

'Our Order and others began in England in 1846 and set up, for the first time, a network of education for Catholic girls which was very important. What wasn't anticipated was the enormous attraction that religious Orders would have. Previously, if you had wanted to become a nun you had to go abroad and never came back. Viewed in the long term, it is phenomenal how many women, often working class, contributed in a secret, invisible way to the restoration of the hierarchy and Church in England.'

*   *   *

Henry Ford said history is bunk. L. P. Hartley said the past is a foreign country, and whichever way you look at it it's hard to grasp. The historian Fred Parsons once observed that everyone knows one historical fact and it's always wrong: Canute did not get his feet wet in an attempt to reverse the tides; the Duke of Clarence did not drown in a butt of Malmsey; Nelson did not say 'Kiss me, Hardy'; and the Reformation was neither demanded nor welcomed by the mass of the people, for whom the destruction of the monasteries was a tragedy. In Disraeli's *Sybil, or The Two Nations*, the 'stranger' says:

> All agree the Monastics were easy landlords; their rents were low; they granted leases in those days. Their tenants too might renew their term before their tenure ran out: so they were men of spirit and property. There were yeomen then, sir: the country was not divided into two classes, masters and slaves; there was some resting-place between luxury and misery. Comfort was an English habit then, not merely an English word. . . . The Monastics could possess no private property; they could save no money; they could bequeath nothing.

They lived, received, and expended in common. The monastery too was a proprietor that never died and never wasted. The farmer had a deathless landlord then; not a harsh guardian, or a grinding mortgagee, or a dilatory master in chancery, all was certain; the manor had not to dread a change of lords, or the oaks to tremble at the axe of the squandering heir. . . . The monks were in short in every district a point of refuge for all who needed succour, counsel, and protection; a body of individuals having no cares of their own, with wisdom to guide the inexperienced, with wealth to relieve the suffering, and often with power to protect the oppressed.

To the question, 'Yet if the monks were such public benefactors, why did not the people rise in their favour?' Disraeli's 'stranger' responds:

They did, but too late. They struggled for a century, but they struggled against property and they were beat. As long as the monks existed, the people, when aggrieved, had property on their side. And now 'tis all over . . . and travellers come and stare at these ruins, and think themselves very wise to moralize over them. They are the children of violence, not of time. It is war that created these ruins, civil war, of all our civil wars the most inhuman, for it was waged with the unresisting. The monasteries were taken by storm, they were sacked, gutted, battered with warlike instruments, blown up with gunpowder; you may see the marks of the blast against the new tower here. Never was such a plunder. The whole face of the country for a century was that of a land recently invaded by a ruthless enemy; it was worse than the Norman conquest; nor has England ever lost this character of ravage. I don't know whether the union workhouses will remove it. They are building something for the people at last. After an experiment of three centuries, your gaols being full, and your treadmills losing something of their virtue, you have given us a substitute for the monasteries.

I am no historian either but I subscribe to a theory which holds that the Reformation was the first in a series of loosely related calamities, leading to the Enlightenment, the French Revolution, the Industrial Revolution, the rise of capitalism, Communism and bringing us to where we are now, locked in a post-modernist, closed shopping-mall mentality, blinded by artificial light and breathing artificial air: our human purpose misunderstood and our psychology deformed.

Conclusion: *Quo Vadis?*

> Christianity is a system. It is a consistently thought-out
> and complete view of things. If one breaks a fundamental
> idea within it the whole thing will fall to pieces.
>
> Friedrich Nietzsche

Once upon a time the local church was the House of God and a
refuge for the people. Way back in the Middle Ages, so I believe, it
was not only a place of worship but somewhere to go to get away
from the dirt, damp and discomfort of daily life in the hovel. It
would be brightly painted, adorned with statues and lit by candles;
a pleasant contrast to the bleak darkness of home, yet, because it
was their Father's house, home also to the parishioners. With the
Reformation churches were destroyed or stripped and vandalised.
With Catholic emancipation Catholics were again able to worship
in their own way but at some point in the confusion after Vatican II
things changed again. Certain enthusiasts, doubtless eager to make
the people feel at home, went so far as to rip out the altar and replace
it with a table. Others left it *in situ* and merely put a table in front
of it. Altar rails were discarded, rood screens torn down. Much of
the panoply and splendour was dispensed with, statues were thrown
away and murals painted over. This process is known as re-ordering
and the reasoning behind it, as far as I can gather, was that the people,
the laity, felt intimidated by the ambience and excluded by the Latin,
while their aesthetic sense and their innate puritanism were offended
by the display of icons. They yearned, claimed the innovators, who
like all reformers pretended that the people were behind them, to
play a greater part in the life of the Church, in decision-making and
the day-to-day running of the parish.

Not ever having seen any evidence of this desire in the lay people
I knew, most of whom evinced, on the contrary, a marked reluctance
to spend their spare time bothering about parish affairs and sitting

on councils, I was surprised. Most of the older parishioners felt, not liberated, but deprived by the reforms, and church attendance fell drastically. Thousands had been robbed of the religion they knew and loved. Some progressives admit to a 'small decline', but Stuart Mason tells me that 'in 1960 approximately 80 per cent of Catholics attended Mass and fulfilled their Easter Duties (i.e. confession and Communion) and observed Friday abstinence. In 1990 between 20 and 35 per cent of Catholics attended Sunday Mass, a minute percentage ever go to confession, people receive Communion habitually and without preparation and thanksgiving, and Friday abstinence has been replaced by a "voluntary act of penance" which I have never known any Catholic, including myself, to observe.' A pity about the fish and fasting. Now that we are exhorted to eat more fish for our health's sake and less of almost everything else except beans and broad-leaved greens and brown bread, the Friday rule would have stood us in good stead.

By the way, when Henry VIII forbade the citizens to eat fish because it was a Popish practice he caused a great rise in piracy. The fishermen of England, deprived of a legitimate livelihood, turned to thieving on the high seas. With the dissolution of the monasteries the fish ponds and herb and vegetable gardens of the monks were abandoned; much medicinal lore was lost, and the broad-leaved vegetable went out of style. Henry VIII, with his passion for meat and contempt for lentils, is probably largely responsible for the blood cholesterol levels in the population. He has much to answer for.

I have before me my old Daily Missal, known as the St Andrews; red edges, the pages being tipped with crimson. The Preface begins with a section on liturgical worship:

'When you pray, say: Father[1].' This is the name that from all eternity God the Son gives to His Father, the name that our Lord invariably pronounced with respect and love, the name He silently repeats in the Blessed Sacrament, and that we find constantly on the lips of His Bride the Church.

'You have received the spirit of adoption of sons, whereby we cry, Abba (Father)[2].' The Holy Ghost, as it were, flows forth from the Word in the sacred humanity of Christ and in the Church, bearing us all to the Father on the waves of His divine love.

This fount of living water which springs up in our hearts unto life eternal,[3] refers, no doubt, to the private prayer with which the Holy Ghost inspires His Church and which we call the Liturgy.[4] In this prayer, all members of Christ's mystical body bear an authentic part in that infinite worship of adoration that its Head ceaselessly renders to God: 'Always living to make intercession for us[5],' as the Apostle tells us. Thus the word of the Master is realized: 'The hour cometh when the true adorers shall adore the Father in spirit and in truth[6],' which St Anselm explains as meaning that they will render a filial worship to God in the Holy Ghost and in union with Christ the Son of God. St Paul says: 'By Him (i.e. our Lord) we have access both in one Spirit to the Father[7].' All the properly sacerdotal formulas said by the celebrant at the altar (Collect, Secret, Preface and Postcommunion) are addressed to the Father through the mediation of the Son in the unity of the Holy Ghost. That is to say, that under the influence of grace attributed to the Holy Ghost we are united with Christ as a man, as our priest or mediator in order to honour the Father in whom the whole blessed Trinity may be said to be implicitly contained, since from Him the Son and the Holy Ghost proceed.

It is 'through Christ that we go to God[8].' Therefore all the Church's prayers conclude with the words 'Through Jesus Christ our Lord'; and the Canon of the Mass ends with the formula: 'Through Him, and with Him, and in Him, be unto Thee, O God the Father almighty, in the unity of the Holy Ghost, all honour and glory, world without end. Amen.'

[1]St Luke 11.2.   [2]2 Rom. 8.15   [3]St John 4.14   [4]From the Greek, a word signifying: 'a public act'.   [5]Heb. 7.25.   [6]St John 4.23 [7]Eph. 2.18.   [8]2 Cor.

The Latin, in which the priest said Mass, is translated on each page into English and was easy to follow once you got the hang of it. My copy, if shaken, disgorges holy pictures bearing messages from various nuns and lay people: the custom of exchanging 'h.p.s', as they were known, was a pleasant gesture of goodwill, requiring less trouble than the writing of postcards. There are also a few letters tucked inside the cover, one from the late prioress of a Carmelite convent and one from the late Leonard Cheshire VC. These letters are cheerful and amusing, full of life and hope and an easy grace stemming from a confidence of belief and an unselfconscious charity which is not apparent in the *unco guid* of today. I am sure that there are still many virtuous people, both religious and lay, but their manners are not so pleasing and with the exception of a few notables they are too concerned with making an impression. Many lay people are over-eager to exhibit their sense of community and togetherness, and the new-style nun, not being instantly recognisable by her habit, is wont to display excessive friendliness in order to prove her commitment and can be a nuisance.

Before the changes I would go to Mass with my missal and chapel veil, a small type of mantilla which could be stuffed into a pocket when it had served its purpose of covering the female head according to the dictates of St Paul. Wherever the church was, the form of the Low Mass was the same, from the grandeur of the cathedral to the bare simplicity of the convent chapel. On special occasions we had High Mass with the magnificence of sacred music and ritual, Gregorian chant, exquisite vestments and the time-hallowed movement and gesture of priests and servers. It was easy to pay attention to the proceedings, for each moment held meaning and purpose. Familiarity bred not contempt but reassurance. There was a sense of occasion, and a profound reverence emanating from the altar and echoed by the congregation, because you were in the presence of something of eternal importance. It was quite hard to let your attention wander, since each part and detail of the Mass was imbued with significance. The innovators claim that in the old days nobody paid any attention, but they lie. Doubtless there were some who knew little and cared less what was going on but they were in the minority. The priest officiated with his back to the people, addressing God.

In every Catholic church hung a red sanctuary light signifying the presence of the Blessed Sacrament. The altar, which contained the relics of saints, stood against the east wall and the sanctuary was separated from the body of the church. There were statues of the saints, the Stations of the Cross, candles and flowers and an all-pervading odour of incense. It was by these things that you recognised a Catholic church anywhere in the world and it was in this atmosphere that Catholics knew themselves to be at home. When Mass was said in Latin then no matter what your nationality or mother tongue you knew where you were unless you were hopelessly inattentive. There were confessional boxes where you could unburden your conscience and be absolved of your sins, and it was incumbent on priests at any time to hear a penitent who felt he could not wait. There were numberless aspects and signs of Catholicism which are now out of favour and likely to be forgotten if they are not swiftly recovered. In place of the old it seems in many cases that we have a new Church.

In the *Catholic Herald* of 3 December 1993 an article by Father John McGowan distressingly entitled 'Power to the People of God' begins: 'I believe the re-ordering of churches is fundamentally important for the future life of Catholicism. It has nothing to do with fashion or trends, but rather with education.' He writes: 'When I was a child I was taught that the Mass was a sacrifice and something between myself and God. It was a very private business. Since then there has been Vatican II with its fresh insights and understanding. There has been a rediscovery of the importance of the gathering, the coming together, and the Mass as a shared meal.' He says that the tabernacle should not be the focus of attention 'because each time we come together on a Sunday we are re-enacting the Last Supper'. Together with the Protestants he seems to have disregarded the concept of the Sacrifice on Calvary and recommends that the tabernacle be 'put somewhere else. Somewhere dignified like a side-chapel.'

Many priests have been over-influenced by new approaches to biblical scholarship which owes more to the German Lutheran than to Roman Catholic tradition. Some Protestant scholars proclaim that the Gospels are myth, not history, while one of them holds (as I did when I was thirteen) that Christ Himself was a historical fiction. C. S. Lewis wrote: 'The undermining of the old orthodoxy has been mainly the work of Protestant divines engaged in New Testament criticism.' Michael Dummet, the Wykeham Professor of Logic at Oxford, has written, 'The monolithic Church was never a reality, and is not an ideal: but the divergence that now obtains between what the Catholic Church purports to believe and what larger and important sections of it do believe, ought, in my view, to be tolerated no longer; not if there is to be any rationale for belonging to that Church; not if there is to be any hope of reunion with the other half of Christendom; not if the Catholic Church is not to be a laughing stock in the eyes of the world.' Michael Walsh, the librarian at Heythrop College, writes, 'Scratch any Roman Catholic short of professors of divinity, and you are quite likely to find him or her a Pelagian on grace and an Apollinarian on the divinity of Christ.' If this is so then they have been misled. Walsh seems to think it of no significance, appearing to hold that error does not matter as long as we get more ecumenical.

It is customary, when speaking of Vatican II, to say with a certain

212 Serpent on the Rock

look on the face – an expression compounded of sober fidelity and open-mindedness that its intentions were good. The damning phrase 'well-meaning' springs to mind. It is, I am told, the first Church Council to be convened without the express purpose of refuting a current heresy. Nobody has given me a good reason why it *was* convened. It would be flippant to suggest that time hung heavily in the Vatican and it is probably a matter of excommunication to wonder aloud whether it was not the Holy Spirit but the spirit of the age which inspired the Council. Not so much *Heilige Geist* as *Zeitgeist*. Paul VI said, 'If the world changes should not religion also change?' I would have thought that the obvious answer was 'No'.

One of the insights in Parkinson's Law is that people in authority feel they must make changes in order to justify their position. As the journalist Gwynne Dyer pointed out, no one on his retirement is showered with honours because he made no changes. The urge to mend that which is not broken is a primary cause of social decay, disruption and unrest.

The message of Vatican II, for whatever reason, appears unclear. It is permissible, even among the committed, to say that some of its documents give an impression of ambiguity. One of its stated aims was to enhance the ministry of the laity and bring the people to greater awareness of the Body of Christ of which they are members. All that seems to have happened is that people who used to think of themselves only as Catholics have been encouraged to regard themselves as something different and rather special – the Laity, the People of God – a group which before Vatican II had been denied its full rights. The Council appears perhaps inadvertently to have acted in the role of barrack-room lawyer, stirring up dissatisfaction and unrest where none existed or had cause to exist. It contrived to disseminate the view that the people were oppressed and excluded by an élite and remote priesthood from a full and proper dignity and participation in the liturgy. Until this was suggested I doubt whether many Catholics felt thus deprived, but it was fashionable in the 1960s to regard almost everyone as an oppressed minority.

I have before me a CTS pamphlet snappily entitled *Vocation and Mission of* THE LAITY *in the Church and in the World Twenty Years after the Second Vatican Council*. It was published in 1985 in preparation for an International Synod of Bishops due to convene the following year and manages, somehow, to state the obvious while confusing the issue. Under the heading 'The Teaching of the Second Vatican Council on the Laity' it reads: 'The Second Vatican Council has given the Church a very rich doctrinal, spiritual and pastoral heritage on the subject of the laity. Its documents splendidly testify to the wide-ranging and deep reflection of the Council Fathers on the nature, spiritual dignity, mission and responsibility of the laity in the Church and in the world.' This doubtless makes gratifying reading for the Fathers; it goes on:

Of particular interest are the following documents:

– the Constitution *Lumen gentium* develops its teaching on the laity in the ecclesiological context of the People of God: the laity, in fact, are 'the faithful who by baptism are incorporated into Christ, are placed in the People of God, and in their own way share the priestly, prophetic and kingly office of Christ, and to the best of their ability carry on the mission of the whole Christian people in the Church and in the world';
– the Decree *Apostolicam actuositatem* highlights among other things the active and responsible participation of the laity in the salvific mission of the Church as 'special and indispensable' to them: 'Indeed, the Church can never be without the lay apostolate; it is something that derives from the lay-person's very vocation as a Christian';
– the Decree *Ad gentes* underlines the importance and indeed the irreplaceability of the laity in the missionary activity of the Church: 'The Church is not truly established and does not fully live, nor is a perfect sign of Christ unless there is a genuine laity existing and working alongside the hierarchy';
– the Constitution *Gaudium et spes* portrays the involvement of the laity as a significant and decisive moment in the Church's relationship to the contemporary world.

It is difficult to discern anything startlingly new in these pronouncements, although one is surprised to learn that until the Council Fathers treated us to their wide-ranging and deep reflections Catholics were assumed to have been unaware that by baptism they 'were incorporated into Christ'. The pamphlet tells us about the 'new and magnificent horizons for the laity' opened up by the Second Vatican Council, how its teaching 'has clearly and vigorously re-presented the ecclesial nature and role of the laity' and how from this has come 'the development of a greater awareness of belonging to the Church and participation in her salvific mission'. Nowhere does it mention the full in congregations, the dearth of vocations, the disillusion and bafflement, the sense of betrayal felt by millions of Catholics in the wake of Vatican II, although it does admit to a few 'problems':

> problems which require spiritual and pastoral discernment capable of taking up, confirming and developing the intrinsic values, while at the same time being able to single out and remove the dangers involved in the recent experiences of lay participation in the ministries of the Church. In reality, in certain situations in some local churches there exists the tendency to restrict apostolic activity to ecclesial 'ministries' only, while interpreting them according to a 'clerical image'. This can involve the danger of confusion in the correct relationship which must exist between clergy and laity in the Church. It can also lead to an impoverishment of the salvific mission of the Church herself, called as she is – in a special way by means of the laity – to carry out this mission 'in' and 'for' the world of temporal and earthly realities: 'The primary and immediate task (of the laity) is not to establish and develop the ecclesial community – this is the specific role of the pastors – but to put to use every Christian and evangelical possibility latent but already present and active in the affairs of the world.'

Nowhere have I found any evidence of Vatican II having had a beneficial influence. In place of the old rigours we have sentimentality, confusion, untruth, meaningless talk of 'renewal' and 'improvement', and 'sharing' and 'caring', where once these were taken for granted and practised in a specifically and recognisably *Catholic* fashion.

As Paul VI lamented, a few years later, it provided an inbuilt agency for Satan to enter and stifle the fruits of the Council. Pope John XXIII had proclaimed that Vatican II would open the windows of the Church to the world and great gusts of fresh air would flow in. All that seems to have happened is that someone of unsound architectural mind and uncertain grasp of structure opened up the floodgates letting in a tide of sewage.

The most marked difference between Catholicism and Protestantism was always that Catholics gave the impression of *liking* God, of approving of Him. They liked His friends, the saints and the angels, and they dearly loved His mother. They filled his churches with beautiful and costly things, and very often with things conspicuously lacking in artistic merit, but the intention was the same. They held festivals and processions to His greater glory and rejoiced in His worship. They enjoyed making a fuss of Him and kept reminders of Him in their houses; icons and statues, holy water stoups and shrines. Many of them went to church not only on Sundays but during the week to say the Rosary, or kneel before the Blessed Sacrament. God was real to them and they had a constant sense of His presence, invoking His help in every aspect of their lives and seeking His support in their reversals and tragedies. The Protestants do not give the same impression. 'Superstition,' they howled at the Catholic. The more extreme, a grim and gloomy group, always gave, rather, the impression of resenting His existence and the necessity it imposed on them of behaving well or resigning themselves to eternal damnation. Catholics also fear damnation but are less pessimistic than the more Calvinistically inclined. With the new diversity of approach many Protestants sing and dance in their churches, clapping and raving in the nave, but they give no sense of being aware of the awesomeness and majesty of God. Nor, now, do many Catholic congregations. The feeling is 'Let's party'. Adherents of this new move, as far as I can gather, are seeking to prove that they 'delight in every aspect of creation' and are spreading the Good News, that God is present in each and every one of us and the more we leap about and smile the more evident this will become to the unconverted.

There were a number of Protestants involved in Vatican II, and despite the denial their influence appears to have been great. They do not apparently find the New Mass offensive: a terrible indictment. More surprising, another person, Archbishop Bugnini, who is alleged to have had close Freemasonic connections, was also highly influential in the proceedings. It was this desperate fellow who recommended that the tabernacle should be separated from the high altar. He has been described as the evil genius of Vatican II.

Stuart Reid in the *Sunday Telegraph* of 27 February 1994 writes of the New Mass:

In 1984 Cardinal Ratzinger, Prefect for the Congregation of the Doctrine of the Faith, spoke of 'a progressive process of decay' within the post-Conciliar Church.

Opposition to change has come mainly from lay people: the professionals — the bishops and priests — have a vested interest in the new product. But lay opposition often misses the point, since it is concerned almost exclusively with aesthetics. It is, of course, true that the dog English and the mincing, participatory rubrics of the *Novus Ordo* are hard to stomach. But this is not principally a matter of aesthetics; it is a matter of theology. What is wrong with the new Mass is not that it is in English, but that the English is a mistranslation, and therefore perversion, of the Latin. Anarchy has been institutionalised.

Some of the mistranslations are so infantile as to seem hardly to matter. Thus *Credo* (I believe) becomes 'We believe' – i.e. We, the people, believe. Others matter greatly, however. For example, *sed tantum dic verbo et sanabitur anima mea* (say but the word and my soul shall be healed) becomes 'but only say the word and I shall be healed' – i.e. the hell with soul, we're talking whole person here; *peccata mundi* (sins of the world) becomes 'sin of the world' – i.e. one world, one sin: we are all guilty; and, in the consecration, the elitist *pro multis* (for many) becomes, or became originally, the user-friendly 'for all men' – i.e. we may all be guilty, but we are all saved.

Not only is 'all' for 'many' patent nonsense (since the part cannot equal the whole); it is also a departure from St Matthew and the explicit teaching of the Council of Trent, as well as from Cranmer's Prayer Book, the Alternative Service Book of 1980 (itself a spin-off from the Council), and the Puffin Children's Bible. Even the 'modern world' has rejected it. Soon after the Mass appeared in English, sensitive priests noticed that Jesus was being made to use sexist language. Therefore, with arch self-righteousness, they adopted a more acceptable line: 'for all men *and women*'. Really hip priests made it 'for *all women* and men'. Now the text has been revised again, so that the words are simply 'for all'. No doubt this has gratified the animal rights activists, as well as the inclusive language people.

The loss of style, the dilution of any distinctive Catholic flavour, was apparent is some of the churches and chapels I visited in my recent investigations. One monastic chapel was particularly striking: it had been carpeted, the table laid with a tartan cloth, and rows of plastic stacking chairs had been arranged in a semicircle, while the tabernacle had been moved to one side. It now resembled a funeral parlour or possibly a dentist's waiting-room or hospital cafeteria. The assumption behind the designer's intentions (for the hand of the designer was evident) had clearly been that an unreconstructed chapel was a chilly and unsympathetic place with frightening undertones of mortality, a place not entirely consonant with human expectations of comfort and cheeriness: a place acknowledging the existence of God without paying due deference to man's fears and reservations. The designer had gone to some pains to brighten it up and disguise its true purpose, to deny the uncomfortable fact of a possibly demanding God, as the funeral parlour tries to sweeten the unpalatable fact of death. As I gazed around enquiringly the priest said, with a note of apology in his voice, that they held a lot of conferences at the monastery and the participants liked it this way. But Father – I said – there must be a million rooms suitable for conferences in this building; why pick on the chapel? He gave me no satisfactory answer and I concluded, charitably, that the situation was probably similar to that pertaining in a private house, where no matter how many rooms there are the occupants invariably gravitate to the kitchen, because that is the heart of the home. I later discarded this interpretation as untenable: it seemed more likely that the participants were imbued with the popular sense that they were the people of God, God was within them, and they were entitled to use the chapel for any purpose they pleased.

The possibly strangest innovation I am aware of is one I have seen only in photographs. In Armagh Cathedral, adjacent to the altar there stands a sculptured representation of what appears to be the Horns of Hathor. It seems to be about fifteen feet high, and if anyone knows what it is doing there I would be grateful if he'd tell me.

* * *

A group of American writers were once discussing religion (this was some years ago when it was still considered a topic to which the self-respecting intellectual could address himself) when they came to the subject of the Eucharist and the question of transubstantiation versus consubstantiation. After a while one poet remarked, 'Well, if it isn't the Body and Blood of Christ then the hell with it.' Transubstantiation, for those who have forgotten or possibly never knew, was the word used to describe the process whereby the Host, the wafer, becomes, at the moment of consecration by the priest, the Body and Blood of Christ, an unbloody renewal of the sacrifice at Calvary. The Protestants detest this concept, holding that the Communion rite is no more than a memorial of the event at the

Place of the Skull. Many Catholics also now get shifty at the mention of the word transubstantiation, seeming doubtful not so much of its theological as of its philosophical and scientific connotations. It is, sadly, increasingly hard for those with modern intellectual pretensions to adhere to the tenets of faith which they fear are not consonant with the latest state-of-the-art theories. Intent upon progress, which implies change, they neglect to take into account that there are matters which are eternally true yet beyond verification. This may seem too obvious to state but it is surprising how many supposedly independently minded people are slaves to fashion and swayed by the spirit of the age.

Luther, who was, on the evidence, more than a little nuts, said: 'I affirm that all brothels, murders, robberies, crimes, adulteries are less wicked than this abomination of the Popish Mass.' He observed of the Canon which is central to the Mass: 'This abominable Canon is a confluence of puddles of slimy water, which have made the Mass a sacrifice. The Mass is not a sacrifice. It is not the act of a sacrificing priest. Together with the Canon, we discard all that implies an oblation.' The most fervent ecumenicist would find it difficult to reconcile this view with that of, say, Pope Urban VIII, who said: 'If there is anything divine among the possessions of man, which the citizens of Heaven might covet (were covetousness possible for them) it would certainly be the most Holy Sacrifice of the Mass, whose blessing is such that in it man possesses a certain anticipation of Heaven while still on earth, even having before their eyes and taking into their hands the very Maker of both Heaven and earth. How greatly must mortals strive that the most awesome privilege be guarded with due cult and reverence, and take care lest their negligence offend the eyes of the angels, who watch with envious adoration.'

Article Thirty-One of the Thirty-Nine Articles ('those wondrous little particles') states that the Mass, as understood by the Council of Trent, is a 'blasphemous fable and a dangerous deceit'. Doctor Berger, a Lutheran sociologist of all people, has pointed out that 'The Liturgical Revolution – no other term will do – is a mistake touching millions of Catholics at the very core of their religious belief. Let me only mention the sudden abolition and, indeed, prohibition of the Latin Mass, the transposition of the officiating priest from the front to the back of the altar (the first change symbolically diminished the universality of the Mass, the second, its transcendent reference) and the massive assault on a wide variety of forms of popular piety. . . . If a thoroughly malicious sociologist, bent on injuring the Catholic community as much as possible, had been able to be adviser to the Church, he could hardly have done a better job.'

*   *   *

I try to be open-minded and receptive as I follow up the different strands of contemporary Catholicism – which is now, in many cases, a misnomer, so I use the term loosely – but the enterprise and my approach to it sometimes conjure up an image of a person attempting, for the first time, one of those impossible American sandwiches: no single human being could possibly eat all of it, it is full of unexpected and incongruous ingredients and as you sink your teeth in one end unexpected bits emerge and fall out at the other. The impulse is to forget the whole thing, throw it in the bin and take a nourishing vitamin tablet instead. The temptation is sometimes overwhelming: it is again possible, as for a time it was not, to find a Catholic church where the Mass is conducted in a proper and dignified fashion, where the sense of awe and holiness is undiminished, and it would be pleasant and easy to go only to these and ignore the excesses prevalent elsewhere. But I have another image – a person going about the dreary, miserable and often sorrowful business of living in the world, yet confident in the knowledge that there is a haven, a home where all is ordered and right and implicit with consolation. Then he sees that that home is in disarray, the wreckers have been in and wrought destruction and before he can rest he must at least make some attempt to tidy up, to mend the furniture, replace the windows, wash the dishes and make up the bed. It would be idle and sinful simply to sink down in the ruins and craven to abandon it to others in the hope that someone else would sort it all out. I feel like the mouse who has been elected to bell the cat.

I once went with Beryl Bainbridge on a train to Poland. It was all her fault as she refused to fly. We were locked in a carriage with access to neither food nor water and after a while we ran out of matches. We had cigarettes but nothing to light them with; a uniquely frustrating situation. (At the risk of sounding like a Church of England clergyman I will say that this reminds me of the state of the western world – some of us know that God exists but we have no means of utilising that knowledge.) After thirty-eight hours of wakeful discomfort punctuated by even more uncomfortable naps we tottered on to the platform at Warsaw. It was, I reflected, the sort of journey which causes you to arrive at your destination closely resembling your passport photograph. I feel the same way at the end of this quest.

Often I found myself in uncharted territory in an almost dreamlike state of disorientation, in an atmosphere so unfamiliar that it seemed unreal. New or re-ordered churches of Lutheran barrenness, all Catholic culture, all tradition lost. Clown-like priests vainly trying to be 'with it', women flitting round the altar, lay Ministers of the Eucharist handing out the Host, guitars twanging in the aisles, clapping, hugs and handshakes and never a hint of awe or reverence. The innovators have intruded upon the secret places and destroyed the mystery, the peace and the beauty. They have made false what was true and rejected holiness in their terror of space, of silence, of the unknowable, the abject fear of facing God alone. Like those who have ruined the deserted places with picnic sites and signposts, 'Welcome to the Wilderness', they have missed the point. Fear and a concomitant pretence that there is nothing to be afraid of make a disastrous combination. The denial of the nature of God is more dangerous even than the refusal to accept human nature for what it is. We have been overtaken by a cosmic neurosis, an attempt to redefine mankind and human experience in terms more acceptable to our sense of *amour propre*, have submitted to the delusion that God exists only within ourselves, for the paranoiac personality cannot tolerate the existence of the good 'other', the suspicion that goodness exists independently of itself, and it must either kill or subsume into itself that 'otherness'. It could be thought of as envy – envy of what arrogant yet fearful humanity suspects may exist but cannot understand. Nor can it tolerate contemplating the serenity of belief which it cannot or will not share. The fear of God has become literal and the response has been to misinterpret and deny His message and attempt to make it palatable to all and sundry: on no account to frighten the children. The sweetening and dilution lead to heresy, to a nervous reversal to what *can* be understood. The result of doubt and fear and of unacknowledged pessimism is strident acclamation of the human and denunciation of the numinous.

The human race has always had a tendency to hate God. It crucified Him, after all. Now it is trying to convince itself that He does not exist or that, if He does, He is indulgent to and indeed identifies with its every whim, even the most sinful. We have no trust and will not face the dark for the fear that it is endless.

I cannot see how anyone with any self-knowledge, anyone who is not a psychopath, irrevocably vain or mentally unstable, can hold a completely favourable and optimistic view of mankind. Not on the evidence. Yet the more we see of atrocity, corruption, crime and cruelty, the more people maintain that they are the result of socio-economic causes, of tyranny or religion, as though these forces arose independently of mankind and man himself was blameless. Few people with pretensions to intellectual respectability believe in the devil, and the concept of Original Sin is considered outdated. On the principle that once all the possibilities and probabilities have been examined and discarded then what remains, no matter how unlikely or unwelcome, must necessarily be the case, I find belief in the devil and Original Sin inevitable. And just as the optimist will claim that the world in its loveliness is a foretaste of Heaven (if he goes so far as to believe in Heaven) so may the pessimist suggest that in its vileness it prefigures Hell.

It is a measure of the arrogance and ignorance of our 'civilisation' that because we deem ourselves to have 'progressed' from the Dark Ages we imagine this to be a sign of the 'improvement' of mankind, supposing that those who appear to be lagging behind will eventually catch up and come to emulate, if not resemble, us. Being creatures of limited brain and tunnel vision we can only evaluate what we have done (necessarily in self-congratulatory terms), and persuade ourselves that we are on the right lines and will 'progress' even further.

I prefer God to man. I think this is permissible – the Decalogue requires us first to love God and then our neighbour; it is not, however, fashionable to say so. Lest I should be thought misanthropic I should explain that on the whole I am well disposed to almost everyone I know, although there are many with whose opinions I disagree. I am seldom censorious about their behaviour and include in my acquaintance murderers, thieves, adulterers, wine-bibbers, etc., who are often better company than more sober and respectable citizens. I once even went for a walk with a tax inspector. In common with all sane people I hate deliberate cruelty above everything, but apart from that my expectations are not high. When too much in the presence of my fellows I have to seek recourse to solitude.

Isabelle de Charrière, who was born in 1740, grew disillusioned with human nature, having lived through the French Revolution. She wrote in a letter, '"My arse", said Voltaire, "is very natural, but I am careful to wear breeches." I am afraid that humanity may be all arse.'

Osbert Sitwell observed that human beings display 'the identical combination of flaming pride and meek submission that in the animal world distinguishes the camel', and this, I think, is fair. We trust in our reason, in our purely human abilities, until something goes contrary to our plans, at which we sink to our knees whining that it is the fault of fate, the state, God or just someone else. We do not adapt well to adversity, seldom accepting it as the will of our Maker, but seeing it as an undeserved evil.

I feel shifty when I hear the words 'See these Christians, how they love one another', for I have come across many Christians whom I have found more detestable than any Marxist or maypole-hopper, and I love many non-Christians quite as much as those co-religionists I find not intolerable.

Several times in the course of this 'quest' I have felt that I was losing not only my mind but my faith and that I worshipped a different Deity from the one recommended by certain enthusiasts. The conception of the Lord of Hosts, the Ancient of Days, is hard to reconcile with the figure some perceive as a sort of divine quartermaster or super-social-worker concerned only with granting their every wish, from perfect personal happiness to the immediate provision of a new washing machine or a parking space. This god I came to refer to as Auntie Elsie, seeing him as an over-indulgent maiden aunt, susceptible to flattery and emotional bribery, yet capricious and petulant when feeling insufficiently appreciated or admired. He belongs more to magic and wish fulfilment than to religion. Nor do I recognise Christ the King or the Saviour of Mankind in the Caspar Milquetoast or Che Guevara figure that others invoke, wishy-washily complaisant or rigidly partisan. I ought to say that I accept the possibility that they might be correct in their perception and approach and I an infidel, but that would be taking humility beyond the bounds of reason and into the realm of self-indulgence, vanity and untruth: there is no real virtue in affecting to be stupider than you are or in pretending to respect views which you inwardly consider to be mistaken.

I have been told that I should end on a hopeful note but am finding it difficult in the present climate of foolishness, of ungrounded optimism, of error and artificial *bonhomie*, of worldwide mayhem and chaos, and no one to lead us, for those who would do so in truth and fidelity to God are ignored or derided. I keep thinking of the tale of the rabbi, alone at night in the synagogue: he sees God sitting in a corner, his head in his hands. 'My Lord,' says the rabbi, 'what are you doing here, your head in your hands?' 'I'm weary, Rabbi,' says the Lord, 'weary unto death.' If I were God I'd feel like that, but fortunately I'm not. The gates of Hell shall not prevail. That promise was the only hope I could see until I remembered the moment in the Creed at which we kneel, at the words *et homo factus est* and realise that God so loved us that he lived on earth and died for us. This reminder of the absolute reality of self-sacrificial love, of total goodness, is all we can hold on to in a climate dedicated to the *pretence* of fellowship and loving-kindness, to schmaltz, self-conceit and heresy.

Much of my acquaintance will be glad to see the last of this book, for I have thought of little else for a long time, and even when it's finished I shall go on thinking about what I have found and wondering about what has been lost. Somebody once said to his friend, 'Can't you talk about anything else but God?' And the friend responded, 'What else is there?'